Films of Fury

THE KUNG FU MOVIE BOOK

By Ric Meyers

Emery Books

Emery Books (emerybooks.com)/an imprint of Eirini Press
510 Long Hill Rd., Guilford, CT 06437

Copyright © 2011 Richard Sam Meyers
All rights reserved. No part of this book may be used or reproduced in any manner whatsoever without prior written permission from the publisher except in the case of brief quotations embodied in critical reviews and articles. All inquiries should be addressed Emery Books/Eirini Press, 510 Long Hill Rd, Guilford, CT 06437.

Covers design by John Agostini, Stephen Sloan of Upon Animation, and Greg Spalenka. Book design by Denise L. Meyer.

> Library of Congress Control Number: 2011920922
> ISBN: 978-0-9799989-4-2
> I. Meyers, Richard, 1953-
> II. Title: Films of Fury: The Kung Fu Movie Book
> > 1. Moving-pictures—Plots, themes, etc.
> > 2. Hand-to-hand fighting, Oriental, in motion pictures
> > 3. Martial arts movies
> > 4. Kung Fu movies

Photos reproduced courtesy of: Cannon Films, Circle Releasing Corp., Columbia Pictures, Sony, Tristar, Well Go USA, Magnet, Eternal Films, National General Films, New Line Cinema, New World Pictures, Ocean Shores Limited, Seasonal Films, Tai Seng Entertainment, Warner Brothers Inc, WW Entertainment, World Northal, Mike Stone, Golden Communications Company Limited.

Bruce Lee is a registered trademark of Bruce Lee Enterprises, LLC. The Bruce Lee name, image, likeness, and all related indicia are intellectual property of Bruce Lee Enterprises, LLC. All rights reserved. www.brucelee.com.

DEDICATION

As ever, to my masters (Art, Vincent, Bill, Karen, Stephe, Rick,
Don, Avi, Uncle, Feng-San),
mentors (Jeff, Warren, Alice, Jim, Brian and Al),
and friends (Steve, Don, Bill, Chris, Mike, Melissa and Kate).

ACKNOWLEDGEMENTS

The kindness of friends and associates has been invaluable during the past thirty years of study, starting with Amy Harlib, Bill Palmer, and Karen Palmer, whose research contributions helped fuel the original 1985 book *Martial Arts Movies: From Bruce Lee to the Ninjas*.

Covers design by John Agostini, Stephen Sloan of Upon Animation, and Greg Spalenka.

Great thanks, past, present, and future, also go to:

Lou Israel and Zita Siegel of World Northal (a.k.a. WW Entertainment); Raymond Chow and Russell Cawthorne, of Golden Communications Ltd.; Jackie Chan, Willie Chan, and Solon So, of Jackie and Willie Productions; Sammo Hung and Bojon Productions; Tsui Hark and Nansun Shi, of Film Workshop; John Woo, Michele Yeoh, and Terence Chang; Peter Chow and Fannie Ng, at Peter Chow International; Curtis Wong, Sandra Siegel, and all the fine folks at Curtis F. Wong Enterprises; Helen Soo, Frank Djeng and Tai Seng Entertainment; Jackson Hung and Matthew Tse of Ocean Shores Video Ltd.; Jonathan Ross and Alan Marke of Channel X Ltd.; Miss Choi Suk-kuen of the Hong Kong International Film Festival; Rudy De Blasio and Rick Sullivan, of Theater Management Associates; Bill Connolly and Martial Arts Movie Associates; Pak Chan and Superior Oriental; Robert Tam and the Sun Sing Cinema; Ronald Lee and NYUE; James Veronico and Crash Cinema; A&E's Biography; Alan Goldberg and ABC News Productions; Asian Cinevision, New Line Cinema; Patty Keung and Patrick W.L. Chow of Celestial Pictures; AnimEigo, Michael Stradford of Sony/Tristar; Rick Stelow and Alisa Grant at Drunken Master; Grady Hendrix and Paul Kazee of Subway Cinema; Mark Osbourne, John Stevenson, and DreamWorks SKW Animation; Andrew Heu-

Films of Fury

bner and Nickelodeon Studios; Eddie Ibrahim and Gary Sassaman of the San Diego Comic Con; Jason Ebner and Danielle Tokunaga of San Jose FanimeCon; Andrea Beasley Brown of MADCAP Theaters Phoenix AZ; Mark Setton, Tom Ward, and the University of Bridgeport Martial Arts Degree Program; Dave Cater and Inside Kung Fu magazine; Tai Chi Alchemy, Sedona AZ; Snow L. Chang and the Meiman Qigong Culture Center, Taipei, Taiwan; Shin Lin at the University of California at Irvine; Tom Coleman, Andrew Robinson, Andrew Corvey, and Lux Digital Pictures ; Fact-checker supreme Lana Zukowski; David Owens and the Japan Society; Merlin David and Samurai Video; Greg Yokoyama and Video Action; Renee Witterstaetter, Caroline Vie, Jean-Marc Toussaint, Larry Bensky, Seaton Chang, Rolanda Chu, David Chute, Fredric Dannen, F. J. DeSanto, Vincent Lyn, Tim Kwok, Alfred Cheung, Clyde Gentry III, Gere Ladue, Victor Lim, Kenn Scott, Gine Lui, Larry Hama, Linda Sampson, Joe Ragus, Mark Schreiber, Van Washington, Tom Weisser, Laurine White, Michael Avon Oeming, Jeff Yang, and Denise L. Meyer (not necessarily in that order).

CONTENTS

Introduction   9

Preface   13

Chapter 1: Kung Foundation   17

Chapter 2: The King of Kung Fu   37

Chapter 3: The Shaw Standard   69

Chapter 4: The Clown Prince of Kung Fu   115

Chapter 5: The Clown Prince's Court   153

Chapter 6: Woman Wushu Warriors   169

Chapter 7: Jet Powered   197

Chapter 8: Gun Fu   225

Chapter 9: Kung FU.S.A.   239

Chapter 10: Kung Futures   287

THE TOP 100 KUNG FU MOVIES 1966 - 2010   315

Selected Index   337

INTRODUCTION

Third time's the charm?

Martial Arts Movies: From Bruce Lee to the Ninjas was published in 1985. It was updated in 2001 as *Great Martial Arts Movies: From Bruce Lee to Jackie Chan and More.* And now there's this. So why a third volume on the same subject (fourth, if you count *The Encyclopedia of Martial Arts Movies,* to which I only contributed existing, previously-published, reviews)?

Well, obviously, there are more martial arts movies now than there were in 2001 ... but maybe not enough to warrant a whole new book. The real reason is two-fold. First, Lux Digital Pictures asked me to write a kung fu film documentary. Naturally, now that *Films of Fury: The Kung Fu Movie Movie* is near completion, a tie-in book version was karma kismet. But the more pressing, real, reason that I jumped at the chance to write this is that I know more now ... and not just about movies, either.

Kung fu is so potent that you need only know around five percent to teach it for the rest of your life. I knew the movies, sure, and I had studied martial arts since the late seventies, but it wasn't until 2002 that I seriously started practicing Chinese kung fu. By sheer serendipity I met world heavyweight taichi push hands champion Stephen Watson, who set me on a road to semi-illumination with the greatest sifus I have ever known ("when the student is ready, the teacher will appear," he told me).

With each technique and form, every film I had seen took on deeper dimensions. There's a reason "kung fu" translates as "hard work" or "concerted effort" rather than "martial arts." Turns out that kung fu is, first and foremost, a supra-human method of self-improvement ... with the ability to negate or terminate an attack as an organic side-effect.

As I began to learn the internal, external, physical and mental components of kung fu, every cinematic sequence I viewed or reviewed changed, as if going from silent to sound, black and white to color, or 2D to 3D. I collected medals and trophies for a year or two, until tournament ennui set in. Then I got down to the serious business of reassessing everything I ever saw or did.

Finally, in 2008, *The Kung Fu Movie Movie* came knocking, and with it, a chance to bring all my experiences and education together. As of this writing, I haven't seen the final cut of the documentary, so I don't know if it holds together. But this book is one hundred percent my baby, with all the flaws and favoritisms that entails.

It's unavoidable that this book will recycle some sections from my first two (or three) stabs at the subject, and, obviously, narrows their focus. Gone is the chapter on Japanese chambara/samurai/ninja films. My love for *Zatoichi the Blind Swordsman, Kyoshiro Nemuri/ Son of Black Mass, Lone Wolf and Cub/Baby Cart/Shogun Assassin*, and *Shinobi No Mono* remains unabated, but now you don't need forty pages to figure that out.

Also, given this new book's structure, a strictly chronological tale would be difficult. However, as you'll notice that the timeline jumps back and forth a bit, especially at the beginnings of chapters, I've endeavored to create a decent through-line, which, as you keep reading, will hold you in good stead.

Ideas will be fleshed out (hopefully), points will be made (and reiterated), and horizons may be broadened (or narrowed), as each chapter builds on the last, and, hopefully, vice versa. Veteran readers may also notice less emphasis on plot descriptions. They made sense back when few of these films were available, but now, thanks to the web, all may be watchable, so you can figure out most of the stories yourselves.

Now for the names. A lot can be lost in the translation. Since this is my book, I'm writing the names and titles as I've come to know and love them. Although the "Liang" in Liu Chia-liang is

Introduction

equivalent to the "Ric" in "Ric Meyers," I am not, as the Internet Movie Data Base does, going to refer to him as Chia-Liang Liu ... not when I know him as Liu Chia-liang. That is also the Cantonese version of his name. His name to Mandarin speakers is Lau Kar-leung, but I know him best by his Cantonese name, so that's the one I'm using.

That brings up another point. In my previous books, for clarity's sake, I eliminated the hyphens and capitalized everything (Liu Chia Liang, for example). But I think we've progressed enough that I can type the names as they originally were. If that leads to confusion — especially with the likes of Jacky Wu Jing, etc., I apologize. But the reason it's not Jacky Wu-jing, is that Wu Jing is his name. "Jacky" is his Western name, which he got to choose and tack on himself. My book; my rules.

Now for the dates. As much as I possibly can, I will list the date of the film's first showing, in whatever country that showing happened to be. Although Jackie Chan's *Supercop* premiered in America during 1996, I'll be listing its origin as 1992, which is when *Police Story 3: Supercop* first showed up in Hong Kong.

In any and every case, I'll attempt to emulate my kung fu film idols: keep it moving and keep it entertaining. As one grasshopper to another (or, as my literary sifu referred to me, as one "pale piece of a pig's ear" to another); let us carry on, with style.

Ric Meyers
December 2010

PREFACE

Now it's time for some deep background. Hold onto this stuff, it'll come in handy.

First and foremost, Chinese kung fu is a combination of external martial applications and internal powering and/or self-healing applications, where internal energy (chi) and calm are always more powerful and effective than muscle power and malice.

The following kung fu styles have developed over years, even centuries, and are constantly evolving—being fine-tuned and personalized to better suit their students' sizes, shapes, lives and times.

To list all styles would be tough, considering how many families and films create their own, but it's always exciting to see sifus (Chinese teachers) and/or senseis (Japanese teachers) using different forms against each other, then adapting to the other's style, and improving upon it in order to triumph.

But remember, kung fu is not really a matter of win or lose, it's a matter of learn or not learn. So saying, here are…

THE TOP "TEN" KUNG FU FILM STYLES & STYLINGS

"Animal" styles (Crane, Eagle, Leopard, Mantis, Monkey, Snake, Tiger, etc.): Created from extensive study of the creatures they are named for, these techniques adapt the way beasties fight into human terms.

Baqua: The "eight diagram palm" technique, derived from Taoist precepts, and incorporating "Taoist circle walking" to create remarkable power.

Chi Na: A gripping, hold-based technique, very roughly equivalent to Japanese judo, but with the added benefit of internal power strengthening each move.

Choy Li Fut: A long-arm style with a strong power-and-balance-building stance. Stances are often overlooked, but are vitally important as literal power bases. With the correct stance you can harness the energy of everything around you.

Dragon: A fearsome form that combines four Shaolin animal styles (crane, leopard, snake, and tiger) into a bone-pulverizing technique that is rarely seen in reality, let alone film (it's usually replaced by the apparently invulnerable, most likely fictional, iron skin style). But it is discussed and feared.

Drunken Style: A potent addition to any technique, it gives the impression of inebriation but helps the user be endlessly malleable and adaptable.

Hsing-I: A technique that incorporates time-tested physical methods to gather, channel, and recharge internal power during battle.

Hung Gar: A combination of tiger and crane styles, and one of the most visually powerful techniques.

Phoenix Eye: An internally powered pinpoint technique, identified by the use of an extended foreknuckle. You'll know it when you see it, and if you watch a lot of classic kung fu films, you'll see it a lot.

Taichi: One of the most sophisticated, subtle, and deceptive techniques, combining internal healing with devastatingly effective external power. Most learn only one-half of the art, robbing its literal translation, "balance," of meaning.

As I tell my students, if you only know half of what you should,

Preface

you'll always be half of what you could.

Wing Chun: Created by a woman of the same name, it emphasizes simultaneous, up-close, defense and attack.

Legendary Weapons: Swords (of many sizes, widths, and lengths), spears, axes, hammers, poles (aka staffs or "bo"), tridents, shields, three-section staff, and the chain whip (a linked series of blades).

You're now suitably armed and ready. Don't worry about checking back here. I'll remind you of these techniques, and more, in the coming pages.

As always and ever, we still know that being a kung fu film fan can be a lonely vocation, so feel free to email with any questions or comments to Ric4kungfu@gmail.com, and check out www.ricmeyers.com for the latest and greatest.

Enough ado. Let's begin.

CHAPTER ONE
KUNG FOUNDATION

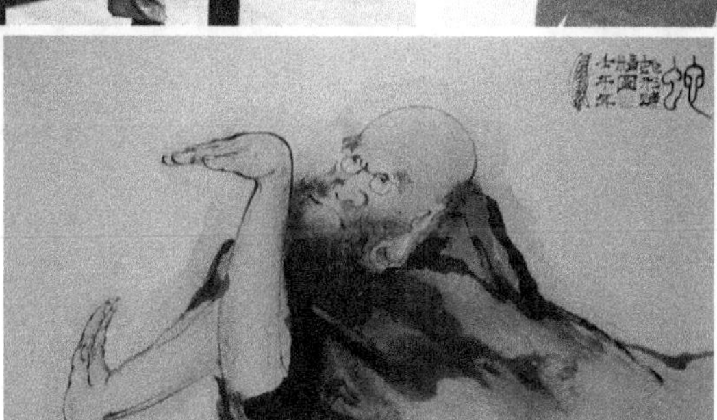

Picture identifications (clockwise from upper left):
Kwan Tak-hing in *Dreadnaught*; The Shaolin Temple; Peking Opera; Kwan Tak-hing as Huang Fei-hong; Dat Mo; Kwan Tak-hing fights Li Hai-sheng in *The Magnificent Butcher*.

Kung Foundation

This is all hearsay. Chinese history in general, and kung fu history in particular, is notoriously questionable. Since many (I daresay most) think of kung fu as a martial art, the contentiousness that dogs the question of "who, or what, is better," extends to the system's source and inspiration as well. Although the Chinese culture, arguably, created written history, as well as, unarguably, many other cultured pursuits, you'd think that the creation of kung fu would be well documented.

You'd be right, and wrong. There's a reason the yin-yang symbol is so identified with kung fu pursuits — because the "right" answer is usually a flowing mix of several answers. Just as in life, kung fu is a series of "ands" rather than "ors." On the one hand, kung fu history is extremely well-documented … after the fact, by many whose intentions might not have been the most objective. On the other hand, kung fu creationism is full of fascinating, fun fables of wise masters and philosophic students.

Ultimately, the ancient admonition of "learn mother nature, learn human nature, learn your own nature, and then you are truly ready to learn kung fu," extends to the study of its origins as well. There are certain immutable truths in terms of these natures, and a strong, smart, serene, and steady, generations-long, study of how we move and why we act the way we do would naturally lead to a time-tested system of self-improvement, health, and knowledge … with the ability to consummately defend ourselves coming as an unavoidable side effect.

Thankfully for this volume's existence, China had such a generations-long era to create this study, and, once created, the inclination to develop it, and, perhaps more importantly, personalize it. Not surprisingly, other countries and cultures also found much to appreciate in human/mother nature, but most of them seemed to decide to use it against others and/or to greedily better their positions, as opposed to improving themselves. Thus was martial arts born.

However, "kung fu" does not translate as "martial arts." The simplest, generally accepted, translation is "hard work." A more ornate definition that I appreciate is just about the only thing the misbegotten *Forbidden Kingdom* (2008) got right. There, Jet Li's "Silent Monk" character states that kung fu is a "concerted effort toward a specific goal."

Each student then gets to decide: what is that specific goal? A few chose wisely. Seemingly most decided the goal was to defeat others. As the young Bruce Lee character says in *Ip Man 2* (2010) when asked why he wanted to learn wing chun: "To beat up people I don't fancy (he is told by the venerable title character to come back when he was older, and, hopefully, wiser)." So, with that ego-stroking decision as foundation — which acknowledged human nature without really challenging it — several industries were created: kung fu schools, and more pertinently to this endeavor, kung fu movies.

"The problem with kung fu," Fred Weintraub, producer of *Enter the Dragon* (1973) told me, "is that it is fantasy. Once someone shoots someone else, everybody understands it. That's reality. But when somebody does fantastic martial arts, that's fantasy. You never see that in life. You never see that on the news. What you see is people shot and run over. When you're working in martial arts, you're working in fantasy."

Things have changed in the decades since he made that statement, but it still has more than a kernel of truth for our technology-soaked world. To better understand kung fu, it's helpful to better understand the country that created it. Considered the oldest cultured civilization, evidence of Chinese societies dates back to 7000 B.C. But their ancient period dated from around 2500 B.C. to about 200 B.C., during which time they grew accustomed to invasions of every kind, not to mention revolutions, insurrections, intrigue, and war. Even then, there were already great martial legends: Fu Hsi, the Hunter; Shen Nung, the Farmer; and Huang Ti, bringer of fire and music. Already Chinese history was full of complexities, complications, and conflicts.

Meanwhile, however, toiling almost unnoticed by the powers that be, there were family and village elders who were putting their life-long studies of mother nature and human nature to increasingly good use. Somewhere, someone was discovering that if he, or she, put a finger, or needle, on one spot it could cause personality-changing pain. But if he, or she, put that finger, or needle, just a hair's breath to one side or another, it could ease pain.

Galloping out of the ancient era was the Han dynasty, which stretched about four hundred years — from 200 B.C. to 200 A.D. Within hard-won governing walls, a certain ruling logic was in effect: a leader was chosen from the ruling family, and other members of the same family succeeded that person when he died. Simple to decide, hard to enforce. The Chinese had big families, and the infighting to become leader was ornate and often deadly.

Also, craziness wasn't restricted to the royal family. Constant wars were being waged to take over China from both outside and inside. Different families wanted to create their own dynasties, and different Chinese wanted to create different Chinas. Even so, Chinese government was becoming more structured at the end of the Han dynasty. The central government was located at the capital, with a chancellor, an imperial chancellor, and a commander-in-chief advising the emperor.

Out in the field, as it were, were nine ministers of state, each supported by a staff of directors and minions. In addition, there was the Department of Agriculture and Revenue, and the Lesser Treasury. Throughout this organization were various officials, secretariats, and even eunuchs. None of these people were immune to the emotions that are the stuff of great motion pictures such as lust, greed, pride, and envy.

Meanwhile, on the other side of the equation, some people sought mental and physical peace in the pursuit of Taoism and Confucianism. Scholar/philosophers Lao-tze and Confucius may have been contemporaries in the fourth or fifth centuries, but both apparently developed a way of life that emphasized simplicity, humility, harmony, wisdom, and the acceptance of both human and mother nature in an insightful, personal, forgiving manner. The two may have even found it sadly amusing how followers and politicians would ultimately attempt to put the two philosophies in conflict to see which would become the more influential.

Back on the other side of the tracks, the Han emperor gave parts of the country to his relatives as kingdoms. Agencies and armies were everywhere, especially because warring nomads in central Asia, called the Hsiung-nu, kept attacking from the north. As 200 A.D. neared, things just got worse and worse. China was divided, and dynasties came and went with alarming frequency. Because of this, the period from about 250 A.D. to 600 A.D. was known as the Six Dynasties.

Now there was a mess. Although Taoism promoted simplicity and Confucianism spotlighted ethics and education, both were reinterpreted by followers, users, and abusers to fit their means, ends, and times. And the times were turbulent. Then came Buddhism, an Indian system of behavior founded on enlightenment and the desire to eliminate suffering by eliminating desire. There was much more room for abuse and corruption of this creed than the less difficult teachings of Lao-tze and Confucius. The basic problem with eliminating desire, of course, is that it can't be done, because it's part and parcel of human nature.

But within the seeds of this mess blossomed the *Romance of the Three Kingdoms*, a Chinese novel written by Luo Guanzhong, based upon the turbulent years at the end of the Han Dynasty, when the kingdoms of Shu, Wei, and Wu vied for supremacy — lasting from around 170 A.D. until the uniting of China in 280 A.D. As influential to entertainment as this huge book was, even more potent was the creation of "Jiang Hu," initially mentioned by a poet somewhere in the 9th century, but cemented, like the *Romance*, in the 14th.

The Romance of the Three Kingdoms can be wildly compared to *Gone with the Wind*, in that they concentrated on civil strife within their respective countries — only the Chinese epic was far longer and served as source material for far more plays, books, poems, and movies. Jiang Hu, however, was a concept — an alternate universe of "rivers and lakes" (its exact translation) roughly relatable to America's "wild west" ... only this "wild east" was full of swordsmen and women all vying for power, lust, love, and happiness in a "martial art world."

Beyond this simplicity, Jiang Hu can also be fully recognized by fans of comic books, which predominantly exist in the "Marvel Universe (Spider-Man, Iron Man, et al)" and the "DC Universe (Superman, Batman, et al)" — which are recognizable variations of America, only filled with flying, swinging, individually costumed superheroes. Such was also the case in Jiang Hu's martial art world, complete with esoterically named, outfitted, skilled, and weaponed supra-heroes. This creation led to thousands of "wuxia," aka "heroic chivalry" stories, and hundreds of movies.

Outside the writers' windows, however, the Sui and T'ang dynasties (approximately 600 to 1000 A.D.) were really picking up the action. The Sui dynasty reunited northern and southern China, but collapsed from overextending itself. The T'ang dynasty saw the creation of the Shaolin Temple, and, thereby, semi-officially marked the sorta start of kung fu. Of course, kung fu, in many forms, was already well established. The more militant kind was alluded to in artifacts as far back as 2700 B.C. Confucius, the son of a soldier, was supposedly well versed in battle.

But outside the temple walls all sorts of court intrigues were going down, resulting in many lives being ruined or ended. Several of the emperors were truly perverse and depraved, creating all sorts of situations the Shaolin monks could fight. Life went on as usual in the royal court, with everyone stabbing each other in the back, front, side, or wherever a blade might fit. Everyone jockeyed for power, including the courtesans and concubines. One, Empress Wu, was so good at power games that she rose from being just one of the emperor's women to deposing the rightful heir to become empress herself.

None of this happened — not the reunifications or deposings — without all manner of bloody complications. Empress Wu managed to hold on until she was eighty years old and then handed the empire over to a rightful heir, but he was poisoned by his wife, who tried to become Empress herself. She, however, was outclassed by Wu's daughter, who got her brother to the throne, and tried to run the country through him. She, in turn, was foiled by her brother's rightful heir, who took over in a coup that resulted in her "suicide."

Things improved considerably (at least as depicted in modern cinema) with the coming of the Sung dynasty. The Sungs united a deeply fractured China, known as the Ten Kingdoms, into a Northern Sung and a Southern Sung. The Northern Sung consolidated and instituted reforms (which didn't quite take). The Southern Sung had a sophisticated political structure, which led to legal problems and clerical corruption. Overpopulation didn't help either. Already the Chinese numbered in the millions.

Then there was Genghis Khan. He led the Mongolian horde, who had decided to take over China. The Northern Sung made a deal with the Mongols, and for forty years, waited until the time was right to take out the Southern Sung. Khan's sons, Mangu and Khublai, marched down in 1250, and, by 1268, Mangu was dead and Khublai was attacking. Within a dozen years the Mongols controlled the entire Chinese empire.

Kung Foundation

Thus began the Yuan dynasty, a less-than-one-hundred-year reign marked by resistance fighters and espionage. It was not a happy time. Most Asians are deeply concerned about their pride — their "face" — and this era marked a great loss of face. All that changed in the mid-1300s. Bad government led to rebellion. The Mongols were pushed north, and the Ming dynasty started in the south.

There were clan intrigues, gang battles, threatening western Mongolians, threatening far eastern Manchurians, threatening Japanese, and internal warlord conspiracies. There was also *Journey to the West*, a landmark novel published anonymously sometime in the late 1500s. It told of a Tang Dynasty Buddhist monk's pilgrimage to India, but featured a scene-stealing character who was to become a cornerstone of Chinese kung fu fables: the Monkey King.

Otherwise known as Sun Wukong, he is a mischievous, clever, rebellious anthropomorphized simian who has a way with the kung fu pole. His powers and character so delighted so many that he has since been the source for adventures in every entertainment medium, from Peking Opera through cartoons to movies. He was certainly a great character with which to escape from the trials and tribulations of Ming Dynasty life.

Things came to a head in the mid-1600s, when the Manchus combined with bandit leaders to take over China and institute the Ch'ing (aka Qing) dynasty. This was yet another roughly three-hundred-year reign that created great change, and magnificent fighters to survive those changes. It contained at least one, if not several, Shaolin Temple destructions, forcing the surviving monks to create new kung fu forms. It was also a time of remarkable foreign contacts. The early Ch'ing emperors had relations with Russia, Tibet, Turkey, Nepal, Burma, Thailand, Vietnam, and Korea. They also had some trouble with Rome and Christianity.

All those residents and visitors were probably entertained via the Peking Opera, a traditional form of theater that combined music, singing, acting, mime, acrobatics, and choreography (both dancing and kung fu). Arising in the 18th century, and fully developed in the 19th, it revolved around a set repertory of increasingly familiar romantic, comedic, dramatic, and martial plays which were judged by the quality of the exacting, nuanced, performances, as well as the complex and colorful make-up and costumes. Peking Opera, now also referred to as Beijing Opera, established theatrical traditions which remain influential in Chinese cinema.

In Peking Opera there are great heroes, but also great villains. In Chinese history, one great villain was the British East India Company. It wanted the wealth that China reserved, so to open its shipping lanes, they sent opium. Once introduced, it could not be gotten rid of. A booming smuggling trade sprang up, and the demand was so great that it even strained national silver supplies. The leaders in Peking and the walled city of Canton said they wanted opium out. England wanted the silver that opium brought. In 1841 the British attacked.

By 1846 China was open to the British, the French, and the Americans. Anti-foreign feelings swelled in Chinese hearts, leading to some very nasty goings-on … what with British heads impaled on spikes and all. The central areas of anti-Anglo feelings were Kwangtung and Canton. Pirates and bandits were everywhere, taking white people's heads. In 1857 the British and French occupied Canton and started moving toward Peking. The Russians joined them.

By 1860, things that had come to a head came to a boil. There were Taiping rebellions and Muslim rebellions marking political and religious unrest. The more confusing things became, the more widespread was the corruption. All the out-lying areas (Nepal, Burma, and the like) were falling under British control. Meanwhile, Japan was getting into the act, coming into conflict with China over the sovereignty of Korea. Things got so bad between China and the "gweilos" (foreign devils) that the government leased Hong Kong to the British for ninety-nine years to serve as an import-export way station. It was basically a liaison between the fractious powers.

Things boiled over in 1900. This was the infamous boxer rebellion, where a zealous army of anti-foreign revolutionaries depended upon what they called the "Righteous and Harmonious Fist" to face down the gweilo guns. You can imagine how well that turned out. A form of "concerted effort" toward a goal of health and balance was monkey-kinged by the blind hopeful into a mythically invulnerable form of self-offence.

Actually, it's little wonder. For centuries, kung fu students had been internalizing and personalizing handed-down knowledge, making alterations as needed for their own size, shape, and temperament — as well as that of their loved ones. The Ling family fashioned ling gar (Ling Family Fist). The Hung family designed hung gar (Hung Family Fist). A woman named Wing Chun developed, well, guess what, to suit herself and her friends. The Chen family and Yang family, among others, devised their personal variations on taichi (which, in itself, means "balance").

On the inside, astonishing things were happening. But, on the outside, all the unknowing, unhappy, people could comprehend was that amazing things could be accomplished if you just followed the right teacher. The insecure and self-hating amongst them used that desire to their own advantage. On June 20, 1900, all-out war was declared for "support of the Ch'ing and extermination of foreigners." By 1901, China was no longer under its own rule and the populace who could be humiliated were humiliated.

For the next decade, China suffered all manner of indignity: foreign intervention, civil war, and Japanese invasion, among others. Finally, in 1912, the Republic started to take shape. The National Assembly was created, populated by mostly revolutionaries. But just because they were revolutionaries didn't mean they were any less insidious than their power-hungry ancestors. Dirty deeds were the order of the day. Yuan Shih-k'ai convinced the Assembly to declare him president, then promptly disbanded the Assembly and instituted a dictatorship.

But Yuan died in 1916, and members of the government battled amongst themselves to see what sort of country China would become, imperial or democratic. When the smoke cleared, there was the Nationalist party and the Communist party. By 1922, most of the influencing nations agreed to allow China to find its own way, and from there on in, it became a battle between Chinese regions — mostly north and south.

China's story was full of "no-win" scenarios. There were many times during its eras when both sides of an issue were "right," allowing modern filmmakers to picture all kinds of heroes: Ming, Ching, Manchu, Shaolin, or others. The 1930s were equally rich in stories. The Nationalists had established a new order, which lasted from 1928 to 1937, even though they warred with the Communists most of the time.

What brought them together was an outside enemy: the Japanese. For years, the Japanese ravaged China, committing atrocities that the Chinese still can't quite comprehend, let alone get over. This has always been a vital aspect of Chinese kung fu movies: hatred of the Japanese. It wasn't until relatively recently that a Japanese was pictured in a favorable light in a Chinese movie. For the most part, they are pictured as the worst kind of cowardly, arrogant, dishonest, and foul creatures imaginable.

By 1939, things had stalemated somewhat. The Allies threw in some five hundred million dollars to aid China in her fight. Sadly, the fight wasn't just with the Japanese; it also continued between the Communists and the Nationalists. On December 7, 1941, that all changed again: Japan bombed Pearl Harbor. America was angry now, which didn't help the Nationalists. As World War II dragged on, bringing poverty and inflation with it, the reigning Nationalist

Kung Foundation

government fell completely out of favor.

Once the war ended, Chinese civil war raged until 1949. It was Chiang Kai-shek versus Mao Tse-tung, and Mao won for the Communists. October 1, 1949 marked the establishment of the People's Republic of China, while Great Britain still ruled Hong Kong until 1997 (the Nationalists fled to Taiwan and created the Republic of China, which still has a troubled relationship with the mainland). So, now that we've established where all the kung fu films' stories come from, we can get down to the history of the movies themselves.

Up until the last few decades, the kung fu film story was really the Hong Kong kung fu film story — the People's Republic didn't really make a bona fide non-propaganda action epic until 1981. Although many films were made in Thailand, the Philippines, and most especially Taiwan, few were of any note. In fact, I once recognized a Taiwan movie star working as a busboy in a California restaurant. He remembered appearing in about seven hundred movies in the twelve years he toiled as an actor. That was more than a movie a week! When I asked him what he was doing working as a busboy, he replied, "The pay is better." So you can imagine the quality of those seven hundred movies. There were exceptions, of course, but those will be dealt with in good time.

In any case, there seems to be a slight disagreement concerning which was the first Chinese kung fu movie. The Hong Kong International Film Festival lists it as *Thief in the Car* (1920). *Martial Arts Movies* magazine listed it as *Monkey Fights Golden Leopard* in an article by James Seetoo. This was a 1926 silent film about the Monkey King, taken from *Journey to the West*. However, most English-speaking fans of the genre consider it to be *The Burning of the Red Lotus Temple* (1929). It hardly makes any difference, really, since the 1930s and 1940s were rife with nebulous martial arts-influenced films. The one thing they all reportedly had in common was that the kung fu wasn't very good.

These movies all shared an artificiality that reduced the effect of whatever kung fu was included. Even so, the films from 1920 to 1949 are interesting in terms of how they relate to the later movies, and for how their colorful titles compare to their somewhat staid presentation. For instance, there was *How Wu Song Killed His Sister-in-Law* (1927), *Bloody Fights* (1933), and, most importantly, *The Adventures of Fong Sai-yuk* (1938) ... important because this latter film is the first to feature credited kung fu choreographers (Ho Si-kit and Ng Mei-lo).

We'll be seeing a lot more from Fong Sai-yuk, but, in the meantime, the reason movies were being made at all was that Hong Kong was westernized. That is, they were more modern and less restricted than their mainland Chinese comrades. These areas were also overpopulated, and stricken with all manner of social ills that progress can create. Therefore, they were in far more need of entertainment. Up until 1949, this entertainment was highly stylized theater and cinema, mostly based on ancient traditions, presented in a Peking Opera-esque manner — much in the way that early American sound movies were little more than filmed stage plays.

But then a director named Hu Peng heard about a healer and kung fu teacher named Huang Fei-hong (aka Wong Fei-hung). Born in 1847 (and died in 1924), Huang Fei-hong was the son of one of the famous Ten Tigers of Kwangtung (a group around which several movies have been made). Other than the fact that he practiced medicine, was expert in many forms of kung fu, and excelled at a sport-contest called lion dancing, not much is known about the fellow.

Wu Pang rectified all that by starting a marathon film series that comprised eighty-five feature films over a twenty-year period. *The Story of Huang Fei Hong, Parts One and Two* (1949) was only the beginning of a phenomenon which was to become the foundation of the modern kung fu film. Up until then, most movie martial arts feats were totally ludicrous and completely inaccurate (a problem that still afflicts most bad kung fu movies, namely most of those that appeared in the United States following Bruce Lee's death).

Men leaped higher than trees, women flew through the air for hundreds of yards, and fighters did endless somersaults. The actors in the Huang Fei-hong movies insisted on realism in the all-important action scenes. For the first time, kung fu was the heart of the film, not just a peripheral ingredient. The need for accuracy became vital in order to honestly portray the leading character's life. It also didn't hurt that the lead actor was so similar to the character he portrayed.

That actor was Kwan Tak-hing. Born in 1906, he became an actor in Cantonese opera, but more importantly, he was an accomplished lion dancer and martial artist. He initially studied Hung boxing, which goes several steps further than hung gar. While the latter melds two forms — the tiger and crane styles — Hung Fist, as it is also called, melds all five Shaolin animal styles with the horse, elephant, and lion techniques. From there, Kwan became a proponent of the white crane style. All these styles are based on the human body and mind, as well as the way animals defend themselves.

As the films progressed over the decades, Kwan became proficient in all the areas Huang himself was known for. Huang seemed dedicated to mastering the most esoteric, difficult skills — such as the Iron Wire and Tiger Vanquishing Fists as well as Huang's trademark "Shadowless Kick," which Kwan seemed to delight in showing throughout the series. Kwan himself was the creator of what is now known as the Omni-Directional Gangrou Fist.

So director Wu had the character and the actor. And while the honorable legend of Huang and the charming personality of Kwan were vital, it took more than those to make the series a success. First, these were pictures about a beloved personage in happier times, so they became a nostalgic preserver of particular pastimes, such as "vying for firecrackers" — another sport-contest in which a bunch of red sticks were fired into the air so different kung fu school teams could battle for possession when they fell. Whichever team held the most sticks at the end of the tournament won.

But vying for firecrackers paled in comparison to the pride felt by the school that won the lion dancing contests. A hallmark of Chinese life, these tournaments pitted teams of athletes who performed with ornate, colorful Chinese Lion costumes. It is the skill of the dancers beneath the costume that imbues the rippling dragon-like body and heavy, puppet-like lion head of the outfit with character. Maneuvering this lion in competition with other lion dancers can call for the greatest skill a martial artist possesses. In this area Kwan was a master, making the many Huang movies that involved lion dancing a visual delight.

But the nucleus of the Huang Fei-hong films was kung fu ... and not just the external, martial variety. Unlike his contemporary film series competitor, Fong Sai-yuk (aka Fan Shiyu), a hot-tempered Shaolin renegade, Huang Fei-hong was first and foremost a healer, who spread wisdom and traditional Chinese medicine from his famed school/clinic known as Po Chi Lum. Although he would be disappointed in his students whenever they were undisciplined, he rarely angered and would always teach that the highest form of kung fu was not to fight.

Of course, his many envious, greedy villains would always force the issue ... to the delight of audiences who preferred the real thing to the artificial, theatrical feats portrayed in years past. For the record: there were apparently five basic Kwangtung schools of kung fu teaching at the time — the Hung, Liu, Cai, Li, and Mo Schools. They taught the ten major fist forms, based on the movements of the crane, elephant, horse, monkey, leopard, lion, snake, tiger, and tiger cub. In addition, there was training utilizing the eighteen legendary weapons of China, which included staffs, spears, and swords. From there the possibilities seemingly become endless.

The Huang Fei-hong movies of the era made use of many of these possibilities, in addition to showcasing the subtler, but just as important, concept of "wu de" — which means "martial virtue." As usual, Chinese action films concentrated on savage tales of vengeance, characterized by a plot that had rival martial arts schools in conflict with one another due to pride or greed. This tried-and-true plot is still being overused today, but the Huang Fei-hong movies introduced an honorable martial artist who sought to use kung fu for health and self-defense only. He was a chivalrous, considerate saint of a man who was always patient, humble, and eternally on the underdog's side.

Wu Yixiao, a Cantonese opera writer, scripted the first four films, but Wang Feng is generally credited as being the main influence on the series, since he wrote, as well as directed, many of the most popular. But this was truly a partnership between the actors and the crew. Although choreographers Leung Wing-hang and Yuen Siu-tin were credited with the lion's share of the series' action scenes, Kwan was said to have choreographed most of his own battles with his main opponent, Shih Kien (best known as the evil Han in 1973's *Enter the Dragon*). Together, they created believable bouts that remain the series' high points. Almost every major modern kung fu director was influenced by, or actually worked on, these motion pictures.

The best of them, like *Huang Fei Hong Vied for the Firecrackers at Huadi* (1955) and *How Huang Fei Hong Vanquished the Twelve Lions* (1956), not only displayed fine martial arts but Huang's wisdom, courage, restraint, morality, and intelligence as well. Although there were some other martial arts films during the 1950s and early 1960s, the Huang Fei-hong movies practically monopolized the market. By 1956, twenty-five of the year's twenty-nine kung fu pictures starred this hero.

These films were in the cinemas practically every month, and there were some years when the only kung fu movies were the Huang Fei-hong ones. Just about the only other film series that was any kind of competition at all concerned the aforementioned Fan Shiyu (aka Fang Shih Yu aka Fong Sai-yuk), an eighteenth-century, fiery-tempered master swordsman and bare-handed fighter who was trained at the Shaolin Temple. There were about sixteen films concerning this legendary young man over the same two decades the Huang movies reigned.

The reason why the genre didn't flourish sooner is obvious. Just like the great dance movies of Fred Astaire and Gene Kelly, great kung fu is not easy to fake. It can, and has, been done, but it is rarely convincing unless the actor is also, not coincidentally, a good dancer. It takes years of dedication and discipline to perform kung fu well on-screen, no matter whether you are a martial arts student, a Peking Opera alumnus, a gymnast, an acrobat, a dancer, or an actor. And if you don't perform kung fu well it is painfully evident to the audience.

Still, the Hong Kong film industry wasn't very artistic during the 1950s and 1960s. Seemingly, just about the only man who seemed to know what to do with a camera was King Hu — an epic filmmaker who toiled in Taiwan. He probably was the best action filmmaker China had ever seen, but far from the best moviemaker. This is not as fine a distinction as it might first appear. The "film" aspect of entertainment is technical. The "movie" is emotional. King Hu's films, including his masterpiece, *A Touch of Zen* (1966), concentrate far more on character interaction and cinematic technique than on the niceties of the kung fu.

"I have no knowledge of kung fu whatsoever," the director said in a 1989 interview. "My action scenes come from the stylized combat of Peking Opera." To Hu, kung fu was dance, and was treated as such.

There's hardly any action in *A Touch of Zen,* but plenty of mood and symbolism — not to mention three distinct endings — within its three-hour running time. Rumor has it that the studio was so impressed with the first ninety minutes, but so unhappy with its inconclusive ending, that they asked for a more fight-oriented finale. King Hu showed what could be done cinematically with what the Chinese movie industry had to work with, but essentially his films were magnificent visual elaborations of legends and stage plays.

But one of the most important reasons kung fu films did not flourish earlier is a fascinating sociological one. The Hong Kong Chinese had their hands full with surviving. After the turbulent dawn of the 20th century, they contended with the Boxer Rebellion, Japanese invasion, civil war, and World War II. Once the Communists took over the mainland and the somewhat supercilious British took over Hong Kong, movies were the last thing on the breadwinners' minds.

As far as 1950s Hong Kong society was concerned, the only people who had any free time would be spoiled housewives, and their hard-working husbands didn't want them ogling handsome hunk heroes at the local cinema. So the local movie industry felt inclined to have women playing their male movie action heroes (which is something, considering that they hadn't allowed women to even play women's Peking Opera roles for quite some time).

The result were cute, interesting, but hardly convincing tales of heroic chivalry that held back Hong Kong action cinema for nearly a decade, as the rest of the world produced stirring masterpieces. By the 1960s, the South China audience was finally ready for real kung fu action, and a few folk were ready to give it to them ... with a vengeance.

CHAPTER TWO
THE KING OF KUNG FU

Bruce Lee is a registered trademark of Bruce Lee Enterprises, LLC. The Bruce Lee name, image, likeness, and all related indicia are intellectual property of Bruce Lee Enterprises, LLC. All rights reserved. www.brucelee.com.

Picture identifications (clockwise from upper left):
Bruce Li in *Dynamo*; Jason Scott Lee in *Dragon: The Bruce Lee Story*; Mike Stone, James Coburn, Chuck Norris and Bruce Lee; Bruce Le in *Cobra*; *The Dragon Dies Hard*, Brandon Lee in *The Crow*.

The King of Kung Fu

Bruce Lee remains the man who has brought more people to kung fu in general, and kung fu films in particular, than anyone else in the world. He is personally responsible for introducing kung fu to the Western world, and for forging the modern kung fu film. Through his life, he did more to educate Americans to kung fu's benefits than anyone. Through his death, he has done more to clarify its detriments. Through his legacy, he represents the full spectrum of kung fu's physical possibilities, as well as its mental limitations.

It was his superlative martial arts ability and canny filmmaking knowledge that galvanized audiences everywhere. But it is also Bruce Lee, simply by being deprived of the opportunity to mature, who set a trap for the kung fu film that it is still in the process of escaping. Everyone in the industry is compared to him, or forged himself in, and out, of his image. Decades after his untimely death, he remains a universally known cinematic icon. Simply put, without him, this book probably would not exist.

It started November 27, 1940, when Lee Jun-fan was born to Lee Hoi-chuen and his wife Grace in San Francisco. Since he was born in the United States, the hospital requested an Anglicized name. Supposedly, it was the supervising doctor, Mary Glover, who suggested "Bruce." He was born into a family that included two older girls, Agnes and Phoebe, and an older brother named Peter. Soon he had a younger brother as well, Robert. To his siblings, Bruce was better known by the name Lee Yuen-kam (an adaptation of his birth name).

Their father was a well-known actor for Chinese audiences on both American coasts as well as in Hong Kong. Just three months after his birth, Bruce joined his father onstage, in a production of *Golden Gate Girl*. When the family returned to Asia soon after, Bruce continued his thespian ways ... while starting a few new distressing ones as well. He was a thin, small, and somewhat sickly child, prone to nightmares and sleepwalking. Compensation came in the form of energy. He always seemed to be moving, never satisfied with being still. Friends and family remember Bruce as an extremely positive, assured youth, and his assurance became brazen as he grew.

His progress was marked by appearances in Hong Kong movies, starting just after World War II, when he was six years old. The director of one of his father's films was impressed by Bruce's attitude and cast him in a small role for *Birth of a Man* (1946), which was also known by the title *The Beginning of a Boy*. Only a year later, Bruce was already starring in films such as *My Son A-Chang*, in which he played the title role of a street-smart kid trying to get ahead in the sweatshop world of Hong Kong. As was fairly common at that time, he was given a movie star name: Lung, or Siu Lung, which means "Dragon" or "Little Dragon."

Even at the age of seven, Lee's screen persona was strong. He was a clever, capable, but short-tempered little ruffian who specialized in the scowl, the pout, the stare, and the slow burn. This character served him on the streets as well. Ignoring the lessons of his films and his family, Lee, in his own words, "went looking for fights." By the time he hit his teens, he was already well equipped to handle those fights. He was a natural dancer, becoming quite proficient in the cha-cha, and his natural grace lent itself to wing chun, the physically economical, but extremely effective, martial art he decided to follow.

Created by a woman of the same name, wing chun was popularized by Yip Man, a venerable teacher who proved to the rest of the male-chauvinistic martial art world that the technique could more than hold its own against hung gar — then one of the most prevalent styles being taught in Hong Kong. The story goes that Bruce sought out Yip Man to start his kung fu journey, but even his esteemed sifu (teacher) could not quell Lee's contentiousness. Some nights he would dance; other nights he would scour the streets for a fight.

The King of Kung Fu

Often he would do both.

Lee read voraciously, and was notably near-sighted. He was known for practical jokes, which became serious if he was personally challenged by his victim. Often, it was no fun playing with Bruce Lee; his desire to win seemed almost obsessive. Some said that even when he lost a street fight, he would find a way to make it seem as if he had won. Others said that he would return to the victor again and again, eventually winning by either learning enough or simply wearing down his opponents by attrition.

And all the time he exercised and trained — seemingly wanting not only to convince himself that he was the best, but to actually be the best. He rapidly became aware of the Chinese place in the post-war world, which cried out for a Chinese Superman. Bruce Lee wanted to be that Chinese Superman. The tragedy of his ultimate fate was to be played out on a minor scale in the Hong Kong of 1959. The more famous Bruce Lee became as a teenage movie actor, the more uncontrollable he became in real life.

Things came to a head with the premiere of his most successful film of that time, *The Orphan* (1959). Although Wu Chu-fan was the ostensible star (playing a teacher who lost his family in a Japanese air raid), Bruce all but stole the show as Ah Sam, an orphan who survived as a street thief. Again, all the acting skills that were to lead to his superstardom were well in evidence. Lee's emotional intensity was compelling. He portrayed frustration beautifully, as on-screen schoolmates laughed at his lack of education, and his peers were embarrassed by his bad manners. When he finally fights back, threatening his teachers and fellows with a knife during class, it is a cathartic scene that Lee plays to the hilt.

Ah Sam returns to his gang, which masterminds the kidnapping of a rich man's son, but Sam can't forget the kindness of his teachers. He returns when Wu Chu-fan, playing Ho See-kei, discovers that Ah Sam is his own long-lost son — separated from him in the aforementioned air raid. Repentant, Ah Sam leads the police to the gang's hideout and single-handedly saves the kidnapped boy. The film concludes with Lee tearfully begging forgiveness from his father, teachers, schoolmates, and ancestors.

On-screen, Bruce Lee begged forgiveness. Off-screen, he begged from no one and gave no quarter. Things were getting so difficult for his family that Bruce went back to America. The story goes that the Shaw Brothers Studio — the most powerful movie company in Hong Kong (see next chapter) — offered him a contract … which his mother forbade him to take, all but banishing him to the United States, praying that education there would straighten him out. So, at the moment when Bruce Lee was to gain his greatest success, he was forced to retreat.

The exile, self-imposed or not, had served its purpose. Bruce Lee was a stranger in a strange land at the age of eighteen, forced to work all the harder to excel. At first he enrolled at the Edison Technical High School in Seattle, but moved on to the University of Washington. His energy did not lessen, but at least it was directed. Lee worked in restaurants for awhile, but soon began teaching kung fu, aka gong fu. Bruce's wing chun had been built on a foundation of taichi (aka taiji, aka tai chi, aka tai chi-chuan), which had been taught to him by his father.

Taichi is a greatly misunderstood style and is represented by the yin-yang symbol. Even though that symbol pictures two ever-swirling, interchanging sides, it seems as if the majority of students only learn one-half of the art — the internal, "dance-like" form. Although powerful enough to be effective, it's like vacuuming the house with the cleaner unplugged. True taichi is a balance of both internal, healing applications and external, martial applications. Combined with the practical effectiveness of wing chun, Lee had much to build upon. He thought deeply about his skills and developed them further while attending the University of Washington.

The King of Kung Fu

Lee's exhaustive research led to his writing the insightful *Chinese Gung-Fu: The Philosophical Art of Self-Defense* in the early 1960s. But by 1964, the demons that had led him to the Hong Kong streets were now pointing him toward Hollywood.

1964 was a particularly important one in Lee's life. He married Linda Emery, moved to California, and met Ed Parker, Chuck Norris, Bob Wall, and Mike Stone. The latter quartet were all at the Ed Parker International Karate Championships. "He did a demonstration there, and I won the grand championship in the heavyweight division," Stone told me. "Afterward we went out for a Chinese dinner. We would work out together one day a week. I would work out with him one day, Chuck Norris would work out with him another, and so would Joe Lewis." He had much to teach these martial arts champions. All their skills were Japanese in origin. Bruce opened the world of Chinese kung fu to them. It was as if men who had only known ice all their life were suddenly introduced to the benefits of water.

All three men would become influential in the American martial arts movie market, but it would be Bruce who created the market the other men would enter. The man who put Lee's foot in the door was Ed Parker. He had filmed Bruce's performance at the internationals, and showed them to his student, Jay Sebring, who, in turn, showed them to William Dozier, who needed a "Kato" for the show he was planning to produce in 1966. Dozier was riding high with the success of *Batman* (1966-1968), a series that camped up Bob Kane's famous comic-book character. The ABC-TV network wanted another silly superhero to follow on the "Caped Crusader's" heels, and Dozier chose George W. Trendle and Fran Striker's popular radio character — the somewhat generic masked master crime fighter known as *The Green Hornet*.

Behind the mask was Britt Reid, created by Trendle and Striker as the grandnephew of John Reid, better known as the Lone Ranger (also created by Striker and Trendle). Fortunately for Bruce Lee, Dozier did not eliminate the character of Britt's Asian manservant and chauffeur, Kato (originally Japanese but made Korean in movie serials produced during World War II). Kato piloted the Green Hornet's heavily armed and high-octaned supercar, "The Black Beauty," through battles against crime. Dozier wisely decided to downplay the camp aspects of the *Batman* show for his new baby, but the network had other ideas.

Much to Bruce's satisfaction, he passed a now-famous screen test and was cast as Kato — forever changing the character to Chinese. *The Green Hornet* (1966-1967) began production with high hopes and good intentions, but it soon became clear that ABC wanted a brightly colored, cutsie clone of the popular series it had already begun to beat into the ground. The only time the new show took off was when Bruce Lee did. More than the Green Hornet's guns (which shot gas and needles) and his armor-plated car, what sold the show to its young audience was Lee's kung fu.

Whenever Kato got out from behind the wheel and started kicking, the show started clicking. But as Mike Stone noted, "They had to restrain Bruce as Kato, because there was a star." That star was Van Williams, made famous by two previous TV detective series: *Bourbon Street Beat* (1959-1960) and *Surfside Six* (1960-1962). Ironically, however, it was Williams who was Lee's most vocal advocate.

"Both Bruce and I wanted Britt and Kato to be more like partners," Williams told me. But the network turned a deaf ear. Neither campy nor serious, *The Green Hornet* series was cancelled after only one season. But, by that time, Lee had developed his own form of kung fu — Jeet Kune Do — the Way of the Intercepting Fist. What many saw as pure egoism was actually a time-honored tradition of personalizing kung fu to your own personality and physiology. Jeet kune do was only a name, as far as Bruce was concerned — a label which seemingly came to annoy him.

The King of Kung Fu

At first it was known as jun fan gung fu. Then it became the Confucian "Bruce Lee's Tao of Chinese Gung Fu — Using No Way As Way, Having No Limitation As Limitation." By any name, it was Lee's unique, effective method of fighting, which stressed continual improvement and the joy derived there-from. "Practice seriously," he said, "but don't seriously practice." In other words, work for the love of it, and stay flexible.

By the time *The Green Hornet's* stinger was removed in 1967, Lee had experienced a series of both setbacks and breakthroughs. His father had died in 1965, but his son Brandon had been born the same year. He attended his father's funeral in Hong Kong but returned to Los Angeles to pursue stardom. There he attracted a notable stable of students for jeet kune do, leading to schools in L.A., Oakland, and even Seattle. His fame as a teacher led to more television roles, on the likes of *Ironside* (1967-1975), and movie jobs (technical advisor on *The Wrecking Crew* (1969), a 007 satire starring Dean Martin as American secret agent Matt Helm.

He suffered through a somewhat degrading guest-starring role in the 1969 movie *Marlowe,* in which he played a Chinese villain paid to intimidate private eye Philip Marlowe (James Garner) with his superlative kung fu skill — culminating in Bruce doing a kick, straight up, to destroy a light hanging from the ceiling. His demise in the movie was as imbecilic as the lamp kick was impressive. After having his manhood taunted by Marlowe from a precarious position on a balcony ledge, Lee irrationally launches a flying kick, then plummets to his death when Marlowe merely steps aside.

Lee was treated better back on television, as his student, scripter Sterling Silliphant, wrote an episode of the series *Longstreet* (1971-1972) specifically for him. Titled "The Way of the Fist," it portrayed Lee's character teaching the hero, a blind insurance investigator, how to defend himself against a bunch of muggers. Lee spoke eloquently of kung fu and the mental composure necessary to master it. The two portrayals were perfect bookends — one all flash and the other all substance. While few in the United States were overly impressed, Hong Kong was buzzing.

The Green Hornet had premiered there three years after its premiere in the United States, and Lee took the opportunity to promote himself to the Chinese audience. Legend has it that a kung fu display during a HK talk show so impressed Raymond Chow, head of Golden Communications Company Limited (otherwise known as Golden Harvest) that he signed Lee to a contract to do a movie called *The Big Boss,* directed by Lo Wei. The legend was a bit misleading. The more credible story is that almost every major Hong Kong film company bid for Bruce's participation, but after almost a year Raymond Chow secured the actor-teacher's services to make the movie, on location, in Thailand.

Thailand was a warning location. When American producers want to save money, they film in Canada or Mexico. When Hong Kong producers thought they had an iffy proposition, they trundled the cast and crew to Thailand. After all, director Wei had seen better days. Starting his career in the early 1950s, by the time he got saddled with Bruce Lee, he had settled comfortably into the status quo.

The nicest thing you could call mid-60s kung fu films was moribund. Female stars portraying male flying swordsmen were still the order of the day, and, while Huang Fei-hong was still in there kicking, he was doing so less and less. If actual kung fu was being used on screen at all, it was the artificial, unconvincing, sort reviewers Bill and Karen Palmer termed "swingy arms." And, to Lo Wei's mounting frustration, Bruce Lee refused to play along. The director was credited with the script about a young man banished to Thailand to work in an ice factory after his mother had exacted a promise from him not to fight. *The Big Boss* (1971) turned out to reflect many Lee images that would recur throughout his painfully short career.

The King of Kung Fu

The "Big Boss" of the title, played by Han Ying-chieh (who was also credited as the kung fu choreographer, a position he held on many of King Hu's classics) is using the ice factory as a front for drug running. When Lee gets too close to the truth, the bosses first try to buy him off, then seduce him with wine and women, and finally try to kill him. But instead of taking on the bad guys with loads of swingy arms and low, awkward kicks, Bruce adamantly refused to do more than just a few moves. Wei angrily summoned Raymond Chow to Thailand, complaining that the crew had derisively nicknamed Bruce "three kick Lee." Bruce's explanation: "No one would survive more than three of my kicks."

Chow watched the footage. He returned to Hong Kong after instructing Wei: "Do it Bruce's way."

Although Wei and Han still had on-screen credit for the direction and action, the best portions of *The Big Boss* are clearly accreditable to Bruce. After the bad guys kill all his friends, Lee explodes with a barely controlled rage that thrilled audiences. The scene is now considered a classic. Lee finds the drugs embedded in ice. He is surrounded by about twenty knife-, club-, and chain-wielding thugs in the eerie, red-lit icehouse interior. With mounting anger clearly etched on his face, he takes the villains apart in a battle that combines dramatic action with nearly cartoon-like violence (the latter of which Lee only reluctantly acquiesced to).

From that climactic scene, Lee created an uncharacteristically cathartic one. Upon finding his dead friends, he takes a scene to comprehend his heartbreak and responsibility, making the fight-filled finale all the more effective. Lee races to the Big Boss' palatial estate to take on the main bad guy and all his minions. It is on the lawn of the mansion where the two antagonists have a knife fight, showcasing two more Lee trademarks — the wounds that inspire Lee on to greater heights of heroism, and the tension-building pauses that add to Lee's ground-breaking on-screen style.

Films of Fury

When Lee is cut by the Big Boss' blade, he stops, tastes the blood, and moves forward, always letting the tension build. And *The Big Boss* represented the first time moviegoers heard Lee's now trademark animal screeches. All three main filmmakers — Chow, Wei, and Lee — were happy enough with the results to immediately start on a follow-up. The trio were already at work on a second movie when word came in: *The Big Boss* was a gigantic, galvanizing success. Made for only $100,000, it earned five times that much in Hong Kong alone. Bruce Lee was now, officially, a star, and he fully intended to take advantage of it.

Fist of Fury (1972) is again credited to Lo Wei as writer/director and Han Ying-chieh as choreographer … but there's no mistaking who the real big boss was (in fact, Lee made a habit of working on films with directors who never again made anything nearly as good as the movie they made featuring Bruce). This time the crew had the Golden Harvest Studios as home base and a budget befitting their star's talents. Allegedly Lee even called on the services of the great I Kuang, a stunningly prolific and polished film writer, to punch up the script (all puns intended).

The Chinese usually made movies the way some people make cars — on an assembly line. With such a gigantic population to supply, Hong Kong filmmakers in the early 1970s could wrap up a normal production in seventy-two hours, a "big-budget extravaganza" in a week. *Fist of Fury* premiered in Hong Kong less than five months after *The Big Boss*, but proved to be at least twice the picture. It may have cost twice as much, but it made at least twice as much as well.

Lee makes it clear from the very outset that a new age of filmmaking, fight choreography, and screen acting had dawned. When the audience first sees him — playing the now legendary character of Chen Zhen, student of kung fu sifu Huo Yuan-jia — he is so overcome with grief at the death of his master that he leaps into the grave and onto the coffin, clawing and crying. From then on, his body becomes an extension of his character. Set in the Shanghai of the late 1920s, the film depicts a society in which the Chinese are all but spit upon by the occupying Japanese. Using a series of disguises, including a rickshaw driver and, in a delightful turn, a grinning, mincing phone repairman, Lee discovers the murderers and takes them apart.

Within the seemingly simple story, Lee invested a wealth of invention and imagination. But what truly set the film apart was the fierce sense of identity Lee infused the movie with. As great as so many scenes are, the one that changed everything for Hong Kong kung fu films takes place outside a park. There, Chen Zhen is prevented from entering, and made aware of a sign reading "No Dogs or Chinese." A kimonoed Japanese (played by Sammo Hung and Jackie Chan's Peking Opera school classmate Yuen Wah) offers to escort him in ... if Chen crawls between the Japanese's legs like a dog.

Lee levels him, then does a *Marlowe*-esque kick to shatter the "No Dogs or Chinese" sign. I've been told by those lucky enough to have seen the film's original run in Hong Kong cinemas that they had never sensed such a mass triumphant psychological release before or since. But Lee wasn't done with them yet. The climatic moment in a movie filled with climatic moments came when Lee destroys a calligraphy that reads "The Chinese Are the Weaklings of Asia."

The icing on the cake was Bruce's introduction of the nunchaku — two small clubs joined by a short length of chain. Lee supposedly learned the particular nunchaku skill with his star student Daniel Inosanto. However he learned it, he had chosen a particularly cinematic, esoteric weapon with which to dazzle viewers. To see Lee swirl and spin the sticks with ridiculous ease was to experience pure enchantment — despite the fact that the nunchaku is one of the least effective martial art weapons in the arsenal (given its difficulty of true control). It sure looks great though, doesn't it?

Fist of Fury ends by freeze-framing on a tremendous leap by Lee, seemingly right into his persecutors' bullets, defiant to the end. To say the Hong Kong audience went crazy would be an understatement. Unlike Huang Fei-hong, Lee did not turn the other cheek or remain humble and unassuming. He stood up and shouted, "I'm Chinese and proud of it!" Then, perhaps even more importantly (certainly to his eventual international audience), he backed it up with on-screen kung fu skill hitherto fore unseen by anyone.

Seeing even Kwan Tak-hing take on his movie adversaries with rhythmic certainty couldn't compare with Bruce's electric power. No one could. It was like comparing a dancing bear to Fred Astaire. Bruce's kung fu clout, control and command was instantly identifiable as the real deal, and once audiences saw the real deal, they wouldn't settle for less. Seemingly overnight, kung fu cinema convulsed into its first real era.

Lee was not about to rest on his laurels. No more Wei or Han. After creating his own Concord Productions, he struck a deal with Golden Harvest to co-produce his next film — which Lee would star, direct, write, and choreograph (officially). *Way of the Dragon* (1972) opened in Hong Kong just nine months after *Fist of Fury*. Essentially, this is Bruce Lee's last film. It is certainly the only film he completely controlled, and the only film in which his approach was primary. In it he played unassuming, but fiercely patriotic and surprisingly clever, Tang Lung, who travels to Rome to help relatives run a Chinese restaurant.

Although the first part of the movie chronicles largely humorous "stranger in a strange land" confrontations with the locals (including a child and a prostitute), Lee slowly strips his character of his surface naiveté to reveal a supremely capable hero beneath. First Tang Lung shows the other restaurant employees the superiority of "Chinese boxing" in an alley behind the restaurant. But when

The King of Kung Fu

racketeers arrive looking for protection money, the lessons become more pointed. He teaches the derisive, arrogant thugs a comparative lesson in a nicely structured fight that culminates with the reappearance of the nunchaku. Probably the sharpest moment here is when the hoods' leader manages to grab it. At first he seems to think that it will imbue him with some sort of magical power, but he winds up knocking himself out with it.

All this is achieved, essentially silently, and is a mark of Lee's skill as a film director (as is his use — obvious in the Hong Kong edition, but steamrolled by subsequent U.S. dubbing — of different languages ... the Chinese and Italians literally can't understand one another). The next major step forward *Way of the Dragon* takes is in allowing the appearance of guns. Guns could sound the death knell of kung fu movies because no matter how skillful one is, no martial artist can fight a bullet (a lesson the Boxer Rebellioners learned the hard way). Lee confronts that problem in this movie, Kato-style, by having his character make wooden darts that he hurls into his enemies' hands. It is the most unlikely technique in the picture, but at least Lee attempted to deal with this particularly sticky genre drawback.

Tang Lung repeatedly stymies the Mafioso's takeover attempts, so the big boss decides to fight fire with fire — calling in one Japanese and two American martial artists. Two of them, played by Wang Ing-sik and Bob Wall, pretty much take care of the restaurant employees. The final American is flown in especially to take on Tang Lung. It is Lee's old California friend Chuck Norris, in his first major screen role. The two face each other in the Roman Coliseum, using their real skills, with all the graciousness and solemnity of honor-bound warriors, in the most realistic empty-handed martial art fight ever filmed to that date.

Lee smartly infuses this serious, yet exciting, scene with small humorous touches, supplied by a mute kitten that witnesses the fight, and Norris' own abundant body hair. Another change in Lee's approach is in the ending — he is neither arrested nor killed. Instead, it looks as if he will settle down with the romantic lead (played in all three Lee films by the lovely Nora Miao), only to suddenly pack up and go.

"In this world of guns and knives, wherever Tang Lung may go, he will always travel on his own," is the last line. And travel Bruce Lee did. All the way back to America. There, two projects were being created just for him. One was *Enter the Dragon* (1973), produced by Fred Weintraub, who had seen some of the those "swingy-arm" kung fu films, and "loved the last ten minutes, when the hero would take on an army of crooks and defeat them all bare-handed. I was certain a hugely successful American movie could be made.

"I went to Hong Kong and saw Bruce's films," he told me, "and brought one back to show Ted Ashley [then chairman of the board at Warner Brothers]. If it wasn't for Ted, the movie would have never gotten made. I had half the money, but everybody else had turned me down — including other executives at Warners. But Ted asked me what I needed, and then said, 'Go ahead.'"

Weintraub and co-producer Paul Heller cut a deal with Lee's Concord Productions, then worked with Lee and novice screenwriter Michael Allin on the script. Robert Clouse was chosen as director on the strength of the thrilling, brutal fight scenes in the otherwise mishandled *Darker Than Amber* (1970), and, because, in Weintraub's words, "Nobody else wanted to direct the picture except him."

The story was James Bond by way of Fu Manchu. An unnamed espionage agency asks a Shaolin Temple teacher named Lee to compete at a martial-arts tournament in order to infiltrate an island off Hong Kong lorded over by a Shaolin renegade. Lee goes to the island in the company of Williams, a cocky black fighter, and Roper, a gambler — both of whom are in trouble with the law. Once on

The King of Kung Fu

the island, they face the evil Han (named after Han Ying-chieh, perhaps?) — a stereotype with a fake, interchangeable hand, a small army of guards, and a jail filled with drug addicts, slaves, and white slavery victims.

To put it mildly, the script was makeshift. Han is hardly more than Dr. No, and even has a white, long-haired cat like 007's main nemesis, Ernst Stavros Blofeld. The only place the movie excels — in fact, the only place the movie is unique — is in its kung fu and its star. Not surprisingly, getting the project started in a city known for its standard operating racism was no easy task.

Darker Than Amber (1970) star Rod Taylor was considered for the integral role of co-hero Roper, but the versatile John Saxon, an actor who had been toiling in B movies since the mid-1950s, shared equal billing with Lee. Rockney Tarkinton was cast as Williams ... at first.

"Jim Kelly was a last-minute replacement," Weintraub revealed. "He came on the night before the picture was to start. At the last minute Tarkinton said I was taking advantage of him. I disagreed, and that was the end of that. At two o'clock in the morning, I went to see Kelly and said, 'You're hired.'"

Weintraub had Saxon, Kelly, and Bob Wall ready to go. He had also hired Shih Kien, famous as Huang Fei-hong's most consistent adversary, and the "Queen of Kung Fu," Angela Mao, to play Bruce's sister. To give the American audience a henchman they could understand, he cast Yang Sze as the muscular bodyguard Bolo (a name and physique which stuck with him, despite the fact that he was a skilled taichi fighter). What he didn't have, at first, was Bruce Lee.

"For the first three weeks, we shot around him," Weintraub maintained. "Linda Lee, his wife, was the one who kept things going when he wouldn't show up on the set. I think he was nervous. It was his first big film. And he was fighting with Raymond Chow at that time. He was fighting with me, too, but not as much. It was just that he was so nervous. On the first day, he had a facial twitch. We needed twenty-seven takes to get the shot. But then he settled down, and we made the film."

Things ran relatively smoothly, and word started getting around that Weintraub might have a tiger by the tail. "Once we started," the producer told me, "everybody thought Bruce was going to be something, and started sending me scripts in the middle of shooting. There was a man at Warner Brothers named Dick Moore who understood the market, so we worked up a script with Ed Spielman and Howard Friedlander and showed it to Bruce. We tried to do it as a movie first."

That movie was called *Kung Fu* and took place in the Sierra Nevadas of 1868. It tells of the Chinese "coolie" laborers building the transcontinental railroad. Among them is Caine, a half-breed. Almost immediately, the movie flashes back to Caine's training by Shaolin Temple monks, culminating in a final test that has him in a booby-trapped hall blocked by a red-hot cauldron. He escapes the corridor by lifting the cauldron with his forearms, which leaves tattoos of a dragon on one arm and a tiger on the other.

From there Caine travels to Peking, where his blind sifu, Po, stumbles into a royal guard. He's shot for his mistake, and Caine kills the guards and, of all people, the prince. Then he escapes to America and gets a job on the railroad. From there, the script degenerates into a western *Big Boss,* but with one added twist. After Caine leads the coolies in a revolt against their corrupt masters, another Shaolin monk appears to challenge him. It seems the temple was destroyed as retribution for Caine's act, and the monk wants revenge. Caine kills him, bows farewell, and disappears down the road.

"Tom Kuhn, who was in charge of Warner Television at the time, said, 'Why don't we try this as a series?'" Weintraub said. "I said, 'Great. Bruce would be perfect.' We designed the series for Bruce."

According to the "official" network story, Bruce Lee ultimately turned down the offer to star in the series, thinking he wasn't ready yet. Weintraub doesn't remember it that way. "When he didn't get the part," he recalled, "I was stunned. Bruce was heartbroken, and I couldn't blame him."

The late Harvey Frand, who told me that he was the executive who was actually given the unenviable task of telling Bruce in person, didn't remember it the network's way, either. "Ted Ashley wanted Bruce," he said, "but the network wanted someone like William Smith [who, ironically, played the *Darker Than Amber* villain, and was considered for John Saxon's role in *Enter the Dragon*]. We felt that casting David Carradine made for a good compromise. To tell you the truth, I didn't think Lee's English was strong enough yet."

But his kung fu certainly was. In a vain attempt to try to convince the executive what they were missing, Lee kicked a feather off the bridge of Frand's nose without touching his skin. It still wasn't enough. Carradine got the part in the series that ironically succeeded because of *Enter the Dragon*. And *Enter the Dragon* succeeded because of Bruce Lee.

Comedian Margaret Cho concurs. She has always felt that the TV series should have another name. "I hated that show, because the lead actor, David Carradine, wasn't even Chinese," she said in her comedy act. "That show should not have been called *Kung Fu*. It should have been called *That Guy's Not Chinese*."

Lee's Chinese contribution to *Enter the Dragon*, however, was telling. Bruce starred essentially as himself, and supervised all the kung fu — using many of the same stuntman he had worked with on *Fist of Fury*, including, most notably, the pre-superstar Jackie Chan (Jackie had stunted the *Fist of Fury* villain who was kicked across a stone garden, and, in *Enter the Dragon*'s subterranean fight sequence, memorably gets his neck broken by Lee). This was Lee's showcase, and its every fault only served to bolster Bruce's participation. He was truly the best thing about the movie. In that respect, it could not have been a better vehicle for him.

To top it off, he also gave the entire film a heart most weren't aware of. "I don't think anyone else knows this," Weintraub told me back in 1984, "but when *Enter the Dragon* was finished, I completely reedited it. When it was initially done, it was a linear story that started in the United States. But Bruce went back and did the Shaolin Temple sequence. That was his. He did that without me, and I loved it. I took that and opened the film with it. Then I went onto the boat and did flashbacks, which everybody thought I was crazy to do."

For that memorable, important, prologue, Lee introduced the world to Stephen Tung Wai, who played the young man Bruce was teaching. The child actor grew up to be one of the industry's most promising new kung fu choreographers. But back at the time, Lee also called upon his friend Sammo Hung Kam-po, whom he had met when first coming to work for Golden Harvest. At that time Sammo had been the studio's top action director, so he had listened to all the stories about how great Bruce was with some skepticism. On his first day back in Hong Kong from location shooting, Sammo visited the studio offices.

"I walked around the corner, and there he was," Sammo told me. "I said 'You're Bruce Lee?' He said, 'You're Sammo Hung. Wanna fight?' I said, 'Sure!' So we set up right there in the hall. We're getting into position, then suddenly he relaxes, leans over, and asks, 'Ready?' I said "Yeah!' … and the next thing I know, I'm flat on my back, staring up at the ceiling. Bruce leans over and asks, 'How was that?' I gave him a big thumb's up and said, 'Great!' And we were friends ever since … until…."

The "until" was that *Enter the Dragon* prologue. "I was working in Thailand, I think, and I hear from Bruce," Sammo recalled. "He was wondering if I could do him a favor. So I fly all the way back to Hong Kong, and do the fight scene with him." Sammo played

The King of Kung Fu

Lee's adversary in the sequence. But, with the scene over, Bruce, according to Sammo, drove him back to the airport. "And there he hands me around two hundred (Hong Kong) dollars [the equivalent of about twenty-five bucks]," Sammo said. "I said 'What's this? I was doing you a favor. Why are you treating me like this?'" Sammo rejected the token payment and returned to his set, bewildered. It was his first sign that Bruce Lee was changing. "We didn't really talk after that," Sammo admitted.

Bruce, meanwhile, returned to Hong Kong to a tumultuous reception. It was months before *Enter the Dragon* would premiere, but just the very fact that he had starred in an international film after having attained star status from his first three movies put him in superstar category. After years of being ignored and diminished, his every word and deed in Hong Kong was being received with devoted worship. It would seem that Bruce Lee had the last laugh. Weintraub and he were already discussing a second American movie, for which he would receive a million dollars. He supposedly was on the verge of signing a contract with the Shaw Brothers studio to do a period piece; photos to that effect were taken.

But first he wanted to do a project he called *Game of Death*. Lee had been planning it for some time. He had copious notes and already secured much of the cast. Initially it seemed to be a sequel to *Way of the Dragon*. In the company of two friends, Tang Lung is forced to travel to Korea, where he must secure a treasure at the top of a pagoda, guarded by a different type of martial artist on each level. Under grueling, non-air-conditioned, conditions in the dog days of a Hong Kong summer, Bruce filmed three fight scenes — one with Daniel Inosanto, one with Chi Hon Joi (a hapkido fighter), and one with Kareem Abdul-Jabbar.

Lee looked very lean, even wan, in the footage, and rumors circulated about his exhausting schedule and arduous training (including one exercise where he strapped electrodes to a band on his forehead and tried punching in the time between two electric shocks). Tales of his blinding, debilitating migraines were rampant (as were stories about various ways he tried to relieve them). Nevertheless, he soldiered on. More than an hour of nearly finished footage was completed on *Game of Death*, and it was looking like a magnum opus of Bruce's kung fu — smart, humorous, effective, exciting, fascinating, and even deep.

But on July 20, 1973, Bruce Lee died. After he was late to a dinner with Raymond Chow and George Lazenby to discuss making a film with the Australian actor who had resigned the role of James Bond during *On Her Majesty's Secret Service* (1969), he was found in the apartment of actress Betty Ting Pei. His death was attributed to a cerebral hemorrhage, or brain aneurism. None of his fans could believe it, and the hysteria that followed was equally hard to believe.

Some said that he was murdered by envious kung fu masters using the "Death Touch," or poisoned by jealous rival studios. There were tales of his involvement with gangsters and drug pushers. In short, no one could believe that their idol, their "Chinese Superman," had died naturally. He had to have been killed by some sort of insidious supervillain or because of an elaborate conspiracy.

Enter the Dragon premiered in the U.S. during the summer of 1973, then opened in Hong Kong in October. In the meantime, a small distributing company, National General, had secured the rights to present Lee's earlier films to the American public. The movies were dubbed, and the Chinese titles translated. *The Big Boss* was supposed to be called *The Chinese Connection*, and *Fist of Fury* was to be called *Fists of Fury*. But, with the care and consideration customarily reserved for "chop-socky" flicks, the titles were switched. Now *The Big Boss* was *Fists of Fury* and *Fist of Fury* was *The Chinese Connection*. That's how American audiences saw the features, and that's how American audiences still know them ... by the wrong titles. Soon after, *Way of the Dragon* came to U.S. shores as *Return of the Dragon* — promoted, of course, as a sequel to *Enter the Dragon* ... although made before that film.

Bruce Lee was the most successful Chinese star in the world — a month after he was already dead. Still, decades later, people don't believe the "official" cause of his death. They maintain that drugs had to be part of his downfall. While it is impossible to say for certain that Bruce Lee did not use drugs, Fred Weintraub was definite in his opinion: "Let me tell you that Bruce would never put anything into his body that would hurt him. I had him examined at UCLA the week before he died. He was in great shape. He had an aneurism. That happens to people under the age of thirty-five."

Mike Stone echoes Weintraub's sentiments. "I've met several people with Bruce's intensity and, interestingly enough, those people died quite young. But the unique thing about Bruce was that his belief in himself, and the intensity with which he did things, was always at a peak. He had a tremendous faith in himself and a belief in his ability."

Sadly, the Chinese film industry could not let their hero go honorably. They chose to remember him by mounting literally dozens of quickie, rip-off productions that purportedly showed the king back in action, or told his life story. Even the best of these films were pretty bad, if for nothing else than they were being made at all. Asian hackmeisters recruited Ho Tsung-tao, an otherwise credible actor with good martial arts skills, to become "Bruce Li" in a series of undistinguished (but fun) adventures like *Bruce Lee Superdragon* (1974), *Goodbye Bruce Lee, His Last Game of Death* (1975), *Exit the Dragon, Enter the Tiger* (1976), and *Bruce Lee Against Supermen* (1977).

These movies can be entertaining in a ludicrous way. One never knows when a Bruce Lee "clone" will appear behind trademark sunglasses (as in *Exit the Dragon,* when the "real" Bruce Lee asks Bruce Li to solve his murder if he just so happens to get killed in the near future) or when mountain gorillas will rise on their hind legs and fight kung fu-style (as in 1977's *Shaolin Invincibles*).

Following hot on Bruce Li's heels was Bruce Le, originally named Huang Kin-lung. At least Li was a decent performer — an actor who was able to shake his Lee clone mantle in subsequent years to act in better, more respectable, productions. Le is not the former and has not done the latter. Le is a wooden screen presence, sinking any scene in which he isn't swinging his fists or feet. In addition, he seems content to toil in exploitive garbage, trading on both his slight physical resemblance and willingness to go through Bruce's superficial motions. The directors and writers of these travesties manage to sink anything their star can't. Certainly there are defenders and fans of these efforts, but I am not one of them.

Quite possibly the most blatant, shameless exploitation came with *I Love You, Bruce Lee,* known in America as *Bruce Lee: His Last Days, His Last Nights* (1975). Sold as Betty Ting Pei's own statement about her alleged lover's fate, it was actually the esteemed Shaw Brothers Studio's sneering, shabby "settling of accounts" with the "star that got away" and the ex-employee, Raymond Chow, who had the audacity to make it on his own. Starring Betty herself with Li Hsui-hsien (aka Danny Lee) as Bruce, it was helmed by lean, mean action thriller maker (Johnny) Lo Mar as the most obvious of sore-loser-hack jobs, made all the more sad by Ting Pei's willingness to degrade herself. The film pictured her as a hopelessly self-delusional, constantly nude gold-digger with a self-worth issue, and Bruce as an immature, egomaniacal rapist who occasionally gripped his skull in pain.

After trotting out mean-spirited caricatures for ninety minutes, the sympathetic bartender to whom Betty has been pouring out her memories beats up some thugs who want to punish the girl, and tells them to respect Bruce's memory ... which is more than this movie did. But the worst was yet to come. As howlingly bad fun as *I Love*

The King of Kung Fu

You, Bruce Lee was, the ultimate indignity came from Bruce's own studio, Golden Harvest. With about a hundred minutes of footage Bruce had completed before he died, Raymond Chow announced to the world that *The Game of Death* would premiere in 1978.

They had Bruce Lee's notes. They had Bruce Lee's hand-picked co-stars, James Tien and Chieh Yuan. They had the footage. Using the co-stars, they could have created a framing story, and fashioned a film that honored Bruce Lee's wishes. Instead, they jettisoned all but eleven minutes of Bruce's work, and hired Robert Clouse to create what was essentially an entirely new movie ... a patently ludicrous and shameful one.

Using several obvious stand-ins, and some of the most labored camera tricks imaginable (including positioning a stand-in so that it looks like his body is coming from a cut-out picture of Bruce's face pasted on a mirror), Clouse tells the labored, laughable story of movie star "Billy Lo" fighting for his freedom against a crime syndicate who wants to control him ... or something equally absurd. Rather than being a brilliant treatise on kung fu, in Bruce's so-called collaborators' hands, it becomes the stupid story of "Brewce Leigh" fighting an insane actor's agent.

Markedly better was 1981's *Tower of Death,* known in the United States as *Game of Death II*. Directed by Ng See-yuen, who also directed *Bruce Lee, the True Story* (U.S.: *Bruce Lee, the Man and the Myth,* 1976), it starred Kim Tai-chung in the leading role of Bobby Lo, the brother of Billy Lo (Bruce's *Game of Death* character). This time the actual Bruce Lee footage came from scenes edited out of *Enter the Dragon,* with all new dialogue dubbed in. The "real" Bruce Lee appears in only the first half hour, "playing" Billy, who is mysteriously killed, allowing Bobby to investigate. Bob-o is then given a series of eight, increasingly more ambitious, fights, until he reaches the top of the pagoda, where he has an excellent battle with Huang Jang-li, one of the screen's best "leg fighters" (i.e., kickers).

In a bunch of dreadful movies, this one reigns supreme, which, of course, isn't saying much.

Some fans seem to think that *Game of Death* would have been Bruce's ultimate kung fu statement, had he lived. But given that Lee wanted to continue making movies, that opinion is doubtful. After all, he had yet to realize his full potential as an actor, filmmaker, or even as a martial artist. But there is no doubt Lee's honorably realized *Game of Death* would have been far superior to what Clouse, Golden Harvest, and Warner Brothers came up with.

Fred Weintraub put it in perspective. "I miss Bruce. I liked him. We fought, but it was never personal. It was for the film, for art's sake. He knew I cared and that was all that counted. He knew, in a funny kind of way, that I was the only one who cared enough to get him into the international market. Nobody wanted him. In the history of show business, there had never been an international Chinese star, especially not one who was five-foot-seven and not gorgeous. Bruce stood tall. Bruce is martial arts. He made the form work. No matter who you see doing martial arts, you always compare him to Bruce Lee. Say 'cowboy' and you think 'John Wayne.' Say 'martial arts' and the name that pops to mind is Bruce Lee. That makes him one of the few giants in show business. That's the mark of his influence and his genius."

And like any icon, he would not stay down. Decades after his death, he has remained a constant, with books, magazines, posters, re-releases of his films, statues, countless collectibles, and more. At the time of this writing, there is both an amusement park and a Broadway musical being planned. So, naturally, a big budget Hollywood bio-pic was green-lit. The production started promisingly. Rob Cohen, an eclectic and enthusiastic director, and the producer of such popular projects as *The Running Man* (1987) with Arnold Schwarzenegger, set about adapting Linda Lee's biography *Bruce Lee: The Man Only I Knew,* with the Lee family's cooperation. He even

The King of Kung Fu

hired several top jeet kune do teachers to choreograph the film's many real and imagined fight scenes. Then the problems started.

Ironically, most of the people who created *Dragon: The Bruce Lee Story* (1993) probably wouldn't think of them as problems. As far as they may have been concerned, *Dragon* was a critical and financial success, so what could possibly be the problem? There were really only two: finding the bite-size bits of truth amid the total fabrications and wild flights of fantasy, then, perhaps more importantly, honoring Lee's non-cinematic life's work: the creation of jeet kune do.

Dilemma one: how to communicate the anger Lee reportedly felt throughout his life — the anger that made him win any confrontation at all costs. In the case of *Dragon,* the anger was visually manifested as a demon — a demon dressed in what appears to be Japanese, not Chinese, armor. Was this a clever nod to the Japanese villains who helped make *The Chinese Connection* so successful, or Hollywood standard operating racism? You decide.

Dilemma two: the direct power of jeet kune do (like Chinese armor, apparently) is not visual enough. Lee himself always did an exaggerated version of it for the cameras — but not so exaggerated that it would ever be mistaken for the acrobatics of the Power Rangers. Complicating matters further was that a non-martial artist was cast as Bruce. And while Jason Scott Lee (no relation) is an excellent actor, it was somewhat akin to hiring a nondancer to star in a Fred Astaire biopic.

So, while they had such jeet kune do notables as Jerry Poteet on the set, the decision was made: bring in the acrobats. Instead of showing the true power of jeet kune do in an informed, imaginative way, Lee was pictured flipping and cart-wheeling all over the place like some sort of demented pinwheel. That way, the leading actor wouldn't be required to communicate the true artistry of Bruce Lee's kung fu. Not that many American audiences knew the difference. One critic even went so far as to review the movie's martial arts by saying, "Fittingly, fight coordinator John Cheung previously worked with Hong Kong martial arts star Jackie Chan." No, not fittingly. For Chan, as you will read later, purposely patterned himself as an anti–Bruce Lee.

Screenwriters Cohen, Edward Khmara, and John Raffo worked hard to honor Bruce, and there are things to like in the result, but it remains an inaccurate portrayal, and ends with an equally tragic dedication: to the memory of, not Bruce, but Brandon Lee.

The first call came at about four o'clock in the morning. "Brandon Lee is dead," a crew member whispered to me. "He was shot." I couldn't comprehend it. I had only recently met Brandon during the promotional campaign for *Rapid Fire* (1992) — the movie in which he had finally stopped trying to get out of his father's shadow. Instead, he had embraced it, and come out, whole and happy, on the other side.

My colleagues and I had agreed: energetic, goodhearted, and talented, Brandon Lee was the next great hope for the American martial arts action film. But now he was dead — killed in an implausible accident on the set of his breakthrough film, *The Crow* (1994). A crew member quickly and quietly gave me the particulars: they had been working all day and all night for weeks to get the movie done. The production's official "gun wrangler" had already left the production for another job when the film went overschedule. A prop gun, supposedly loaded with blank cartridges, had fired.

In the days to come, a more complete picture was supplied by the local police, who had reportedly taken over the gun-wrangling responsibilities. According to press reports, a hunk of bullet padding — usually used as a wall between the gunpowder and the shell of a regulation cartridge — had lodged in the barrel of the on-set weapon. It was the wadding that was allegedly propelled by the powder of a newly loaded blank.

Some time later, I commiserated with a friend: "If only the actor

The King of Kung Fu

playing his killer had been off by just a few inches." My friend said he knew the actor who had used that gun. "He was a method actor," my friend said with awful irony. "He had been practicing how to shoot to kill for days."

Brandon had died three months shy of the twentieth anniversary of his father's death, and just weeks before the release of *Dragon: the Bruce Lee Story* — a role he was supposedly offered, and which might have saved his life had he not turned it down. But his career had been fashioned to skirt his father's shadow. Brandon was eight when his father died, but he had already appeared with him on Hong Kong TV, successfully breaking a board at the tender age of six.

"Could you imagine what would've happened if I hadn't broken the board?" he asked later. But he had, and despite his best efforts, it set the tone for his entire career. For years he was adamant in his refusal to mirror his father's moves and attitude, wanting to be accepted and applauded for himself, not for a happenstance of birth. Finally, however, Brandon's need for cinematic exposure took precedence over his hopes. Brandon went the way of his father, taking the leading role in a cunningly designed Hong Kong action film *Legacy of Rage* (1986), arguably the best movie of his truncated career. Here, Brandon played a kindhearted, though supremely athletic, construction worker who is forced to slaughter his family's oppressors — but only after he is brutally pushed way beyond endurance.

The true sign of Brandon's acceptance of his destiny came with his next casting choice: to co-star opposite the man whom executives had chosen instead of his father to star in the television series that had been created to showcase Bruce Lee. Brandon played a Shaolin assassin in *Kung Fu: The Movie* (1986) ... which should have been called *Kung Fu: The TV Movie*, since it played on network television. Wherever it played, it remained a fairly pedestrian vehicle, but one well-suited to show Brandon's talent and dedication.

His next starring role was in the cheap and tacky *Laser Mission*

(1989), a U.S./South African/German co-production whose writing and direction reflected its fractured origins. Brandon plays an espionage operative who teams with a tough and resourceful female agent (Debi Monahan) to rescue a laser expert, amusingly played by the always game Ernest Borgnine. It did little more than pay the bills, as did Brandon's next starring vehicle, *Showdown in Little Tokyo* (1991), which blows by in seventy-six minutes. Here Brandon is a wisecracking supporting player to brooding beefcake Dolph Lundgren, as a cop who runs afoul of Japanese-American mobsters.

Once again, it showed anyone who cared to look that Brandon had charisma to spare and was only getting better with each scene. That performance seemed to do the trick, because Brandon wouldn't have to wait as long before his next big break. It came with *Rapid Fire* (1992), the younger Lee's first major studio release, and a canny combination of the star's strengths. Here, for the first time, Brandon doesn't begrudgingly agree that he is Bruce Lee's son, he proudly proclaims it, happily acknowledging his father's influence but letting his own engaging personality carry the day. As before, it was the force of Brandon's charisma, not his fists, that carried this otherwise predictable, unimaginative, and often occasionally dreary movie.

This set the stage for *The Crow* — based on James Barr's bleak black-and-white comic book. The story couldn't be simpler. A rock star is murdered and, a year later, with a crow as harbinger, comes back to wreak vengeance on his killers. Ambitious director Alex Proyas, however, used this story as a clothesline to hang elegant visuals upon, which stayed in the memory long after the rudimentary dialogue and muddled action faded. Basically, Brandon's character lived in a fictional, futuristic, and seemingly post-apocalyptic city of self-conscious sleazeballs, where the only character who doesn't painfully posture and spout film noir clichés is a nice-guy cop played by ex-*Ghostbuster* Ernie Hudson.

The King of Kung Fu

But the excitement (and exhaustion) was palpable on *The Crow*'s North Carolina set, where everyone was inspired by Proyas's vision and Lee's appeal. They knew they had something special and exciting, but they also knew they had to slave to get it done in time for a pressing release date. The mocking "I survived *The Crow*" T-shirts, which were supposedly being planned, turned bitterly portentous on the night of March 31, 1993, when Brandon was shot — just days before his marriage.

The allusions to his father's death continued in the tragedy's aftermath, but rather than being resurrected by stand-ins and tacky camera tricks ala *Game of Death,* Brandon's visage and power were reborn through multi-million-dollar computer special effects, which grafted his face to the body of a stunt double. The final mirthless mockery was that *The Crow,* unlike *Game of Death,* was arguably improved by the rewriting and refilming needed to complete the movie.

Brandon lies beside his father in a Seattle cemetery. In life, they created memorable entertainment. In death, they have forged a tragic dynasty that will never be forgotten. There is little doubt that, had both lived, they would have added much more to the world's knowledge and entertainment. Kung fu, and kung fu films, would have only grown in respect and appreciation. Bruce would have set, then raised, the bar with each production. With age and experience, he would have matured, and then would have communicated that sense of balance and wisdom through his art.

But with his death, taking with it his unique martial art and moviemaking skills, the world outside Asia was left to snigger at clones, bad dubbing, and lost-in-translation ignorance. Even the best of subsequent kung fu films were relegated to critics Roger Ebert and Gene Siskels' "turkey" or "stinker of the week" status on their syndicated movie review TV series through sheer, stubborn unwillingness to learn more.

Why did Bruce Lee die? The truth will never be known for certain, but I have a theory. He pushed himself too hard. Deep in the desire to become the Chinese Superman, he lost sight of himself. As Dirty Harry said, "A man's gotta know his limitations," and Bruce Lee punished his mind and body to the point that it gave in. And, in that light, he represents kung fu's core truth: that a kung fu student's only true enemy is his or herself. Sadly, that was the one fight Bruce Lee didn't get the chance to win.

Presents "FIVE FINGERS OF DEATH" in DeLuxe Color

YOU HAVEN'T LIVED UNTIL YOU'VE FOUGHT DIRTY HO ...AND THEN YOU'RE DEAD! Starring GORDON LIU THE 'MASTER KILLER' A SHAW BROTHERS PRESENTATION A WORLD NORTHAL FILM R

CHAPTER THREE
THE SHAW STANDARD

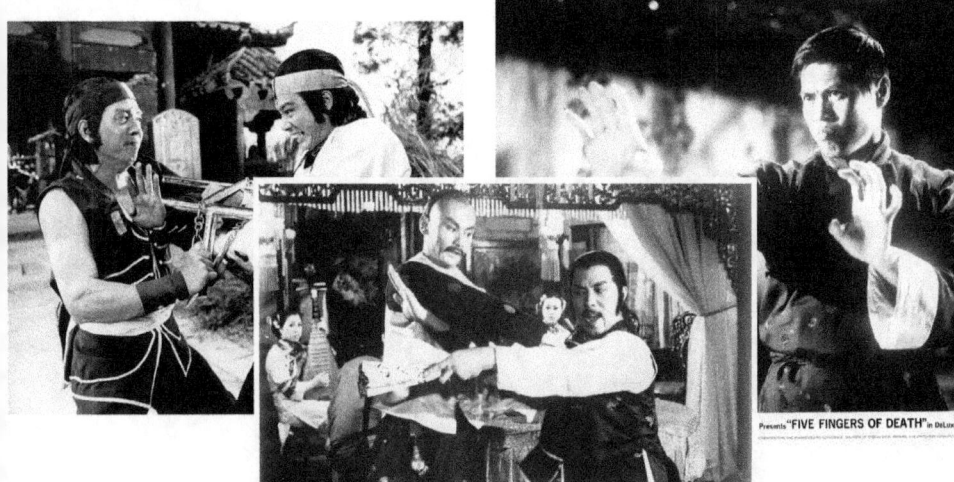

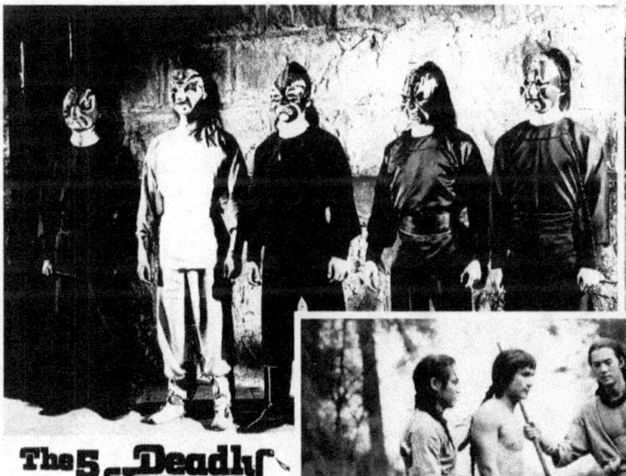

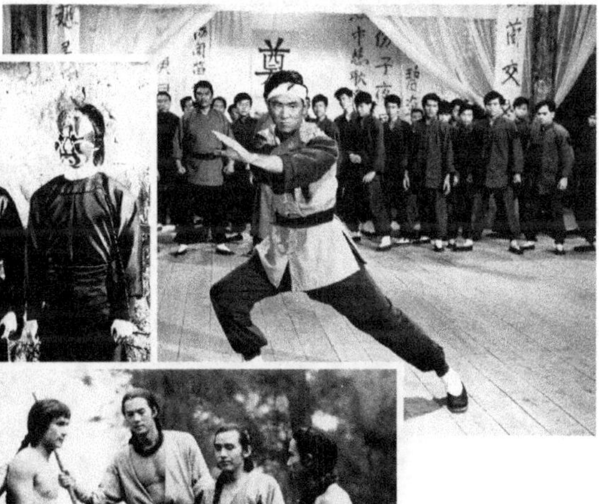

The 5 Deadly Venoms

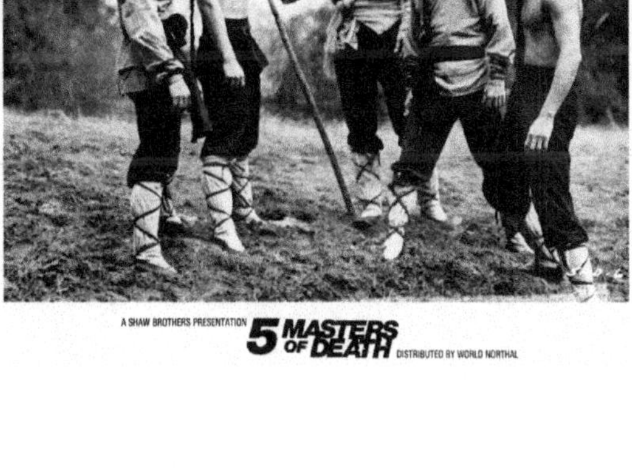

A SHAW BROTHERS PRESENTATION 5 MASTERS OF DEATH DISTRIBUTED BY WORLD NORTHAL

Picture identifications (clockwise from upper left):
Liu Chia-liang vs. Liu Chia-yung in *Legendary Weapons of China*; Liu Chia-hui vs. Wang Lung-wei in *Dirty Ho*; Lo Lieh in *King Boxer*; Jimmy Wang Yu in *The Chinese Boxer*; Meng Fei, Alexander Fu Sheng, Ti Lung, David Chiang, and Chi Kuan-chun in *5 Masters of Death*; Kuo Chui, Lo Mang, Lu Feng, Sun Chien, and Wei Pai in *The 5 Deadly Venoms*.

The Shaw Standard

It's a pleasure to present this chapter. For years there's been the impression that, following Bruce Lee's death, kung fu films lay fallow until the ascension of Jackie Chan. To a great degree that is true ... outside Hong Kong.

But inside Hong Kong, kings of kung fu still reigned, bringing excited audiences some of the best — if not the absolute best — kung fu films ever made. So how did this oversight happen? Because the producers and distributors of those cathartic kung fu movies kept them, for the most part, to themselves, for decades on end.

At the time of Bruce Lee's death, Hong Kong cinema was booming, and the main boomers were The Shaw Brothers Studio. Having emerged victorious some years prior from a cinematic death struggle with main competitor Cathay (aka Motion Picture and General Investments Limited) — following the death of Cathay boss Loke Wan Tho in a plane crash — Shaw Studios made great use of their advantage.

The Shaw Brothers Studio is considered the most venerable in South China, if for no other reason than being in continuous operation for more than eighty years. Starting out as Unique Film Productions in 1925, the company has always been controlled by the Shaw brothers — four siblings who also shared the name Run: Runje, Runde, Runme, and Run Run. While it has long been believed that the latter two monikers were somewhat condescending nicknames given to the youngest brothers by peers impressed with their errand boy skills at another Hong Kong studio, their handles were actually bestowed on them by their father, Shaw Yuh-hsuen, because the name meant "benevolence." In fact, the Runs carried on the family tradition by naming their own sons with variations of "Vee," which means "virtues."

By 1934, the Shaws had already established a full-fledged studio consisting of sound stages, film processing facilities, editing bays, screening rooms, and office space — while also managing an extensive circuit of cinemas throughout Southeast Asia. In the long term scheme of things, World War II was a minor blip as the brothers protected their investment by diversifying in banking, real estate, and amusement parks.

It was in 1949 that Runde finally renamed the operation Shaw Studios, but it wasn't until 1957, when the then-fifty-year-old Run Run Shaw decided to take the reins — that the company entered its golden era. Buying forty-six acres of land in the scenic Clearwater Bay area (for a mere forty-five cents per square foot!), Run Run announced the creation of Shaw Brothers (HK) Limited, and the internationally influential studio we know today was off and running.

It didn't reach full flower, however, until a full decade later when there were editing, dubbing, special effects, and film processing facilities, a dozen sound stages, and more than five hundred full-time writers, technicians, and staff members who worked in three eight-hour shifts, twenty-four hours a day. In addition, Run Run instituted the Shaw Actors Training School, complete with on-lot dorms for the graduates. At their best, the Shaw Brothers Studio could produce forty films a year, or a completed movie, from start to finish, every ten days.

For the next eighteen years, the Studio produced more than seven hundred films (dramas, comedies, musicals, etc.), of which approximately three hundred and fifty were martial art movies (both kung fu and wuxia) — cementing the subgenres, traditions, and stereotypes that the rest of the industry would exemplify, develop or elaborate upon. But no one could match the unmistakable Shaw Brothers "look." It was a lush, hyper-artificial look that bordered on its own sort of "Shaw Reality" — thanks to the studio's huge soundstages and expert technicians who ran the gamut from lighting to set decoration.

By the early seventies, their fame was international. U.S. studio

The Shaw Standard

interest led to a testing of American box office waters with the theatrical release of select, retitled, and dubbed studio fare just prior to the ascension of Bruce Lee (who worked for the Shaw competitor, Golden Harvest Studios, created by ex-Shaw Studio exec Raymond Chow). First, director Chang Ho-cheng's *King Boxer* (1972) became the cleverly renamed *Five Fingers of Death* (1973) in America, making veteran screen villain Lo Lieh the first international kung fu star.

Born in Indonesia on June 29, 1939, with the name Wang Lida, Lo Lieh moved to Hong Kong as a teenager, and miraculously avoided the standard operating racism that favored Hong Kong-born Chinese actors. Despite Lieh's exotic looks, his talent led to him securing both heroic and villainous roles shortly after his Shaw Acting School training. He became such a valued contributor that the studio allowed him the rare freedom to move between their productions and movies made for his own company, as well as independent producers. Lo worked until the end, supplementing his movie career with an extensive Hong Kong television resume. He died November 2, 2002, in Shenzhen, Guangzhou, China, having played a vital part in the golden age, new wave, and beyond.

Following the relative success of *Five Fingers of Death*, Chang Cheh's *The Water Margin* (1972) was hacked into *Seven Blows of the Dragon* (1973), giving U.S. audiences just a whiff of stars David Chiang and Ti Lung's charisma. There was even a fitful co-production with Hammer Films, *The Legend of the Seven Golden Vampires* (aka *Seven Brothers Versus Dracula*) in 1974, also starring Chiang.

All were washed away in America by the Bruce Lee phenomenon, whose 1973 death led to decades of shoddy exploitation, with but one gleaming U.S. exception. By the early 1980s, several years into Jackie Chan's HK reign, when competition between South Chinese movie studios was at its height, Shaw agreed to edit, pan-and-scan, and dub some of its kung fu films for a small New York company called World Northal, who hoped to sell the broadcast rights to independent television stations as part of the "Black Belt Theater" package (aka *Drive In Movie*).

Much to the Studio's reported surprise, these films became a big success in America, leading to five more seasons of the program, encompassing more than one hundred of the studio's best kung fu adventures. The acceptance of the films in the U.S. could not have come at a worse time for the studio. Much of its film unit earnings were reaped from keeping production costs down, which became increasingly difficult as the casts and crews discovered how popular they were in the rest of the world. There was even a rumor that Run Run threatened to fire any actor who gave themselves an English name.

The combination of employees' demands for profit participation, government pressure to break up their production-exhibition connection, and the overwhelming success of Golden Harvest's Jackie Chan led to Run Run's decision to shut his Studio's film units in the mid-1980s. Although the Shaws continued to benefit from its domestic television production and other businesses, Run Run flatly refused to allow a *Black Belt Theater VI* to be compiled, or to release his Studio's films to the burgeoning home entertainment market — despite the extra money it could reap the participants ... although many grumble it was because of that (allegedly the Studio didn't like to share the wealth and was excellent at holding a grudge).

For whatever reason, regardless of national and international demand, the Shaw Brothers Studio library of innovative and important films remained legally unseen for fifteen years. But finally, at the dawn of the new century, the vault doors were cracked open, and remastered digital versions of their influential motion pictures were slowly made available on DVD. Over the next eighty-four months, the films trickled throughout the world, finally making it to America, which still longed for a revisit to its dormant *Black Belt Theater/Drive In Movie*. And, with those films, came information

The Shaw Standard

— information that was also entombed in the Shaw Studio vaults until recently. They revealed a vital, integral part of kung fu film history.

Despite their many successful wuxia productions, Bruce Lee's success rocked the Shaw Studio status quo. Up until then, their kung fu films were of the swingy arm/limp leg variety — emblazoned by the convulsive success of director/writer Chang Cheh. Cheh was born in 1923 but only began his film career after World War II. He started as a scriptwriter but was soon writing, directing, and even scoring films he made in Taiwan. Even when China shut its cinemas to Taiwanese productions, Chang continued to write and direct, only this time for legitimate theater.

Finally, in 1957, an actress named Li Mei invited Chang to Hong Kong to write and direct a film for her. The resulting effort, *Wild Fire*, was something of a box office bomb, but it served to establish Chang in South China, where he explored all his skills by writing martial arts and romance novels, film reviews, and a newspaper column — all under different pseudonyms. He returned to the film industry in 1960, again as a scriptwriter, but with even more success. Two years later, he was invited to join the Shaw Brothers Studio, where he served as chief scriptwriter for five years, churning out more than twenty screenplays in that time. It was at the end of this initial tenure that he really hit pay dirt, by writing and directing *Tiger Boy*, starring (Jimmy) Wang Yu and Lo Lieh, in 1964.

Its success emboldened him to take on the entire basis of Hong Kong kung fu films. It had been twenty years since the end of World War II and all those hard-working husbands now had leisure time too. Besides, Chang liked looking at strong, handsome men, almost as much as he enjoyed watching American films. He especially appreciated the wild emotions of *Rebel Without a Cause* (1955) and the cathartic violence of *Bonnie and Clyde* (1967). He couldn't help but wonder what those two would look like, blended together and projected through a kung fu prism.

The result was *The One-Armed Swordsman* (1967), a truly revolutionary production that changed the way Hong Kong audiences watched movies. This tale of a Jiang Hu swordsman who is forced to chop off his own arm through the hateful machinations of his teacher's daughter (only to learn a new style, complete with a chopped-off sword), was a huge success. When the theater lights came up after the title character successfully wiped out the evil Long-Armed Devil's headquarters, the audience was not the same — figuratively and literally.

After years of Confucian morality and bloodless, unconvincing, stagy fights led by women "disguised" as men, *The One-Armed Swordsman* showed them a tortured antihero who thought nothing of slaughtering his enemies. And after all the abuse he had taken, the viewers went along with the slaughter — in fact, cheered it. And the slaughter was bloody. None of this swinging a sword and having the opponent just fall down stuff. Here, limbs were chopped off, blood spurted, and victims fell writhing.

Suddenly producer Runme Shaw, director Chang Cheh, remarkable screenwriter I Kuang, and star Wang Yu had the first million-dollar-grossing movie in Hong Kong history. And with it, Chang Cheh had established a new tradition that has become known as "yang gang (staunch masculinity)." Chang Cheh's yang gang led to the director being declared the "Godfather of the kung fu film" — creating a separate but equally successful genre to the wuxia flying swordspeople phantasmagoricals directed by such studio stalwarts as Ho Meng-hua (1975's *The Flying Guillotine*), Li Han-hsiang (*The Mad Monk*, 1977), and the aforementioned Chang Ho-cheng, among many others.

Naturally a sequel was called for, and *The Return of the One-Armed Swordsman* appeared in 1969, but not before the director cemented his stardom with two other films during the intervening year —

The Shaw Standard

The Assassin and *The Golden Swallow*, both starring Wang Yu. Both movies displayed Chang Cheh's priorities: manly men giving, and receiving, hyper-violence. The finale of both films find Wang Yu covered in blood — both his own and his enemies. But the actor wanted to boil his own blood.

To that end, he wrote and directed *The Chinese Boxer*, which was released in 1970, a full two years before Bruce Lee got his big Hong Kong break. It established the Japanese-hating, empty-hand martial art sub-genre Bruce revolutionized with *Fist of Fury*. By then, Yu was South China's biggest action star, beating his Japanese enemies into the ground, as well as his Shaw Studio contract. Bolting for Golden Harvest almost the moment *Return of the One-Armed Swordsman* was done, he added insult to injury by making *The One-Armed Boxer* in 1971, followed by what many consider his best movie, *Beach of the War Gods* (1972), which had him taking on the invading Japanese army single-handedly.

Wang Yu (aka Wang Zheng-quan) was born in Jiangsu Province, but little else was revealed in his official biography. Reportedly an avid swimmer and a "skilled student of karate," he showed little martial art skill in his films. Far from classically handsome, his screen persona was dark, small, and furtive. To compensate, he filled his films with slaughter and torment, always taking on dozens of attackers who he could wade through with a stiff chop here and a weak kick there. His action choreography looked more similar to American cliff-hanger serials than kung fu.

After grinding out a bunch of less and less distinguished flicks, the renamed Jimmy Wang Yu replaced Bruce in several internationally co-produced oddities following Lee's death. *A Man Called Tiger* (1973), *The Man from Hong Kong* (1975), and *A Queen's Ransom* (1976) had one thing in common: they were all laughably bad. The latter two also featured ex-007 George Lazenby, and all three also served to display just how good Bruce Lee had been. Wang's on-screen charisma and kung fu were negligible.

Yu retreated to Taiwan and into ultra-cheap efforts designed to trade on his previous successes: *One Armed Swordsman vs. Nine Killers* (1976), *Return of the Chinese Boxer* (1977), and, ironically, his most beloved film in the West, *The One-Armed Boxer vs. the Flying Guillotine* (aka *Master of the Flying Guillotine*, 1975), which heavily influenced *The Street Fighter* video games.

Meanwhile, Chang Cheh plunged on with nary a look back. The director seemed relieved to be done with Wang Yu, replacing him with David Chiang with hardly a blink. It was Chiang, an ex-choreographer and stuntman, who stared in *The New One-Armed Swordsman* in 1971, as well as at least a half dozen more in between. Chiang was part of a show business dynasty. His father was a popular star while his mother was a well-known actress. Eventually, both his brothers, Paul Chu and Derek Yee, would also make their mark in movies.

David was born in Suzhou, Jiangsu Province, on May 11, 1947, and given the name Jiang Weinan. Although educated at Chu Hai College in Hong Kong, no one doubted that he'd follow in his parents' footsteps, and, by the time he graduated he had already appeared in many films, most notably *The Call of the Nightbirds* (1965). Nevertheless, action called to him, and, once on his own, he presented himself as an agile, clever martial arts instructor on film sets. It wasn't long before the personable, stylish young man, then known as John Chiang Dawei, came to the attention of Chang Cheh, who invited him to join the Shaw studio in 1966.

While Chiang may have been even thinner and more diminutive than Wang Yu, his face communicated a more clever, rebellious, and mischievous demeanor than Yu's dark, sour expression. To off-set his stature, Cheh teamed him with a tall, majestic actor named Ti Lung. Born in China in 1946, then educated at the Eton School in Hong Kong, Ti originally went to work as a tailor. But finally, the man born with the name Tan Furong auditioned for a part in Chang Cheh's *Dead End* (1968). One look at the tall, sensitive, intelligent, well spoken, handsome young man and Cheh fell in love. Ti Lung was created and nurtured by Chang, who showcased him in dozens of movies — his sincere, imposing yang suitably served to Chiang's clever, brisk yin.

As the director remembered in his memoir, "Chiang was only [a] supporting actor in (his first Shaws film) *Dead End*, playing a garage repairman, but his 'cool' demeanor was second-to-none. So, in *The Duel* (his second Shaw film), Ti Lung was in the leading role. But in *Vengeance* (his third film), it was Chiang who played the lead...."

Once Cheh decided that David had the "lean and hungry" look he wanted to showcase, the smaller, more angular young man took precedence in the director's films over the increasingly majestic Ti Lung. It wouldn't be long before both men would chafe against Chang's predilections, but five years in "Cantowood" is like an entire career anywhere else.

Once Chang Cheh hit his stride, he started producing films by the seasons — four a year (often with the assistance of such co-directors as Pao Hsueh-li and Wu Ma). Some flicks, like *Vengeance* (1970), were box-office and critical successes. Others, like *The Anonymous Heroes* (1971) were contrived silliness. But soon the pair of stars and their director were known as "The Golden Triangle." It's a mark of Chang's talent and restlessness that he wasn't content to leave it at that.

Spotting a martial arts champion named Chen Kuan-tai, he decided that his forceful presence was made for his movies, and started a string of productions featuring him. Unlike many kung fu film stars, Chen started as a martial artist, not an actor. He began his training at the age of eight, and became extremely proficient in what was known as the "Monkey-King Split and Deflecting Arm" style. So proficient, in fact, that he won the light heavyweight championship at the South-East Asian Chinese Martial Arts Tournament in 1969.

He made his way into movies via *Huang Fei Hong Bravely Crushing the Fire Formation* (the last Huang movie of the early 1970s), but achieved stardom both in and out of the Shaw Studio system — maintaining his vehement streak of independence throughout his long career. By starring in both Ng See-yuen's independently produced milestone *The Bloody Fists* and Chang Cheh's *The Boxer from Shantung* in 1972, his fame, and reputation, was ensured. But it wasn't until Cheh featured all his new stars in 1973's *The Blood Brothers* that superstardom beckoned to all four.

Based on a classic tale, *The Assassination of General Ma*, it told of a lover's triangle between two men and a woman as well as three friends. It is set in the mid-nineteenth century during the Taiping Rebellion and is based on actual people and events. Chiang and Kuan-tai are highwaymen until Lung convinces them to join the Imperial Army. As Lung excels, his lust for absolute power begins to corrupt him absolutely. He has an affair with the Kuan-tai character's wife, then has Kuan-tai killed. Chiang takes revenge for his dead friend on his ex-friend, and then willingly gives himself up and is executed.

Ti Lung's conflicted power-monger was perfectly set off against Chiang's love-sick idealist, with Kuan-tai's desperate nobility trying to span the chasm. The actors were rarely better, but the result was that they no longer required Cheh's tutelage, which was becoming stiff with repetition. The director compensated by filling his subsequent films with a multitude of actors — carefully studying them for future stardom. Meanwhile, he used them to continue making crowd-pleasing favorites.

The Water Margin (1972) and its long-awaited sequel *All Men Are Brothers* (1975) were two more Cheh milestones, based on the classic novel by Shi Nai-an called *Outlaws of the Marshes*, written in the fourteenth century. It concerned the 108 Mountain Brothers — a famous band of righteous mercenaries in the eleventh century (Sung dynasty) who fight bad guys where they find them. But Cheh truly found his niche in 1975 with *Five Shaolin Masters* (aka *Five Masters of Death*) — the fourth in Cheh's Shaolin series, featuring his new discovery Fu Sheng. (Alexander) Fu Sheng was a remarkable actor, having, at different times, been referred to as the Bob Hope, or Jimmy Cagney, or even the James Dean of Hong Kong. He was equally adept as a lecherous comic, a pugnacious, wise-cracking hero, or as a brooding rebel (who, coincidentally, died way too young in a tragic car crash). Like Cagney, he was also a beloved collaborator who elicited nothing but praise from every director and actor he worked with.

As far as Asian critics were concerned, *Five Shaolin Masters* marked the start of Cheh's decline. As far as American fans were concerned, it marked the start of his ascension. Indeed, he no longer seemed to be looking for relevant images. Now he seemed intent on producing one-hundred-percent superhero entertainment. He seemed to stop taking his movies' histrionics seriously and got down to some serious mayhem.

The film was based on a famous story — the Shaolin Temple's destruction and the survival and vengeance of its escaping students. It teamed Ti Lung and David Chiang with Fu Sheng, as well as two more Cheh hopefuls, a ferret-faced martial artist named Chi Kuan-chun and a cute-looking fellow named Meng Fei. Together they take on early eighteenth-century enemies led by actor (Johnny) Wang Lung-wei — a brutish, mustached presence who was to become one of the most versatile villains in the kung fu genre.

Here is a telling distinction of kung fu movies. Wang Lung-wei is not a versatile actor; he is a versatile fighter. It is his particular skill that he can make defeats by everyone from Fu Sheng to David Chiang look believable. When Wang Lung-wei is ultimately defeated, whether by a ninety-eight-pound weakling or a hulking muscle man, Johnny makes it work. He ranks as one of the Shaw Studio's all time greatest villains. To beat him this time, Fu Sheng and Chi Kuan-chun learn the Shaolin animal styles, Meng Fei learns the "rolling" style (a form of wrestling that David Chiang did in *Seven Blows of the Dragon*), Ti Lung becomes master of the bo (aka staff or pole), and Chiang uses the steel whip (he hurls the sharpened point through two men at once during the climactic free-for-all).

Only Sheng, Chiang, and Lung survive at the fade-out, but this film's success was to lead to many other Shaolin movies made by Chang Cheh over the next two years — all featuring Fu Sheng. In a very short time, this personable actor had won over audiences with his boyish, impish charm. Even when playing a serious character, he had a wit and prickly style unmatched by any other action star working. Cheh secured Sheng's future by starring him in *The Chinatown Kid* (1977) and the *Brave Archer* series (1978-79).

The former film was probably one of the best modern kung fu movies made at that time. In it, Sheng plays an impoverished troublemaker who is forced to flee Hong Kong to an obviously backlot San Francisco. There he slaves in a Chinese restaurant, meeting up with a quiet student (Sun Chien). Because Fu is such a good martial artist, he runs afoul of two warring street gangs, led by muscular Lo Mang on one side and sophisticated Kuo Chui on the other. Sheng is seduced by wealth and power, but when Sun Chien's character becomes addicted to the drugs supplied by the gang, Sheng attacks his new bosses, killing all, but dying himself.

The Chinatown Kid was more realistic than most modern chop-socky pictures, and Chang Cheh pulls off one of his cleverest metaphors in the form of a digital watch. It represents the brave new American world to Sheng's naive character, and his actions all revolve around attaining and sustaining the watch. At the end, as he's dying, he offers it to Chien — who takes it. The whole business is obvious, but extremely effective.

Sheng proved his mettle in period pieces directly afterward with *The Brave Archer* (aka *Kung Fu Warlords*) series, in which he played a Sung dynasty hero named Kuo Tsing, who did precious little archery. Hong Kong audiences lapped up these colorful, convoluted epics — full of duels between fighters of at least equal ability, in sumptuous period costumes, on exact, intricately detailed period sets. They were crazy, silly, and, as the series continued through two sequels and an abortive fourth feature, *The Brave Archer and his Mate* (1982), increasingly unfocused. But the *Kid* and the *Archer* were enough to cement Chang Cheh's next career-changing brainstorm.

Using the "team" concept from *Five Masters of Death,* why not film a series of lively kung fu movies all starring the same actors in basically the same roles? Cheh seemed to think that his mistake was using ambitious actors for his first team (Chiang, Lung, Kuan-tai, Sheng, etc.). For his next, he'd recruit lesser stars to ensure greater longevity. Bit by bit, his new team took shape in the Fu Sheng *Brave Archer* and Shaolin series. Then, in 1978, they were introduced, fully formed, in *The Five Venoms* (aka *Five Deadly Venoms*) — a hunk of kinetic kung fu grand guignol.

In this film, set in the fifteenth century, a dying teacher taught five masked students the deadliest forms of "poison kung fu" known: snake, centipede, lizard, toad, and scorpion. None of the students knew each other at the time, but now several had teamed to become criminals. The sifu tells his last student, who knows a bit of all five arts, to find the students and stop their crimes. From this simple premise, Cheh wrought martial arts extremism. The villains practice esoteric, nasty killing styles. They defeat each other with a solid gold, knife-lined casket, pins in noses, knives in ears, as well as their own unbelievable skills. In the finale, when the venoms fight, the heroes literally walk up the walls and stand there. It is all done with bold, unapologetic style.

Thus the new team was born. Kuo Chui (aka Kwok Chun-fung aka Kwok Choi aka Philip Kwok Choi aka Philip Kwok) was always the main hero and always played a street-smart supreme fighter who hid behind the guise of a beggar, transient, or criminal. Born and raised in Taiwan, his father was a comic actor, but Kuo was only interested in action. Soon he was training in Taiwanese Opera as an acrobat and stuntman, where Chang Cheh discovered him in 1973. Because he could do things almost no other Taiwan stuntman could, and was about the same height as Fu Sheng, Chang Cheh brought him to Hong Kong, and made him the leader of what he called "The Third Class" (following the likes of first class man Jimmy Wang Yu, and second class man David Chiang).

Chiang Sheng was known by American fans as "cutie-pie," and indeed he was. Just as small and thin as David Chiang, he almost always played the acrobatic partner to Kuo. Lu Feng almost always played the insidious traitor who lures heroes into his traps. Like Kuo, this duo was also discovered by Chang in Taiwan and brought over to star in Hong Kong. But unlike Kuo, they did not have the luck to make a go of it outside Shaw Studio walls.

While Lu Feng, who was always saddled with the villain roles, was an intensely private man, Chiang Sheng took things more personally. When his work as Chang's co-choreographer and assistant director didn't lead to bigger things, "cutie-pie" reportedly turned bitter and self-abusive. He died in 1991, at the age of forty, of a heart attack. Kuo Chui has been widely quoted saying that his friend was alone, depressed, drinking heavily, and actually died of a broken heart.

Lo Mang almost always played the thick-muscled (and thick-headed) Hong Kong Chinese of the group. Like Kuo, he was able to create a career for himself away from Chang Cheh, but unlike Kuo, he stayed within Shaw Studio walls when the Taiwanese acrobats headed home near the end of the Shaw Studios film unit era. Born

The Shaw Standard

in China, Lo started kung fu training in his early teens, and still takes pride in working out every day. Finally there was Sun Chien, a leg fighter supposedly held back in his career because he was thought to be Korean. In fact, it's reported that he was born in Taiwan (with the name Sun Jian-yuan), where he was recruited by Chang.

Cheh also used a variety of regular actors in secondary roles (including Wei Pai, Yu Tai-ping, and Wang Li, among others) but these five were the main unit for more than a dozen thrillers that were unique in their extremism. The tone was set by their second movie, *Crippled Avengers* (aka *Mortal Combat* or *Return of the Five Deadly Venoms,* 1978). The venerable Chen Kuan-tai played a Ming Dynasty kung fu master driven mad by his wife's death and son's disfigurement (his enemies chopped off the boy's forearms and the mother's legs). Years later, Kuan-tai has taught his son (Lu Feng) the Tiger style and replaced his limbs with metal arms that elongate and shoot darts.

From then on, the wealthy man cripples whomever he doesn't like. He blinds a trinket salesman (Kuo), deafens a blacksmith (Lo), chops the feet off a passerby (Sun), and renders simple a hero who wants to avenge them (Chiang), by tightening a steel band around his skull. The four unite, find a sifu, and learn new kung fu techniques to off-set their handicaps — the footless man even getting remarkably effective metal feet. They crash the villain's birthday party and make sure he, and his son, don't have one to grow on.

There is hardly a believable second in this adventure, but as a kung fu movie it works, as do such following adventures as *The Daredevils* (1978) — an early Republic of China conflict in which street performers avenge themselves on a corrupt general (about the only Venoms film in which the Kuo Chui character dies) — and *The Kid With the Golden Arm* (1979). Here Kuo Chui plays a drunken-style master who aids a hero-laden escort service trying to get a wagon of gold to a famine area during the Ming dynasty.

The ax-, sword-, spear-, and wine-jug-carrying heroes face masters of the Iron Palm (which leaves a black imprint that slowly kills the victim), the Iron Fan (a gigantic, sword-edged, steel war fan), the Iron Head (really, a man with a steel forehead shield), and the infamous Kid with the Golden Arm himself — a master of an art that makes him invulnerable to blades.

To see any of the Chang Cheh movies of this period is not to believe them, but to enjoy them for their kung fu craziness and exuberant bloodiness. When asked why he was depending upon such supposed "ugly" actors, Chang reportedly replied, "They become beautiful when they move."

And move they did. "Mr. Chang himself cannot handle morning shifts," Kuo Chui explained. "Usually we would do an eleven o'clock shift, or a one o'clock shift. He would arrive, at the earliest, say three or four o'clock, because he had to come back at night to write scripts, and do other things. We were actors, assistant directors, martial art directors, wire-workers, and prop-men. I mean, we actually helped with props. We were rather busy all around. As long as it can help, we would do it. In terms of shooting times, we must wrap at eleven o'clock at night. We were always punctual. So it's a steady shift —normally nine hours."

In addition to all his other duties, the director even started searching out new talent while teaming his Venoms with Fu Sheng and Ti Lung for *Ten Tigers of Kwantung* (1979), a Cheh mess which juggled two stories through flashbacks, involved Huang Fei-hong's father and cousins, and had a man's head kicked off at the climax. Despite its entertainment value, the audience was becoming inured to the director's cavalier approach.

That out of his system, Cheh took his Venoms through *The Spearmen of Death* (1980) and *Masked Avengers* (1981). They fought spear-topped flags in the former and particularly nasty tridents in the latter, both about eight feet long. It gave the stars the chance to strut their stuff, but also the director to overuse a particularly harsh sound effect whenever blade entered flesh.

The final complete Venoms movie was *House of Traps* (1981), which pushed all Chang Cheh's concepts to the razor's edge ... literally. In the Sung dynasty, an evil man hides incriminating evidence in a death-filled pagoda and hires kung fu criminals to guard it. Kuo Chui is the "Black Fox," a tarnished knight-errant who signs on as a guard, but actually intends to secure the evidence for honorable Judge Pao (an actual Sung Dynasty lawman who also figured in the original *Five Venoms* film). But first heroes and villains alike must be sliced, diced, and slaughtered by the place's spike-growing doors, spear-hurling walls, arrow-shooting panels, ax-swinging beams, and most impressively, razor-lined stairs.

By then the Venoms themselves had pretty much had it. There had been some jockeying for space, leading to some films featuring just a few of them, which, in turn, led to a sad realization. Their careers compromised by Chang's increasingly repetitive, diffident approach, Kuo, Chiang, and Lu returned to Taiwan in 1982 to make the politically-incorrectly-titled *Hero Defeating Japs* (aka *Ninja in the Deadly Trap*), leaving Lo Mang behind to help Cheh make his last great movie (while Sun Chien reluctantly jumped ship to work for other Shaw Studio directors).

Five Element Ninja (aka *Super Ninjas*, 1982) starred new discovery (Fourth Class man?) Chien Tien-chi as a virtuous member of a white-clad kung fu school victimized by a jealous, rival kung fu school who hire ninja to make sure the good guys don't win their up-coming challenge. After poisoning the heroes' sifu, who must isolate himself for a month, the ninja issue a new challenge. Expecting the usual, each noble warrior arrives at the predetermined location, only to be massacred by sun ninja using blinding, booby-trapped shields, wood ninja disguised in a forest, water ninja who use liquid as hiding places, fire ninja who burn their ill-equipped adversaries, and earth ninja who disembowel from below (leading to a show-stopping moment when a wounded kung fu student steps on his own hanging intestine). Lo Mang plays an honorable student left to guard his sifu, but foolishly allows in a supposedly abused woman, who's actually a kunoichi (female ninja) spy.

This is an outlandishly entertaining, strongly structured, thriller. The second section of the film portrays the ninja attack on the heroes' headquarters, the immolation of the sifu, and the crucifixion of Lo Mang on his teacher's barricaded door. The third section shows Tien-chi coincidentally finding another sifu in the outlands who just happens to be an expert on the shinobi no mono (shadow warriors). There he turns the surviving hero and three other students into ninjabusters(!).

The fourth and final section is ludicrously enjoyable as the ninja challenge is recreated — only this time by kung fu fighters who know what they're up against and are prepared to fight sun, wood, water, fire, and earth with sun, wood, water, fire, and earth … or, in this case, with a specially made version of what looks like a six-foot long Swiss Army knife. The finale explodes as Tien-chi sacrifices his life in order to literally tear the ninja master in half. When asked why, he understates, "I don't know … I guess I was obsessed."

It was as if the director was answering his growing group of critics and dissatisfied customers. Tired, burned out, and at the mercy of his diversions, Chang Cheh continued working, but made increasingly disjointed, dismissible and even sad films like the aptly-titled *The Weird Man* (1983) the accurately-titled *Attack of the Joyful Goddess* (1983), and the unfortunately-titled *Dancing Warrior* (1984).

Even his anniversary film, *Shanghai 13* (1984) — designed to reunite many of the stars he made famous over his career (including Jimmy Wang Yu, Ti Lung, David Chiang, Chi Kuan-chun, Chiang Sheng, Lu Feng, and Cheng Tien-chi, among others) — was embroiled in a rights dispute that kept the inexpensive, but fun and fight-filled, film from ever being shown in Hong Kong or legally released on DVD.

Happily Chang Cheh lived long enough to see his great films rediscovered and rechampioned — taking his rightful place as the "Godfather of the kung fu film." He wrote his memoir shortly before his death in 2002 at the age of eighty, concluding, in part, "'It's easier to advance than to retreat' is the way of self preservation and ease of mind … it takes a talent to spot a talent … (and) it also takes a talent to judge a talent." His talent was undeniable.

The most important talent he spotted went on to become the master of kung fu movies. Liu Chia-liang (aka Lau Kar-leung) was born in 1936 and grew up in Guangzhou until his family moved to Hong Kong when he was twelve. His father was Liu Zhan, a well-known hung gar teacher who ran the Hua Chiang Martial Arts Society schools. Liang's dad was the favorite student of the esteemed Lam Sai-wing (better known by kung fu film fans as "Butcher Wing"), who, in turn, had been the favorite student of none other than the real Huang Fei-hong himself.

So, was it any wonder that Liang excelled in this martial arts family and that he got his start in motion pictures in Kwan Tak-hing's Huang Fei-hong series? Like Brandon Lee, Liang was first reluctant to toil in his father's shadow, but he was so bullied at school that his father convinced him to start learning the family style at the age of seven. Not surprisingly, Liang took to it like a duck to water — especially when his father always connected martial arts to "martial virtue."

In a short time, Liang's learning became insatiable. His main style was Hung Style Boxing (hung gar, Hung Family Fist), but he also soaked up eagle's claw, wing chun, choy li fut, baqua, taichi, qigong, and others — to the point that, if he was shown a style, he could immediately replicate it. Thanks to his father, his father's teacher, and his father's teacher's teacher, Liu Chia-liang intrinsically understood that kung fu was a combination of physical logic and psychological understanding. And then experience taught him that serenity powered strength — both inner and outer strength.

The same was true of filmmaking. At that time, there weren't enough skilled stuntmen to do anything but real martial arts in the Huang Fei-hong films, especially since Kwan Tak-hing came from a background of Cantonese opera. Although he resembled the real Fei-hong, Hing was not very familiar with Hung Style kung fu, so Liang, his father, and Shih Kien (who played the predominant villain in the series) slowly taught him on set. Naturally, Liang was soon featured as a character on screen — usually that of an arrogant punk. But already he knew he wanted more.

"I wanted to be a director as soon as I entered the industry," he was quoted as saying. And the best way for an ambitious kung fu man to do that was through action choreography. He made his first official foray into the job on the independently produced *South Dragon North Phoenix* (1963), where he met Tang Chia — the man who was to become known as the "action director's action director." Born in 1938, Tang had been working in show business since he was fifteen. His martial arts training in Peking Opera performances led to kung fu work in early Chinese cinema.

Liang and Tang were impressed by each other's skills, so they agreed to team up. It was perfect timing. There were so few knowledgeable choreographers that their talents were regularly in demand. Within two years, they joined the Shaw Brothers Studio. They started collaborating with a few directors, but soon zeroed in on Chang Cheh. After all, the three seemed made for each other. Cheh admired and appreciated good kung fu, but knew little about it. But he wanted someone who could create on-screen kung fu that matched the quality of his concepts and dramatics.

Liang was so good at it that he was soon promoted to the then-new rank of "action director." Whenever there was a fight scene,

The Shaw Standard

Chang would step aside and Liang would take over, placing the camera, instructing the cast and crew, and even saying the magic words, "camera, rolling, cut." Liang and Tang worked with Chang on virtually every film up until 1975, contributing substantially to Cheh's success. By then Liang had also been instrumental in establishing a Shaw Studio kung fu training program and developing the skills of every action star the studio promoted. So it was probably inevitable that Liang's desire to have total control of his work would lead to friction. It finally came to a head after *Disciples of Shaolin* (1975).

For years, apparently, Cheh did what he could to keep Liang from being given his own film. For, as Liang quoted: "'colleagues are like enemy nations.'" In other words, if someone knows you are that good, why would they want you competing with them for the same audience? Finally, on the set of *Marco Polo* (1975), Chang Cheh and Liu Chia-liang went their separate ways. Tang Chia eschewed the director's chair, satisfied to remain choreographing films for other Shaw Studio directors.

Tang's work was prized for its inventive seamlessness and versatility. Chia seemed as comfortable working with two actors as he was with two dozen, and was equally adept at empty-hand fighting as he was with virtually any legendary wushu weapon. He was also known as an exceptional collaborator, willing to work closely with the director rather than insist that his fight scenes be filmed traditionally. The results were movies that pushed the envelope of classical wuxia.

Liang, meanwhile, was sick of studio politics. In fact, he was even threatening to tear up his Shaw contract and go to Los Angeles to open martial arts studios with Tan Tao-liang (aka Delon Tam, the star of such enjoyable independent films as 1977's *Flash Legs*, and 1980's *The Leg Fighters*). But famed Shaw Studio producer Mona Fong finally gave this essentially untried, unknown talent his own movie. There was method to Mona's seeming madness. Bruce Lee had shaken up cinema, the city, and the box office with his realistic, convincing, and believable kung fu. Of all the people working in the industry, the one person who might match him, kick for kick, technique for technique, was Liu Chia-liang. Ironically, it turned out that Liang had known Bruce very well when they were both kids.

"Bruce Lee was passionate about kung fu," Liang said in an interview. "It was his life. He introduced it to the whole world. But he was missing something. That was the 'wu de' (martial arts philosophy) and the 'xiu yang' (self-control). He hit to hurt, for the pleasure of the strikes. He was too much a Westerner. The traditional Chinese courtesy was alien to him. When you watch his movies, the violence and the power of his blows can't be missed. For us, the principle is 'dian dao ji zhi' (to use chi to power the strike, using 'soft' to support and complete the 'hard').

"Someone is really strong in kung fu only if he's able to do that. Bruce Lee was limited in his knowledge. Likewise, his 'zhaoshu' (gestures) were also limited. But there were elements derived from aikido, tae kwon do, karate, Western boxing — all that, with a little Chinese kung fu. And Bruce was very smart. He was a superb actor. He applied himself diligently, and when he practiced kung fu, he gave it his all."

Liang admired Bruce, but did not want to epitomize him. So, instead of a straight-out kung fu thriller, he started his directing career with a then-unheard-of "kung fu satire" called *Fighting God* in Hong Kong and *The Spiritual Boxer* (1975) in the United States. He filmed it in a month with a cast of unknowns (save for cameos in the prologue by friends Ti Lung and Chen Kuan-tai). A kung fu comedy? The studio thought he was insane. But it made over a million dollars — an almost unheard-of amount at that time, especially by a first time filmmaker. Master Liang had cemented the kung fu comedy genre.

Given that encouragement, Liang finally felt it was time to show his peers what he could really do. It was time to put all his kung fu on screen and balance it with his love of martial virtue. It paid off in his second film, *Challenge of the Masters* (1976), which established his reputation for making a traditional concept seem brand new. In this case, it was the Huang Fei-hong movies. Liang had seen them all, been in a bunch of them, and figured it was about time that someone made movies about the character's youth — the all-important genesis of the ultimate Confucian hero.

The film started on a striking note — one that would be repeated throughout the director's career. The credits played over a stark soundstage. There was no attempt to make the environment realistic. It was a huge white expanse with two towers of Chinese calligraphy around which two fighters practiced their forms and stances. The fighters were Chen Kuan-tai, portraying Huang's teacher Lu Ah-tsai, and Liu Chia-hui (aka Lau Kar-fai aka Gordon Liu), the adopted brother of the director, playing Huang Fei-hong.

For years, many thought that Hui was Liang's real brother, but it was not so. "I don't belong to the Liu family," Gordon told me, "but when I was nine years old I started to practice at his martial art school. His mother liked me very much and treated me like her son. Then when I was about twenty years old I joined their working family. That's when I changed my name. My real name is Sin Kam-hei. At first I had no interest in shooting any movies. I started as a messenger, at night I studied accountancy, and then I worked as an accountant for two years."

But that all changed when Liang gave him the leading role in *Challenge of the Masters*. The whole film was a family affair — both blood and adopted — with Hui as the star, the director playing the villain, and his real brother, Liu Chia-yung (Lau Kar-wing), playing the policeman who dies trying to capture the killer. But, more important than merely the plot, Liang used it as a vehicle to introduce a strong current of martial virtue into his movies, and set out to make a film that was actually about the relationship of a kung fu student to his or her sifu.

As such, probably the most important piece of dialogue in the film was "Forgive man and forebear. Never forget humility and kindness. That's the way real kung fu should be." Of course that doesn't mean that evil people should go unpunished. In film after film, Liang showed that by seeking to better your own kung fu, you will be able to correctly show those who would do harm the error of their ways.

What truly set Liu Chia-liang apart was that his films were really all about kung fu. His were the only ones in which the kung fu couldn't be removed without negating the movie. In every other director's filmography, the kung fu could be replaced by guns, or swords, or boxing, or whatever. Not in a Liu Chia-liang film. That's one of the reasons he's the true "Master of the Kung Fu Movie."

He cemented his reputation in his next film, which has stayed with anyone who ever saw it. *Executioners from Shaolin* (aka *Executioners of Death*, 1977) was nominally about the surviving temple monks taking vengeance on Pei Mei (played by Lo Lieh), the white-browed hermit, who betrayed them. But it was actually about the creation of hung gar, the Hung Family Fist. It contained ample amounts of the things that made Liang famous: screenplay wit, cinematic inventiveness, and superlative kung fu.

One of the film's highlights is on the wedding night of Shaolin survivor and tiger style kung fu master Hung Hsi-kuan (played by Chen Kuan-tai) with crane stylist Fang Yung-chun (played by Queen of Shaw Studio kung fu Lily Li). In their honeymoon haven, she sets him a challenge. If he can open her crane legs with his tiger style, he wins. But once he eventually does, and their son, Hung wen-ting (Yung Wang-yu, star of *The Spiritual Boxer*) grows up, the film explodes into repeated attempts to defeat Pei Mei's consummate iron skin kung fu, using such esoteric, fascinating devices as a metal statue with rolling pinballs that symbolize the monk's moving internal weak point.

But only when the son combines his father's and mother's techniques — creating hung gar — does the villain get his bloody comeuppance. *Executioners from Shaolin* succeeded grandly on an emotional, kung fu, and box office level, so Liang pressed his advantage by suggesting his next film be even more unusual.

"No one had ever done a movie like this without a love story," Gordon Liu maintained. "But in this film, the love story was with kung fu."

36th Chamber of Shaolin (aka *Master Killer*) remains a milestone in the industry and a central classic of the genre. Although book-ended by the now stereotypical tale of a young man escaping persecution by learning vengeful kung fu at the Shaolin Temple, it's actually anchored by an extended set of training sequences, taking up almost a full hour of the film's 116-minute running time.

Yu Te (Gordon Liu) is taught the meaning of many things at the temple, having to discover much about himself before he even enters the first of thirty-five chambers of learning and enlightenment. He discovers his own balance, lightness, and intelligence before he is subjected to the tortures that pass for training. To build up his arms, he carries water in heavy buckets, but knives are attached to his forearms so that if he lowers his limbs he will stab himself in the side. He must hit a gigantic bell with a sledgehammer that has a twelve-foot-long handle to strengthen his wrists. He must smash hanging weights with his head to build his skull strength. He must endure and master all of that and more before he actually starts to learn to fight. Then he must become skilled with his hands, feet, and weapons.

To the surprise of his teachers, he excels in all thirty-five chambers within five years and is offered the sifu-ship (lead teacher's position) of any one of them … that is, until another high-ranking monk, played by Li Hai-sheng (another well-known genre villain), suggests that they fight. If the newly dubbed San Te can defeat his double butterfly-swords-style, then he can choose his chamber. In his first two tries, San Te is soundly defeated. Wandering in the bamboo forest nearby, he invents the three-sectional staff — three thin wooden poles approximately two feet long, each joined by a short length of chain. With this he defeats the two short swords of his opponent and is allowed to choose his chamber.

Instead, he suggests instituting a thirty-sixth chamber, a place where other young men could be trained to resist Manchu treachery. The remainder of the movie moves San Te out of the temple, where he takes revenge on his family's killers and recruits the first thirty-sixth-chamber students. Many Western viewers wonder why so much emphasis is placed on incidental characters during these climactic sequences, but Eastern audiences know that each of these men San Te comes across are actually famous historic characters — including some who had been portrayed in previous Liang films.

36th Chamber of Shaolin was an amazing movie. It was the training sequences that made it fascinating and involving. It also secured Liu Chia-hui's stardom. Although wiry, babyfaced, and, when playing a Shaolin monk, bald, Hui had the internal power and acting chops to cement his legacy. The same was true of Liang. Just as he had before, rather than continue to grind out the expected, he changed his approach.

Shaolin Mantis (aka *Deadly Mantis,* 1978) marked David Chiang's only appearance in a Liu Chia-liang film. His very presence marks this movie as a change of pace, and, of course, his kung fu never looked better. In it, he plays Wei Feng, a Ching dynasty official who investigates a suspected family of revolutionaries. His presence there leads to a romance with the head of the household's granddaughter, played by Huang Hsing-hsiu, which results in marriage. Only then does he discover the proof of the family's treachery and has to fight his way out, with the help of his newlywed wife. She dies during their escape, leading Feng to develop the mantis fist so that he can go back and disembowel the grandfather, played by Liu Chia-yung.

Although up until that moment the film is the usually entertaining Liang mix of character development and precise, dazzling martial arts, he distinguishes the film with its ending. Although soundly cheered by the imperial court, Feng is poisoned by his own father for helping the traitorous Chings suppress the Chinese people. Liang had neatly and surprisingly skewered another genre tradition by pointing out the yin-yang aspect of Chinese history. In this movie, David Chiang played a heroic *villain*.

But the director had more in store for his amazed audience. Just when the studio thought he couldn't be any more revolutionary, out comes *Heroes of the East* (aka *Challenge of the Ninja* aka *Shaolin vs. Ninja*) the following year. Here was a kung fu movie in which no one was seriously hurt, let alone killed. Gordon Liu Chia-hui (with hair this time) plays Ho Tao, a wealthy, young, modern man who marries a Japanese girl in an arranged ceremony. The couple's only problem is that they differ in terms of which country's martial arts are superior.

The wife, Kun Tse (Yuko Mizuno), is played as some sort of inconsiderate, stubborn, semi-lunatic who throws martial arts tantrums even when her husband consistently defeats her techniques. She finally resorts to ninjutsu to "win." Tao firmly condemns what he considers this "art of cheating," suggesting that the goal is to learn at all costs rather than win at all costs. Naturally, his wife throws a hissy fit and runs back home to be consoled by her teacher (Shoji Kurata). When Tao writes a baiting letter (which is suggested by his comedy-relief servant), the Japanese family misunderstands and sends their best fighters to challenge him.

"I think that was my most memorable film," Gordon said. "Liu

Chia-liang hired seven Japanese people to shoot it with me, but six of the seven did not know anything about acting. They only knew how to fight! There was swordplay, karate, judo, wrestling, weapons ... and they were all senseis, not actors! With actors, we can communicate with each other; 'Hey, we're only filming and not really fighting.' But these senseis really fought. Every morning at [the start] of our ten o'clock shift, I would arrive to find the Japanese already down there, training. Oh, how scary that was. It was like we were preparing for a real fight. But, finally, later, I realized that they were just very serious about what they were doing, and not looking to beat me up. Now *that* was memorable."

From there on it's one long bout, with each of the Japanese confronting Tao on each successive day. Initially, he overcomes a samurai swordsman with a Chinese taichi sword, and then he goes up against a spear man, a karate fighter, a tonfa pro (almost all TV cops use modified tonfas instead of nightsticks), a nunchaku expert, and an Okinawan sai master (the sai is a small trident with the center spike longer than the others) before facing Kurata's ninja-crab skills. In the end, Tao has his now-understanding wife back, and defeats all the fighters — but also gains their respect through his adherence to Confucian, as well as Jiang Hu, ways.

Audiences were delighted by Liu Chia-liang's ability to extend the kung fu genre beyond its traditional limitations, so they readily accepted a movie that featured sympathetic, non-insidious Japanese. Although they were the bad guys of the piece, their villainy came from misunderstanding and a lack of communication, not the kind of cruel hatred that marked the Japanese villains of Lo Wei's, Chang Cheh's, and Jimmy Wang Yu's films. Under the guise of a so-called simple kung fu film, Liang had created a classic that was instrumental in making him and Gordon superstars in Japan as well.

Finally, the director stepped back with his first sequel. *The Spiritual Boxer Part II* (1979) was an enjoyable kung fu comedy showcase for the star, Yung Wang-yu. Even so, the director added one more ingredient to the mix, which would serve as ample inspiration to his peers — Chinese supernatural mythology. Other directors would do more with the comedy and horror aspects he pioneered, so Liang decided on another tact — one which really only he could pull off.

The title *Dirty Ho* (1979) never fails to elicit Western giggles, although it refers to the sneaky disposition of title character, Ho Chih, rather than a grimy prostitute (a literal translation of the Chinese title is something like "Lazy-head He"). Beyond that unfortunate title, this Ching dynasty classic is one of the landmarks of kung fu choreography. Liang uses the story of how an incognito prince uses street people to protect himself from the assassination of plots of a jealous brother as a showcase for some of the cleverest, most complex, kung fu ever captured on film.

Prince Wang Ghing-chin is played by Gordon Liu Chia-hui (again with hair), but the street-thief and con-man title character is played by Yung Wang-yu, who helps establish the film's class-warfare themes and superb action direction in their first scene together — where the prince secretly makes a female musician (Kara Hui Ying-hung) appear to be a consummate fighter through unnoticed manipulation. As impressive as that scene is, it has nothing on the subsequent fight sequences.

Next comes an assassination attempt in a wine bar. The wonderful Wang Lung-wei plays a killer connoisseur, who, with the help of his assistant server (Hsaio Ho), attempts to murder the prince while serving esoteric wines named for the kung fu styles they then attempt to kill him with. The prince protects himself and foils their plans, also using the same techniques, in such a way that no one in the wine bar, including Ho Chih, is aware of what's happening. This is a milestone martial arts moment that remains one of the finest kung fu scenes ever conceived and executed.

During another attempt on his life in an art shop, Wang's leg is injured, so the duped con man and the prince must overlook their societal ranking to serve as each other's literal and figurative crutches. Together they battle their way back to the emperor's palace to face the corrupt general who is masterminding the attempts (Lo Lieh). Beyond the wealth of brilliant kung fu on display, Asian film critics were especially impressed with the climax, in which the prince, now done with Ho's help, literally tosses him away in the finale's freeze frame.

Dirty Ho revealed another facet of Liang's achievement. It was in this picture that the director's ability to impart character and personality simply through movement became clear. Although Liang had already shown how interested he was in character and story development through images and dialogue, here he openly demonstrates his choreographic genius. A viewer can tell what a character is like simply by the way he does kung fu. Liang adds and subtracts subtle flourishes of movement to achieve this effect. It is wonderful.

Liang put his own face on the line in *Mad Monkey Kung Fu* (1979). Although he had been featured in *Challenge of the Masters*, here he was playing a major role. It was that of a turn-of-the-(twentieth) century performer, who, with his sister (Kara Hui Ying-hung), travels from town to town performing monkey-style kung fu. Lo Lieh plays a cliché: a lustful, evil rich man who frames Liang's character, Chen Po, for rape, then breaks the man's hands, and, on top of all that, takes his sister as his concubine. The sister is killed when she discovers the frame-up, while Chen Po teams up with a pickpocket (Hsaio Ho) to take revenge. Designed as a star-making showcase for Hsaio, a spotlight on monkey style, and another insightful rumination on the student-sifu relationship, it succeeds abundantly on all fronts.

Next, the director decided to put his unique spin on the very nature of sequels. *Return to the 36th Chamber* (1980) looked like a sequel, acted like a sequel, and satisfied like a good sequel, but the

The Shaw Standard

audience-challenging trick was to accept Gordon Liu Chia-hui, not as Priest San Te, but as a con man impersonating San Te, until the real San Te (played here by Ching Chia) puts him to work making a bamboo scaffold to repair the Shaolin Temple's chambers. The satisfying finale shows Gordon vanquishing his friends' persecutors via kung fu he learned through natural osmosis, rather than traditional punch-and-kick training. No wonder the term "kung fu" actually means "hard work."

Following that, Liang decided to try to do for Hui Ying-hung what he did for Gordon and Hsiao. The result was the delightful *My Young Auntie* (1981), clearly the director's take on a kung fu *My Fair Lady*. Kara played a naïve girl from the country who gets caught in a family dispute over an inheritance. This seemingly simple plot is used by Liang as an examination of the generation gap as well as conflicts between educated city slickers and uneducated country bumpkins. A highlight comes when the title character tries to update herself, only to have to fight in a slit gown and high heels ("Oh, those shoes!" Kara told me with a laugh).

Into this seemingly simple plot the director has mounted more wonderful scenes of "secret" martial arts — as in a ballroom sequence where everyone fights in costume — and added exquisite touches, such as the Westernized boy (Hsaio Ho) who constantly uses American slang and profanity incorrectly. The shining star of this movie, however, is Hui. Although she was featured in Liang's three previous films (as well as in *Clan of the White Lotus* aka *Fists of the White Lotus*, directed by Lo Lieh as a sequel to *Executioners From Shaolin* in 1980) this was her first starring role and the one that won her the Hong Kong equivalent of a Golden Globe award.

"He was nice," Kara said of Liang. "He taught me everything. He taught me how to use the camera, how to use film, and how to make movies. He gave me many chances and created stories just for me." And he wasn't through yet. His next film was *Martial Club*

(1981), his final statement in Huang Fei-hong films. Liu Chia-hui again played the youthful Huang, but not before Liang himself pops up during the credit sequence, instructing the audience on the traditions and styles of the lion dance. The film then opens with a lion dance performed by Hui and his partner (Mai Te-lo).

It unfolds as a classic story of kung fu school versus kung fu school, complete with impressive battles and challenges, but the film is basically a setup for its final fight. The evil school has hired a northern Chinese stylist (Wang Lung-wei once again) to defeat Huang. Instead, the pair test each other's skills in an extended fight in a long alleyway that gets narrower and twists. This is an amazing fight scene, displaying a range of styles and techniques, as well as subtle moves and grandstand plays. It is a testament to Liang's, Hui's, and Wei's talents — which are prodigious. The Wei character winds up winning, but he never intended to kill the young man. He merely wanted to see what he could do and was duly impressed. At the close he strongly suggests that the bad guys clean up their act. This was a special movie for Wang Lung-wei ... he finally got to play a good guy.

But it was all a prelude for Liang's next film. More than once, you may notice that when a kung fu star gets to a certain age, he or she becomes interested in capturing his or her kung fu skills at their optimum. This invariably results in an extraordinary film, and *Legendary Weapons of China* (aka *Legendary Weapons of Kung Fu*, 1982) is no exception. In fact, I've often referred to it as the quintessential kung fu film.

First, it is about kung fu. It is not a western with kung fu, a love story with kung fu, a comedy with kung fu. If kung fu did not exist, this movie could not have been made. Second, it is about kung fu *films*. If the martial arts movie genre didn't exist, neither would this picture. On the surface it is about the end of the kung fu era in China. Foreigners (gweilos) have invaded and occupied China, causing the kung fu (or pugilist) schools to unite in order to devise a style to counter their most dreaded and powerful enemy: the gun.

Glorious years of self-improvement have ended ... perhaps even having been for naught. Weaklings with guns could defeat the mightiest fighter, and only one sifu is willing to admit that: Lei Kung (the forty-six-year-old Liu Chia-liang). Naturally, all the other schools put a kung fu hit out on him, lest his contention get to the ears of the enemy. But these are no ordinary schools. The Pugilists are a divided sect of the dreaded "Mosha" (aka Maoshan) — the predecessors of, and inspiration for, the Japanese ninja ... only they don't have the psychological yoke of the ever-corruptible bushido code of honor to hamper them. These Chinese "magician-spies" are feared to this day and rarely spoken of ... even by the filmmakers who cautiously picture them. In this film, they include a group who can control their students via voodoo-like dolls, as well as a vast array of blades, bombs, and chi.

To find Lei Kung, who has gone into hiding, the schools send Kara Hui Ying-hung, Hsaio Ho, and Gordon Liu Chia-hui. Complicating matters is a *Spiritual Boxer*-like kung fu charlatan played by Alexander Fu Sheng in total Bob Hope mode, who impersonates Lei Kung in several memorable scenes. The kung fu complications and comedy Liang wrests from setting the characters off each other like pinballs is a joy to behold, until the Hui Ying-hung character finally finds Lei Kung, who is disguised as an old woodcutter, and convinces him to start honing his rusting skills to confront the killers stalking him.

In several consummate confrontations, Lei Kung defeats his pursuers, gaining their respect in the process. Only then does the truth emerge. Kung's own brother (played by Liang's own brother Yung) had arranged the hunt simply to ingratiate himself with the government, the kung fu schools, and the brothers' own clan. At the end, the two face each other outside a temple at sundown to do battle with all eighteen legendary weapons of China. This extended sequence is, not surprisingly, a masterwork, with each of the weapons and empty-hand techniques identified with titles on the sides of the screen. Even then, Liang takes special care to show that even the most insidious of techniques can be defeated if you use your brain as well as your body.

Lei Kung's skill, even rusted, combined with his honorable nature, defeats his evil brother every time. Although Lei Yung begs his brother to kill him rather than expose his plot or leave him with this dishonor, Lei Kung turns his back on him, letting him live with his guilt and shame. Happily, the film was a great success, not only for Liang and company, but his new protégé Alexander Fu Sheng as well. Fu's legs had been broken on *Heroes Shed No Tears* (a 1980 production directed by prolific wuxia specialist Chu Yuan), and fans were concerned that he'd never be the same.

Thankfully, Sheng's "official" comeback film, *Treasure Hunters* (aka *Master of Disaster*, 1982), laid that fear to rest. Directed by Liang's brother, Liu Chia-yung, and choreographed by the Liu family, this charming, funny, exciting film was to broaden Fu's persona for the rest of his career. *Treasure Hunters* was, essentially, a kung fu "road" picture, with Fu as Bob Hope and his real-life younger brother, Chang Chan-peng, as a Bing Crosby type (minus the singing, of course).

Having immortalized his kung fu skill in no uncertain terms, Liang challenged himself again with a full-fledged kung fu comedy ... with mixed results. *Cat vs. Rat* (1982) was similar to Steven Spielberg's *1941* (made three years earlier) in that it confused humor with loud, strident chaos. Fu Sheng and the elegant, rakish Adam Cheng Shao-chiu (who Gordon Liu directed to far better effect in one of only two movies he helmed, 1981's *Shaolin and Wu Tang* [the other was 1973's *Breakout from Oppression*]) played madcap rivals and neighbors who each wanted wealth and fame.

The Shaw Standard

Unable to settle on a cohesive tone in that merry mix-up, Liang challenged himself to do a decent modern-day film by reversing the theme of *My Young Auntie*. This time Liang himself played a kung fu teacher stuck in old ways, while Hui Ying-hung played a Western-educated hipster who wanted women's lib, baby. *The Lady is the Boss* (1983) was the result, and it was a pretty painful, campy, overwrought mess — only elevated by Liang's superlative kung fu.

Unsatisfied with these last two efforts, Liang collected his crew and started to create a deadly serious film about the Tartar betrayal of the Yang family on a Sung dynasty battlefield. "That was so terrible," Kara Hui Ying-hung told me. "It took us nine and a half months to film because of all the problems. First there was script trouble, Fu Sheng had problems with his wife, and Liu Chia-liang was injured during the filming of *Cat vs. Rat*, which he finished just before."

Even so, advance word was excellent. This was going to be Liang's return to form, and Fu Sheng's return to drama. Then disaster struck. Three months into filming, on July 7, 1983, with his younger brother driving, Alexander Fu Sheng died in a car accident at the age of twenty-nine.

"Liu Chia-liang always filmed the action first," Ying-hung explained, "then filmed the drama, so when Fu Sheng died, he had terrible problems. They were very close. Fu Sheng was Liu Chia-liang's first disciple. After he died, we stopped shooting for three months." But, finally, in honor of his fallen friend, Liang returned to the set.

Not surprisingly, the completed *Eight Diagram Pole Fighter* (1984) was Liang's angriest film. It was also undeniably thrilling, and, incredibly, the only one of the Master's movies that was included in the Hong Kong film critics' list of "The Top 100 Chinese Films." As the credits roll, Chang Chan-peng, Hsaio Ho, Liu Chia-yung, Yung Wang-yu, and Mai Te-lo's characters all graphically die beneath the

Tartars' swords and spears on an artificial indoor set which gives the scene even more of a nightmarish quality.

Only Liu Chia-hui and Fu Sheng's character survive, but the latter is driven insane by his brothers' deaths and his father's sacrificial suicide in the face of trusted peers' betrayal. He returns home to his mother and two sisters, screaming and contorting. His brother is almost killed by the invaders, but a hermit (Liu Chia-liang) gives his own life to help him escape. Hui takes refuge in the northern Shaolin Temple, where his practical killing ways conflict with the monks' peaceful leanings. They practice pole fighting on wood and steel mockups of wolves — the actual counterparts of which often harass the temple.

"Kill them," says the betrayed ex-soldier.

"Defang them," instructs the Shaolin abbot (played by the versatile Kao Fei).

With the Fu Sheng character insane, the mother (Lily Li) sends her eldest daughter (Hui Ying-hung) out for vengeance. At this point the Fu Sheng character completely disappears from the picture.

"Fu Sheng's character was supposed to go back to the battlefield, reclaim his father's sword, and convince Liu Chia-hui to leave the Shaolin Temple so they could take revenge on the Mongol traitor who slaughtered our family," Kara explained to me. "Then Fu Sheng died in the car accident, and they had to change the story so my character would be in danger, so Hui would leave the temple."

Ying-hung runs afoul of the traitorous general (Ku Ming) and Tartar leader (Wang Lung-wei) at an inn, where they hold her hostage. That does the trick. Hui pole-fights his Shaolin sifu to a standstill using the eight-diagram style (which leaves an impression of an "8" on the floor), then marches to the inn to take on all his family's persecutors at once. Awaiting him is a pyramid of coffins filled with his bound and gagged sister as well as sword-wielding killers. Hopelessly outnumbered, he still almost manages to free his sibling

The Shaw Standard

before being overwhelmed. Just as it seems his death is a certainty, his Shaolin brethren arrive.

"We will not kill," says the abbot. "Merely defang the wolves."

What follows is the most disconcerting fight scene Liang ever staged, where the monks, using a great variety of techniques, rip out the Tartars' teeth (a set actually being wedged into a monk's bald skull at one point). Hui personally drives the two main antagonists' heads through the sides of coffins, where their skulls are crushed and throats slit, before marching into the hills, never to be seen again.

Following that, Liu Chia-liang was never quite the same. His penultimate film for the Shaw Brothers Studio was *Disciples of the 36th Chamber* (1985), which returned Gordon to the San Te role, but was actually another showcase for Hsaio Ho, who played the infamous Shaolin hothead Fong Sai-yuk. Although an interesting combination of *Master Killer* and *Animal House* (1978), audiences could surmise that Liang's heart just wasn't in it. But his head and body weren't done … not by a long shot.

Meanwhile, his studio colleagues had their own rice to fry. Although Chang Cheh and Liu Chia-liang were clearly the pillars upon which the Shaw Brothers Studio's kung fu film crown rested, there were others whose contributions were telling — the most prominent being the aforementioned Chu Yuan … for quantity, if not for quality. At the height of his powers at Shaws, he was lauded for being able to work on eight films at the same time. It's not surprising, therefore, that his filmography, although substantial, ranged from the sublime to the ridiculous.

Born in 1934 and educated at the Faculty of Chemistry within Sun Yat-sen University, he ultimately followed in his actor father's footsteps and entered the film industry. Not only did he find it to his liking, he even found it easy. He rapidly progressed from scripting to assistant directing, then started helming entire productions in 1959. By the time he came to the Shaw Brothers in 1971, he had already directed more than seventy films, setting the stage for his unprecedented assembly-line approach. Within five years he had created his most successful and renowned films, starting with *Intimate Confessions of a Chinese Courtesan* (1972) — an impressive melding of a softcore erotic and legitimate kung fu film.

Following that, he established what could be called the "no-trapdoor-remains-unsprung" wuxia sub-genre with *Killer Clans* (1976) — launching an extensive series of like-titled (and like-looking) Jiang Hu tales of inter-family kung fu squabbles in which secret compartments were everywhere and double-crosses were multiplied into veritable quadruple-crosses. That same year he also Shaw-ized an unholy combination of Spaghetti Western and 1940s Hollywood cliffhanger serial into an endlessly malleable series of "sword-slinger" films. In fact, in *The Magic Blade* (1976), he dressed Ti Lung in much the same serape Clint Eastwood wore in *A Fistful of Dollars* (1964) and placed his six-shooter-shaped sword in a holster on his hip.

The final ingredient in Chu's marathon mash-up was novelist Gu Long, whose complex, convoluted wuxia epics served as starting points in the majority of Yuan's multitude of films. By the time Shaws shuttered its film units in the mid-80s, Yuan had made more than a hundred movies for them, the most popular of which was *The Sentimental Swordsman* series (1977-1982) and the most ludicrous of which was 1976's *Web of Death* — where the villain is a big, obviously fake Halloween-decoration spider filmed with color-tinted lenses. Most, if not all, of his efforts were, at the very least, wild, convulsive fun.

Less prolific, but perhaps more important to the genre, was Sun Chung — possibly the most underrated kung fu filmmaker. Probably the reason for this was that he was so versatile. Like legendary American director Robert Wise, he was great at virtually any genre he attempted, and therefore his fame never quite took public root in any of them. In any case, his kung fu films were always recognizable

The Shaw Standard

by his unusually inventive camera work and imaginative approach. Born in 1941, he knew he wanted to work in movies early on, and went to school in Taiwan for it. His first film was a musical (*Wild Girl*) in 1968. His second film was a comedy (1970s *Tops in Every Trade*) and a big hit. That brought him to the attention of the Shaw Brothers.

He hit the ground running, treating the studio like a big toy box. He was most lauded for his crime thrillers, but with *The Avenging Eagle* in 1978, kung fu fans sat up and took notice. Ostensibly a straight-forward revenge tale, Chung elevated it to classic status with a cunning collaboration between his camera crew, cast, and kung fu choreographer (not surprisingly, Sun was the first Shaw director to utilize the Steadicam). Liu Chia-liang's ex-partner, Tang Chia, was Sun's go-to action guy (as, in fact, he was for director Chu Yuan as well), and the two worked beautifully together. The two directors also shared a deep appreciation of actors Ti Lung and Alexander Fu Sheng — using both every chance they got.

With the critical and box office success of *Avenging Eagle,* Sun officially launched an impressive series of fine kung fu films, including *Judgment of An Assassin* (1977), *The Proud Youth* (1978), *The Kung Fu Instructor* (1979), *To Kill a Mastermind* (1979), *The Deadly Breaking Sword* (1979), *Rendezvous with Death* (1980), and *The Kid with a Tattoo* (1980) — all culminating with his landmark *Human Lanterns* (1982), a potent combination of a classic kung fu movie and a slasher, body-count, film.

The director seemed to stumble after that, still making fine films, but ones with obvious aberrations. For instance, his hysterical sequel to *The Kung Fu Instructor, The Master Strikes Back* (1985), is the greatest castration/crotch-shot martial art movie in history. Thankfully he also made *A Fistful of Talons* (aka *Protecting Eagle*, 1983) outside the studio, which remains the best film of "Jackie Chan clone" Billy Chong (the personable Indonesian actor who also starred in such nice Jackie knock-offs as 1979's *Crystal Fist*, 1980's *Super Power*, and the unforgettable *Kung Fu Zombie* and *Kung Fu from Beyond the Grave*, both 1982).

The remaining two major Shaw kung fu creators essentially flew under even the Studio's radar. Ex-actor John Lo Mar's checkered martial art movie directing career essentially began with the ignominious assignment of helming the sad hack job that was *Bruce Lee and I* (aka *I Love You Bruce Lee*, 1976), but he quickly became better known for his comedies and crime thrillers. Every once in awhile, however, he would gather his kung fu friends (including future choreographer superstar Ching Siu-tung) and patch together a story apparently using existing sets and locations. This resulted in several lean, mean, enjoyable fighting films, like *Five Super Fighters* (1979), *Fighting Fool* (1979) *Monkey Kung Fu* (1980).

Then there was Lu Chin-ku. As the Studio grew ever closer to closing its film units, more and more veterans began jumping the sinking ship, while more and more newcomers looking for a lucky break eyed the empty director chairs. Lu came relatively late to the game, but made up for it in flamboyance. Reminiscent of Busby Berkley or Baz Luhrman in his willingness to use a full color palette, wires, trampolines, special effects, and exaggeration, no one could be sure what might happen in his genre films.

Exploding onto the Shaw Scene with *The Master* (aka *3 Evil Masters*, 1982) — the Studio's attempt to fashion its own Jackie Chan-like kung fu comedy — Lu then eschewed trying to copy others' successes and carried on with his own unique visions. With *The Lady Assassin* (1983), *Holy Flame of the Martial World* (1983), and especially *Bastard Swordsman* (1983) and *Return of Bastard Swordsman* (1984), he created his own fabulous fantasy factory. He went out swinging with 1984's *Secret Service of the Imperial Court* (remade as *14 Blades* in 2010), which featured one of his finest moments, immortalized as "The Eunuch Slap."

The Shaw Standard

Liu Yung (playing a psychotic, glitzy eunuch who has taken over the Government) is told the painful truth by a wise old counselor. The eunuch rewards him with a slap across the face ... which sends the old man shooting through the air, across the room, and into an upper wall, before crashing in a bloody heap to the floor — all in the blink of an eye. That's Lu Chin-ku for you (as is the moment in *Return of Bastard Swordsman* when a super-powered warrior grips another under the ribs, causing him to vomit blood like a firehose which paints a gigantic white marble sculpture red).

Finally, there's Tang Chia himself. Although he avidly avoided the director's chair for much of his career, as the epoch of the Shaw Studio film units drew to a close, the opportunity to create his own films became more pronounced. Chia tested the waters with *Shaolin Prince* (1982) and *Shaolin Intruders* (1984) — two elaborate phantasmagoricals that reflected the independent influence of Yuen Wo-ping, who, when left to his own devices, created similar wire-wrought extravaganzas (but more on that later). Although colorful and imaginative, they came as quite a surprise to audiences used to Chia's previous, smooth, sophisticated work.

As the sun set on the Shaw's film units, Chia was no doubt aware that his time in the director's chair was limited, and that his next choice for a personal project could be his last. For whatever reason, *Opium and the Kung Fu Master* (1984) was as different from *Shaolin Prince/Intruders* as *Iron Man* (2008) was from *Iron Giant* (1999). Working in tandem with planner Ling Yun from a scenario by Huang Ying, Chia decided to deconstruct the classic Cantonese kung fu action comedy.

Inspired by a tale of the Ten Tigers of Kwangtung leader's alleged addiction, Chia was going to symbolize the drug culture's insidious influence by letting its presence in his film destroy everything audiences had come to expect from the genre. As the film starts, all the clichés and stereotypes are in place: from the artificial-looking sets to the goofy Cantonese comedy characters to even the Peking Opera-esque "Mr. Spock-style" eyebrows painted on the hero.

But as the title opiate takes hold, audience expectations begin to break down. The comedy becomes tragedy, the love story is shattered, and the student/teacher relationship is turned upside down. Tang Chia himself plays the kung fu master's blind sifu, who is forced to become his doctor and counselor as our hero must survive going cold turkey just in time for the emotional, action-packed finale.

To accomplish his goal, Chia called upon many of his friends. There are no fewer than a half-dozen martial art directors on the film, including, of course, Chia himself, his longtime assistant Huang Pei-chi, as well as co-star Li Hai-sheng (not to mention Yuan Pin, Yuan Hua, and Chiang Chuan). Knowing the end was near may have inspired Chia to give as many associates as much behind-the-camera experience as possible to help them in future endeavors.

And the end was, indeed, near. Liu Chia-liang was in China directing Jet Li's third movie, *Martial Arts of Shaolin* (1986) when the official word reached him. The Shaw Brothers Film Units would be terminated, and those who weren't transferring to the television units were out of a job. The Golden Age of Chinese Kung Fu Films was over. The New Wave had already begun, but it certainly didn't seem as if there was room in it for such veteran workhorses as Chang Cheh and Liang.

Most of the actors would be fine. Shaw's most versatile and honored performer, Ku Feng, was too good not to get work. Having played everything from venal martial arts masters (*Avenging Eagle*) to handicapped cuckolds (as in 1982's *Tiger Killer*), and everything in between during more than two hundred and fifty performances, he was ready for more outside the studio walls. The same was probably true of the kung fu stuntmen, villains, and supporting actors. Wang Lung-wei, Kao Fei, Li Hai-sheng, and the rest would be seen again. Likewise for such major stars as Ti Lung, David Chiang, Chen

The Shaw Standard

Kuan-tai, Lo Lieh, and Gordon Liu.

But the one man who may have made it all possible pretty much disappeared into that good night. That would be the magnificent I Kuang. Born in Shanghai in 1935, Kuang moved to Hong Kong in the 1960s to pursue a successful career as a science fiction and martial arts novelist. Although several of his books were adapted to movies, his first original screenplay was for *The One-Armed Swordsman*, and he rapidly replaced Chang Cheh as the Shaw Studio's top scripter. In addition, his independent contract allowed him to work for other studios and directors — an opportunity he took ample advantage of. Not only did he write the bulk of Chang Cheh's best films, but also those of Liu Chia-liang, and even Bruce Lee. At last count, Kuang has supplied well over five hundred scripts to studios throughout China, and that isn't even including the many screenplays he produced under pseudonyms.

As of this writing, Sir Run Run Shaw, and the Studio he helped create, still lives. Celebrated as a philanthropist, he has donated literally billions of dollars to charities, hospitals, and schools. At the age of one hundred and three, he remains married to Mona Fong, who had been both his mistress and producer of all the Studio's movies.

CHAPTER FOUR
THE CLOWN PRINCE OF KUNG FU

Picture identifications (clockwise from upper left):
Project A; the many faces of Jackie Chan; Jackie Chan in *Police Story 3: Supercop*; *Rush Hour*; Jackie Chan and Simon Yuen in *Drunken Monkey in a Tiger's Eye*; *Drunken Master 2*.

The Clown Prince of Kung Fu

Jackie Chan was born in 1954 with the name Chan Kong-sang (aka Chen Gang-sheng) to a chef father and a maid mother. His parents were poor but steady workers. Until he was seven, his folks cooked and cleaned at the French embassy in Hong Kong. But no matter how hard his father toiled to teach him humility and virtue, Chen/Chan followed in Bruce Lee's footsteps: finding street fights.

Then came the single most meaningful moment in his life: his parents secured jobs at the American Embassy in Australia. Only two problems: they decided not to bring their young son and to enroll him in the China Drama Academy. This benign-sounding institution was an old-style Peking Opera school where, for the next ten years, Kong-sang would eat (not much), sleep (not much), and slave (loads) to learn acrobatics, song, dance, acting, and kung fu under strict, martial discipline.

His headmaster, Yu Zhan-yuan, was half-respected and half-feared. He was a stern taskmaster who was quick to punish and slow to compliment. But at least he was teaching them something useful in the world of Hong Kong show business. That, unfortunately, didn't include reading or writing. While others in the school sought to survive, stay under the radar, or curry the master's favor, Chan dedicated himself to impress.

He soon manifested the personality that shaped his life: that of the textbook abandoned child. Since, subconsciously, he couldn't help feeling that his parents might not actually love him, he set out to make everyone else do it instead. Eventually he gained the nickname "Double Boy," since he tried doubly hard than any one else. That held him in good stead when he finally "graduated" the Academy, only to find no call for Peking Opera performers.

But he had already been featured in movies as a child actor — *Seven Little Valiant Fighters: Big and Little Wong Tin Bar* (1962) and *The Eighteen Darts* (1966) being two of the better known. In 1971, at the age of seventeen, Chan found it the perfect time to use his burgeoning skills. His Academy big brother Sammo Hung Kam-po (aka Hung Chin-pao) was already established as one of the most sought-after action directors, so Chan soon found himself in *The Little Tiger of Canton* (aka *Snake Fist Fighter* aka *Master with Cracked Fingers*, 1971), but, truth be told, he didn't make much of a favorable impression — not with his narrow eyes and greasy little mustache.

He fared much better as an anonymous stuntman — doubling the villain in *Fist of Fury* or getting his neck broken by Bruce Lee in *Enter the Dragon*. "Everybody idolized Bruce," Chan told me years later. "So no one would talk to him. But I asked him if he wanted to go bowling with us after shooting wrapped for the day. He just looked me up and down, and walked away. But then, that night, in he comes and sits down next to me at the lane where we're bowling. He just sits there, watches us bowl for ten frames, then thanks me and goes. It was like the whole place was holding its breath! As soon as he leaves, everybody started slapping me on the back and shaking my hand. He really gave me face that day."

But even Bruce's kindness and Sammo's help wasn't enough to keep the young man gainfully employed, so he joined his parents in Australia, but only found work in construction. Its only benefit was gaining him muscles, and an American nickname. A fellow worker named Jack had trouble pronouncing Kong-sang, so he started calling Chan "Little Jack." Then, when the other workers had trouble pronouncing "Little Jack," they shortened it to "Jacky."

Meanwhile, back in Hong Kong, a hopeful Malaysian film producer named Willie Chan Chi-keung was looking for a way to establish himself. He was duly impressed by Jacky's contributions to such Sammo-influenced films as *Hand of Death* (1975, directed by a promising newcomer named John Woo), and sold the flagging Lo Wei on the idea that this fledgling star was the perfect choice to become the "new Bruce Lee." Jacky, bored by construction work and unable to find contentment down under, was ready to give kung fu films another try. Intrigued by Chan's possibilities, Wei signed Chan to a long-term contract, changed his name to Sheng Lung ("Little Dragon"), and set him immediately to work on *New Fist of Fury* (1976).

This film takes up where Bruce Lee's left off, with the survivors of the kung fu school escaping Japanese soldiers to come across the Chan character. Nora Miao, who was the female lead in the Lee picture, returns to her role, and teaches Jacky what is essentially their idea of jeet kune do — here called Ching Wu. Then he goes back and takes vengeance on Lee's murderer in a rote, lackluster way.

Although hardly inspired, his performance seemed to fit Lo Wei's bill, so he plunged Chan into eight more movies over the next two years. But this was 1976 — the year Liu Chia-liang made *Challenge of the Masters*, Chang Cheh made three Shaolin movies starring Fu Sheng and Ti Lung, and a young upstart, independent producer named Ng Sze-yuen made a surprise hit called *The Secret Rivals*. What Lo Wei was grinding out made money, sure, but otherwise just wasn't cutting it.

Nor was *Shaolin Wooden Man*, Jacky's second 1976 film for Wei's company (directed by Chen Chi-hwa). It was another wooden (all puns intended) kung fu film — with Chan taking revenge for his father's death thanks to the coaching of a handy Shaolin monk. But this was the first film in which Jacky was given a little freedom in the fight scenes. Slowly, he started to find his way. There was little chance to improve in *Killer Meteor* (1977) since Jacky was playing the villain and Jimmy Wang Yu was playing the stolid, limited hero. At least in *Snake-Crane Art of Shaolin* (1977) — a Chang Cheh knock-off also produced by Wei and directed by Hwa — Jacky was back as the protagonist. He was becoming more proficient, while displaying more charisma.

To Kill With Intrigue was next on the treadmill. Lo Wei's company didn't have the money, materials, or even inclination to make great kung fu films. Instead, they relied on Double Boy's eagerness to please. But even a performer of Chan's ability couldn't do enough with terrible working conditions, mediocre scripts, or his producer's desire to maintain his ego's status quo. When this film failed at the box office, Wei all but gave up on Chan … which turned out to be the actor's trump card.

Contractually stuck with Jacky, Wei basically gave him carte blanche on his next picture. Chan took the opportunity to, in his words, "fool around." Seeing that everyone was trying to copy Bruce Lee, he decided to do the opposite. Since Bruce kicked high, Jacky would kick low. Since Bruce was serious at all times, Jacky decided to make faces. Since Bruce never got hurt or made a mistake, well, you know…. Instead of fighting against the inevitable restraints of bad martial arts filmmaking, Chan went with them.

Half a Loaf of Kung Fu (1978) was the first recognizable "Jacky Chan Film." He both had fun with, and made fun of, kung fu film clichés. In the opening credits alone, he lampooned exaggerated sound effects, frenetic editing, wooden men, the famed Japanese film series about Zatoichi the Blind Swordsman, and even *Jesus Christ Superstar*. His inventive, unusual work fell on blind Lo Wei eyes, so it was back to the grindstone for three more uninspired efforts: the 3D *Magnificent Bodyguard* (1978), the Liu Chia-liang *Spiritual Boxer* knock-off *Spiritual Kung Fu* (1978), and *Dirty Ho* knock-off *Dragon Fist* (1978) — all of which Jacky got to contribute his fight choreography to, since Lo Wei didn't seem to care. He had apparently resigned himself to doing the best he could with the rest of this "box office poison's" contract.

But two other people really seemed to care. There was the aforementioned Ng Sze-yuen — once assistant director of Jimmy Wang Yu's *The Chinese Boxer*, and now the creator of the first major independent movie company, Seasonal Films. Ng had been intrigued with *Half a Loaf of Kung Fu*, and saw the glimmer of a market that the two major kung fu film studios, Shaw Brothers and Golden Harvest, weren't really serving.

Then there was Yuen Wo-ping. The son of venerated Simon Yuen Hsiao-tien, a master of stagecraft and northern-style kung fu who personally trained all seven of his children, Wo-ping had seen his father play kung fu villains alongside Shih Kien in the Kwan Tak-hing Huang Fei-hong series, as well as kung fu masters in Chang Cheh's *Shaolin Martial Arts* (1974) and Liu Chia-liang's *36th Chamber of Shaolin* and *Heroes of the East*. As Ng saw something funny in Jacky Chan, Wo-ping saw something funny in his father.

Lo Wei, however, didn't smell anything funny when Ng asked him to loan Jacky Chan to Seasonal for a film or two. All he smelled was money, and traded Jacky over with an ostensible "good riddance." The three men — Chan as star, Ng as producer, and Wo-ping as director — were on exactly the same wavelength. Inspired by Liu Chia-liang's *Spiritual Boxer*, they did it three better with *Snake in the Eagle's Shadow* (1978), a brilliantly conceived and executed "new wave" kung fu comedy featuring Jacky as a hapless, mischievous, well-meaning bumpkin, Simon Yuen as an incognito, on-the-run, consummate snake style practitioner, and Huang Jang-li as a vengeful eagle claw killer determined to wipe out the snake school.

Chan seemed to explode out of the screen with joy at finding his place in the kung fu film firmament, while Wo-ping's directing skills were never more effective. The audience shared their delight throughout, and only grew in exultation when Chan's character develops "cat style" kung fu to defeat the eagle master. The film's success was immediate and almost overwhelming, but the trio were already hard at work on the follow-up.

Drunken Monkey in a Tiger's Eye (aka *Drunken Master*, 1978) proved to the trio, and everyone else, that *Snake in the Eagle's Shadow* was no fluke. In fact, it was the rare sequel that improved on the original in virtually every way. The first masterstroke was to have Jacky play a new kind of Huang Fei-hong — a young, roguish, teenager who came before the august healer. The second was to have Simon Yuen play the legendary Beggar Su, a beloved historical character. The third was to immortalize Drunken Style, which Liu Chia-liang had featured in *Heroes of the East*, but not to this potent effect.

Although essentially a remake of *Eagle's Shadow*, *Drunken Master*'s concepts were streamlined, and this new picture stands as one of the sleekest, flat-out, action-filled kung fu comedies. But quantity of action is not enough. Quality of action and character was the object here, and while Chan's character, nicknamed "Naughty Panther," moved from one fight to another, the imagination that went into creating the wonderful situations is extraordinary. Although essentially one long action sequence (the outlandish training scenes can be considered part of the action), the movie manages to build until the battle between a tiger claw hired killer and the Naughty Panther.

Half the time Panther is being trained (tortured), while the other half he tries to escape ... but is always outwitted by the drunken master who teaches him the "eight drunken fairies" — a style that requires ample portions of alcohol. Chan "graduates" from the training part and moves into the impressive "forms" sequence, before the inevitable and anxiously awaited blow-out finale. There, Panther must save his honorable father from a hired tiger-claw killer (again played by exceptional leg fighter Huang Jang-li), and does so by inventing a new, delightful, amalgamation of the eight drunken fairies on the spot.

This finale was perfectly designed for Chan's skills, and set the tone for the rest of his career's action scenes, because he is a kung fu sponge. In the Peking Opera school, he had learned theatrical wushu techniques. From schoolmate Sammo's productions, he acquired hung gar. From Bruce Lee's sets, he synthesized wing chun and jeet kune do. Then, from Yuen Wo-ping, he infused taichi and

Shaolin animal styles. Finally, he brought his own acrobatic, tradition-changing mentality to the mix, and developed a screen kung fu that was both constantly evolving but still clearly identifiable as his.

Ng Sze-yuen served as shepherd to Chan and Yuen's re-creation, revitalization, and resurrection of the kung fu comedy revolution. *Drunken Master* was an even bigger hit than *Eagle's Shadow*, and Chan went from box office poison to superstar overnight. Simon Yuen, at the tender age of sixty-six, achieved the stardom that had eluded him throughout his forty-five-year career. Ng was happy. Wo-ping was very happy. Chan was even happier. Lo Wei was happiest. Suddenly he had Hong Kong's biggest star under contract for at least one more iron-clad film, and bragging rights that he was the one who had "made" both Bruce Lee and Jacky Chan.

Ng Sze-yuen saw the writing on the wall, and backed away. Willie Chan, Jacky's agent and manager, stepped up. Golden Harvest, still smarting over the loss of Bruce Lee and their fumbling of *Game of Death*, moved in. But while they and Lo Wei haggled over details, the ever-honorable Jacky set to work on *Fearless Hyena*, his final film for his "discoverer's" Company. It followed, in form and function, *Eagle's Shadow* and *Drunken Master*'s lead, with one major difference. This time, Chan called all the shots, proving to his growing group of fans that the previous two films weren't just Ng and Yuen's babies.

Here he plays Lung, the grandson of the last of the Hsin-yi fighters. Like the snake master before him, the head Hsin-yi man is being hunted down, this time by Ch'ing Dynasty General Yen and his trio of killers — all who carry a form of "switch spear," a spear that folds like a switchblade. Crafty, opportunistic Lung sneaks away from his grandfather's forest shack to perform as a martial artist for money. He takes on all comers, disguising himself as a buffoon and a girl, until he inadvertently leads Yen to his grandfather. The old man is killed, but Lung is prevented from interfering by a crippled old sifu (here played by Chan Wai-lau). He takes Lung away to train him in "Emotional Kung Fu," which involves crying and laughing to unleash untapped power.

When the smoke cleared, Lo Wei's bank accounts were considerably fuller, and Golden Harvest had a newly-minted superstar — a "Jackie" of all trades who was always eager to please the new authority figure in his life ... but not so eager that he'd ever let them completely *Game of Death* him. The arrangement was unprecedented: the man they slightly renamed "Jackie" (to differentiate him from the low-rent, box-office-poison "Jacky") had full run of the studio as well as total control of his films — to the point that he could spend as much time and money as he wanted.

"To show respect," Jackie told me, "they even gave me Bruce Lee's old dressing room. Everyone told me it was haunted, so I decided to sleep there to show I wasn't afraid. In the middle of the night I heard a scratching at the door. Even though I don't believe in the supernatural, it took me three tries before I finally swung open the door. It was a stray puppy." Not wanting to share the lost canine's fate, Jackie immediately set about making his ultimate statement in new wave kung fu comedy: *The Young Master* (1980).

To do that, he needed his own team. On his previous films, he had watched with appreciation (and perhaps a little envy) as Yuen Wo-ping worked with his brothers Cheung-yan, Chun-yeung, Shun-yi, and Yat-cho. Having no siblings of his own (that he yet knew about [in later years he would discover that his father was a Chinese spy with a second family]), Jackie set out to create his own. As much as he admired many of his Peking Opera schoolmates, they were otherwise occupied by Sammo, so he called upon stuntman friend Chiang Wing-fat (otherwise known as Mars), and Lo Wai-kwong, to serve as foundation for an ever-growing, ever-changing team of collaborators.

The Young Master was Jackie's "kitchen sink" film, in which he throws in characters and conflicts at will. The plot, such as it is, has him trying to rescue a friend from a life of crime. As he attempts to bring the chief thief down, he keeps bumping into the sheriff (Shih Kien) and his two children (Peking Opera schoolmate Yuen Baio and Queen of Shaw Studio kung fu Lily Li). But that was really just a thin line upon which to hang show-stopping kung fu and French farce-flavored sequences.

There's a sword fight that becomes a complex juggling act, a lion dance, fights with elegant white fans, fights with furniture; and once more Chan dresses as a girl, this time to take out the main villain's cronies (including Li Hai-sheng). Here's where he also cemented his new approach to choreography. As Mars pointed out, what more can you do with only two arms and two legs? So, inspired by another movie idol, Gene Kelly, Jackie added props — not just as weapons, but as integral allies or enemies in the action scenes. Chan not only used his body as an encyclopedia of possibilities, but the environment his body finds itself in. This simple, seemingly obvious, idea led to audience involvement like never before.

Another *Young Master* swerve is that Chan's character is not a good enough martial artist to defeat his enemy (the mighty Wang In-sik). Throughout his last three films, Chan had made it quite clear that he liked torture/training scenes. The things he does to himself on-screen are scarcely believable. In the climactic fight of *The Young Master,* Chan is pummeled unmercifully but keeps coming back for more. He just keeps getting kicked and punched and hurled — sometimes in "dare-you-to-find-any-fakery" slow motion — until he defeats the bad guy simply by surviving.

The last shot of the film shows every part of Chan's body in traction except for two fingers of one hand. With those two bandaged fingers he waves "bye-bye" to the audience. They didn't wave back. Instead they applauded wildly, and in record numbers. It seemed that Golden Harvest's gamble had paid off, and they immediately wanted to take advantage of that ... by doing precisely the wrong thing. Seemingly cowed by Hollywood's international power, they tossed Jackie to the tinseltown wolves with virtually no preparation. They stripped him of his creative power, and he could hardly speak English. Then they saddled him with director Robert Clouse.

It was "new Bruce Lee " time, part two, with nearly the same result. *The Big Brawl* (aka *Battle Creek Brawl*, 1980) was written and directed by Clouse, and starred Chan as a 1930s Chicago resident who runs afoul of a mobster who runs bare-knuckled boxing competitions. Jackie — who had to learn the script phonetically, starting a life-long aversion to learning English — summed up the experience for me thusly: "The script says that I should walk out the door. So I say, 'Look, I can cartwheel to the door, and somersault out.' They say, 'No, just walk out the door.' I say, I can use the chairs and tables to climb and roll to the door, then dive out.' They say, 'no, just walk out.' I was so frustrated. 'No one pays to see Jackie walk!' They said, 'Here they will.'"

They didn't. Jackie got much more mileage (all puns intended) by his appearance with Michael Hui, Hong Kong's top comedy star, in the Golden Harvest-produced, star-studded car chase comedy *The Cannonball Run* (1981). Although he was again encouraged to do stiff-limbed, round-house moves, at least he was able to add the anti-Bruce character touches he had developed. Whether these films helped or hindered his international reputation, Jackie returned to Hong Kong as the crowned heir-apparent to Bruce. His Asian fans didn't seem to care about the relative quality of the American movies — all they knew was that their Jackie was now a worldwide star. Naturally, Jackie immediately set about dismantling it all.

It was a teeth-gritting few years for Golden Harvest. Rather than build upon his kung fu comedies, Jackie rightly decided that he had gone as far as he could in that direction. Only problem was that he wasn't sure what to replace it with. So began a nearly two-year odyssey of trial and error in an attempt to create a new style of kung fu action. First Jackie and company laboriously developed new sports games to replace firecracker-vying and lion dances. One seemed to be a brutal combination of soccer and badminton (a variant of Jianzi), while the other was a truly insane mass race up a bamboo pyramid to secure a bun at the top. Yes, a bun.

Neither of these would ever replace football, which his crew painfully discovered as Jackie set a Guinness World Record for most takes of a single shot — a mind-boggling two thousand, nine hundred times up the effing pyramid. Originally designed to end the movie, the sequence was moved to the beginning to secure a memorable opening. But that left the finale open, and plagued by overspending and overshooting, Jackie finally succumbed to studio pleading and decided upon a fight scene. But Jackie being Jackie, it was no ordinary fight scene.

By then the meandering story had settled upon a simple device: when a love letter goes awry, Jackie's character stumbles upon a gang of thieves who are selling Chinese antiques to gweilo collectors (a plot Chan would reuse constantly). Trapped in a barn with his friend (Mars) and his friend's captive father, the kung fu-lite Jackie must face the kung fu-heavy lead villain (Wang In-sik once more). What follows is the best street brawl-style, realistic kung fu fight thus far filmed, as Jackie is pummeled mercilessly while he goes manic on his opponent. Again, Jackie triumphs through sheer adrenalin, the ability to survive abuse, and his opponent's arrogant inability to counter martial hysteria with concentrated, all-out devastation.

Golden Harvest did the best it could with the unusual, unfocused, sprawling money pit of a movie Jackie handed them. Touting it throughout the long production as *Young Master in Love*, it was finally released as *Dragon Lord* (1982). Not surprisingly, it didn't do as well as they hoped, but, surprisingly, it did much better than they thought it would in Japan — a considerably more profitable market than Hong Kong. For that reason alone, all was forgiven, and Jackie assured his agitated bosses that now he knew what he was doing.

And he did. *The Big Brawl* and *Dragon Lord* experiences had brought into focus what Jackie always thought was wrong with Hong Kong action films. But now he was in a position to do something about it. And what he planned to do was drag the kung fu film, kicking and screaming, into the twentieth century. Precious few kung fu films had been made picturing that era, so Jackie set his new film in 1903. The fighting in *Big Brawl* looked mannered, while the fight in *Dragon Lord* looked frenetic, so Jackie started developing a new, dangerous style of screen mayhem — one that would, for the first time, on purpose, show the fighters hitting the ground.

Finally, Jackie decided to also concentrate on the previously least important aspect of Hong Kong movies — the dialogue. Since all South Chinese movies were filmed silently so that the many languages and dialects could be dubbed in afterwards, what the characters were saying had slowly been reduced to such clichés as "You must be tired of living." The glory of dialogue had been brought home to Jackie on *Drunken Master* where an entire scene consisted of Chan and his "Stick King" opponent (renowned choreographer Hsu Hsia) taunted each other with witty, punny variations on classic kung fu technique descriptions ("Dragon Flicks Its Tail at the Moon," etc.). Ironically, when it was later subtitled and dubbed in English, all that was replaced with "Damn you," and "Eat shit."

Project A (aka *Pirate Patrol*, 1983) also took a while to produce, but it was not from indecision. Instead, it was from the scope of what Jackie was successfully attempting. The title derived from the name of the plan that the Chinese Coast Guard had to clean the harbor of pirates who preyed on foreign ships. Chan played "Dragon Ma," one of the sailors who are constantly at odds with the Chinese police over who should get the bulk of the indecisive government's pirate-busting budget.

The Clown Prince of Kung Fu

A "discussion" of this turns into a barroom brawl where Chan shows off his sharpened skills as actor, choreographer, stuntman, and director. As a result of this fight, and the fact that their boats are sabotaged, the government assigns the sailors to the police force. It seems that the headquarters for illegal smuggling is in a swank nightclub that caters to foreigners and various criminal scum. After trying it the civilized way, only to be humiliated, Jackie and his crew attack in a breath-taking battle that brings home just how serious Jackie was about showing himself and his stuntmen hitting the floor.

But he's not done ... not by a long shot. The film's center is an extended chase/fight scene that's obviously inspired by the silent comedy films of Buster Keaton and Harold Lloyd — only with Jackie's more extreme "damage-wish" — that climaxes with Chan's fall from a clock tower through three cloth awnings that were supposed to split under his weight ... but don't always. The shot was so impressive that Jackie shows all three takes, one after the other, before carrying on with the breathless, elating film.

The climatic sequences take place in and on the pirate's beautifully realized lair, incorporating a wonderful pure dialogue sequence where a disguised Jackie must fast-talk the pirate king (the masterful Dick Tei Wei) that he is who he says he is, when faced with a pirate collaborator (Li Hai-sheng) who knows he isn't. Thankfully this cliffhanger is interrupted by the final battle, as Jackie's few allies (Mars, Yuen Baio, and Sammo Hung) must take on the pirate army. But even after the film ended, Jackie left his audience happy by including outtakes during the end credits — but not outtakes of flubbed lines (as in *Cannonball Run*) ... outtakes of flubbed stunts (including some painful shots of the bar room brawl and clock-tower fall that go horribly wrong)!

Project A was Jackie's first solo kung fu film revolution ... with a little help from his friends. "At the beginning of filming *Project A*,

I was only an actor," Sammo, Jackie's Peking Opera School senior, told me. "But after a year, Jackie had only finished half the movie. Filming did not go very smoothly. So Golden Harvest asked me to take care of the rest of the movie. It worked out okay because I've known Jackie since he was a little boy. If it wasn't me, Jackie wouldn't have allowed it. We finished, and it turned out well."

That was an understatement. It turned out great, and the box office returns reflected it. Jackie was back on top, and had every intention of staying there. But, of course, he hadn't counted on Golden Harvest, Lo Wei, and the rest of the film industry. Lo cobbled together some feeble outtakes and released the execrable *Fearless Hyena Part II* (1983). Another small company took that moment to release *Fantasy Mission Force* (1983), a fun, silly adventure "Jacky" had done an extended cameo in (reportedly as a favor to Jimmy Wang Yu, who supposedly served as Chan's protector in his early cinema years). Then the studio pressed him into *Cannonball Run II* (1984), which was a lesser, but still mildly entertaining, film on all counts.

As if that wasn't enough, Jackie also co-starred with Yuen Baio and Sammo Hung in several Sammo-directed kung fu comedies as pay back for Hung's help on *Project A*. *Winners and Sinners* (1983) and, especially, *Wheels on Meals* (1984) added to Jackie's experience and reputation. Both featured great kung fu, although the latter showcased a classic — a climatic fight with real-life martial arts champ Benny "the Jet" Urquidez that was even more effective and realistic than *Dragon Lord*.

"We filmed it for forty-eight hours straight," Benny told me, "and Sammo asked if I would take a punch on camera. After some thought, I agreed, but told him 'you only get one shot at this.' You can clearly see it in the finished film. That was a lot of work, but a lot of fun, and I think it shows." Sammo concurred, remembering the collaboration with Benny and Jackie as very satisfying and rewarding. But then Golden Harvest reared its head, and back to

America Jackie went for another misconceived misfire.

The Protector (1985) was supposed to correct all the missteps of *The Big Brawl*, but sadly it only replaced one mistake for another. *Brawl* was Jackie and Bruce Lee lite. But *Protector*...? "I make you Clint Eastwood," Jackie told me the film's director (James Glickenhaus) whispered to him. This crude, lewd, stupid modern crime film fit Jackie like a tarp and is painful to watch. But Jackie dutifully slogged through it, establishing another unfortunate Chan American tradition. Rather than try to correct, or even influence, his U.S. directors and producers, Jackie will just do as he's told. He will contribute his knowledge and expertise only if specifically asked to.

But there's one other tradition that this unfortunate exercise cemented. Jackie is never more inspired on what to do right than when returning from an American misfire. First, he filmed additional scenes and recut *The Protector* for its Hong Kong release. Then he decided to do for the modern kung fu film what *Project A* did for the historical kung fu film. Prior to this, kung fu films set in the present were either extremely cheap thrillers in which traditional Peking Opera drama were given polyester trappings (a la Chang Cheh's *The Chinatown Kid*), or campy adventures which ignored the high-caliber realities of modern weaponry (ala Liu Chia-liang's *The Lady Is the Boss*).

This time Chan intended to take everything he had learned about moviemaking, and pour his heart and soul — and his alone — onto the screen. Jackie's story of an obsessed cop trying to bring down a drug kingpin had a sophistication of approach that was light-years beyond anything else. As with *Project A*, Jackie saw to it that much of the film's success came from characterization and plot — two vastly underused ingredients in the Hong Kong film mix. He balanced inventive comedy with emotional drama, making the audience truly care about, and identify with, the characters — something else that had been in short supply in Hong Kong cinema.

Then there's the action: one classic fight after another. First was the shantytown battle, ending with Jackie driving through a hillside village created especially for the film (a scene that was copied, shot for shot, in Michael Bay's 2003 *Bad Boys II*). Then, the double-decker bus fight, starting with Jackie hanging off the back by an umbrella and ending with a scene Sylvester Stallone "borrowed" (using it poorly) in the opening of *Tango and Cash* (1989), where crooks fly out of the braking bus to crash to the road below (sending them to the hospital in real life).

Finally, there's the greatest shopping-mall fight ever filmed. Jackie battles from one side to the other of a real shopping mall (which the crew had from closing at night to opening in the morning), imaginatively using all the store displays in a virtuoso performance that not only rivaled anything that Chaplin or Keaton had done, but Schwarzenegger, Mel Gibson, and Bruce Willis as well. Seeing a man drop off a balcony and hit the floor in 1900's Hong Kong was one thing, but seeing someone (stuntman Fung Hak-on) flip backward onto a shopping-mall's real steel escalator in the present day was another.

Not surprisingly, Jackie didn't spare himself either. He banged himself up regularly (as evidenced by the end credit outtakes), but also seriously burned his hands during the climatic stunt in which he slid down a three-story, lightbulb-strewn, pole to catch the villain (famed director, now actor, Chu Yuan). "They were supposed to be low-watt bulbs," Jackie revealed to me. "They weren't." Even without that oversight, it took hours for him to gather up the courage to actually jump off the mezzanine and onto the pole. "I want to film," he said. "When we're not filming, I worry. 'Maybe I'll get hurt…maybe I'll die.' But when I hear the cry from the camera crew 'Rolling!' I forget everything and just do it."

The thrill of recognition seemed to shoot through Asian audiences, especially since everything was actually being done by the actors playing each role (even occasionally heroines Brigitte Lin and Maggie Cheung). If Jackie Chan had been a superstar before, he was a screen deity now. In two words: game-changing. In another word: universal. Despite there being three different cuts of the film: a basic Chinese edition, a more emotionally complete Japanese version (with character development scenes added to the beginning and the end) and a shortened American edit (that was the hit of the 1988 New York Film Festival), the landmark, influential *Police Story* (1985) works brilliantly in any language.

Jackie, meanwhile, filled his workaholic schedule by appearing in three more Sammo-directed productions. *Heart of Dragon* (1985) was supposed to be their change-up — a straight-on drama of a conflicted young man (Chan) dealing with his mentally challenged brother (Hung). But self-doubt and studio pressure led to Sammo adding three out-of-place fight scenes — great though they were. The climatic fight, in fact, ranks as one of Sammo's all-time greatest.

"I spent most of the movie working on that final fight scene," Sammo told me. "I wanted it to be very different. I wanted it to have incredible style. From the very beginning to the very end of the final fight sequence I used a track camera to create a really exciting, thundering style."

But after that unsure effort, the classmates now known as "the Three Brothers," regrouped for *My Lucky Stars* (1985) — set in Japan to please the burgeoning mass of Japanese Jackie fans — and *Twinkle Twinkle Lucky Stars* (1985), both featuring Sammo, Yuen Baio, and Chan alongside a slightly shifting group of popular comic actors (Richard Ng, Eric Tsang, et al) who spent all their time between a few fight scenes trying to inappropriately touch or ogle girls. Jackie even found time to produce and/or cameo in a few comedies of his own (1984's *Pom Pom* and 1986's *Naughty Boys*).

But when all was said and done, he still had to confront the problem of topping himself. *Lucky Star* member Eric Tsang had the answer: why do something completely new when he could gratify his Chinese audience by doing Indiana Jones one better? For decades, "Cantowood" had an inferiority complex about Hollywood. Rather than create their own soundtracks, independent kung fu film producers had been ripping off the James Bond, *Star Wars*, and Spaghetti Western scores of John Barry, John Williams, and Ennio Morricone for years. When I first visited Hong Kong, the usual reaction to my professed love of the genre was an incredulous "You *like* those things?!"

So the idea of giving *Raiders of the Lost Ark* (1981) a distinct Chan spin was attractive — especially with experienced writer/producer/actor Tsang as director (Jackie had been particularly impressed with his back-to-back direction for 1980's *The Loot* and *The Challenger* — two lively, enjoyable independent kung fu comedies starring David Chiang, Norman Chu, Kao Fei, and Lily Li). Thus *Armour of God* (1986) was conceived, and Jackie threw himself into this anxiously awaited effort. He was riding high, so, naturally, the egomaniacal industry was waiting for him to fall ... but no one thought he would do it literally.

Jackie ignored the nay-sayers, enjoying the worldwide locations where they were scheduled to film — starting with an action-packed prologue in Yugoslavia where the "Asian Hawk," an international finder of rarities, had gone to secure an ancient tribe's idol. "I had just flown in from a meeting," Chan remembered. "Maybe I hadn't had enough sleep." The director was on another location (some say he was busy shopping), but that had never slowed Jackie down before. He and his handpicked team of stuntmen went to work realizing the sequence.

The stunt was relatively easy: jump from a thirty-foot-high wall to a branch, hold on to the tall, thin tree as it bent over from his weight, and drop safely behind a second wall. The scene went well the first time they filmed it — and was, in fact, the version that is seen in the actual movie — but Jackie thought he could do better. The second time the branch broke.

"If the cameraman had tried to cushion my fall, or even just pushed me a little, I would have been okay," Jackie explained on the UK-TV series *Son of the Incredibly Strange Film Show*. "But he grabbed the camera and ran away!" Jackie landed heavily, hitting his head on a rock. "At the time I didn't think it was that bad. But when I looked up I saw my stunt guys and my father crying. Later, when I looked at the film, I saw the blood coming from my ear."

In Hong Kong film, it was customary that when someone gets hurt, even breaks a limb, they just go get it set, administer some Chinese herbs, and return to the set (as Liu Chia-liang did after breaking his leg directing *Cat vs. Rat*). But this wound put Jackie in the hospital for weeks. After hours of operating to remove skull fragments from his brain, the doctors were amazed how quickly Jackie recovered. Chan was left with a coin-sized hole in his skull, covered in plastic, which vibrates when he hums. He was also left with a firm conviction that *Armour of God* must be finished.

Many film industry leeches and weasels were waiting for him to fail, but he would not give them the satisfaction. Besides, Golden Harvest had a lot of money invested in the production, and Chan's work ethic would not let them down. After recollecting the cast (Alan Tam, Rosamund Kwan) many months later (resulting in an obvious on-screen change of hairstyle [some thought Jackie's original "unlucky" hairdo was the supernatural cause of his accident]), Chan restarted the production with himself at the helm and a lot to prove — namely that he still "had it."

He did, but, understandably, *Armour of God* is one of his most makeshift efforts. The plot hinged on the prophecy that if the title weapons — five pieces of medieval armament — fall into evil hands or are destroyed, the world would be plunged into ruin. Well, the armor does get stolen by a money and sex-loving cult, and are destroyed in the finale, but no ruin is forthcoming. Like a good magician, Jackie distracted the audience from that slip with extremely impressive stunts and action set pieces.

While recuperating, Chan had plenty of time to consider the state of kung fu film choreography — especially that traditional Bruce bug-a-boo that saw him being attacked by a circling mob … one at a time. So Jackie designed, developed, and put into action a circular form of kung fu defense that allowed him to take on multiple attackers at the same time by constantly turning, even spinning. He had already played with the multiple attacker situation in *Project A* and *Police Story*, but usually by being more beat up and/or moving faster. In *Armour of God*, he got the better of his assailants by always knowing where they were, and putting his attack in effect even while whirling.

Originally Cynthia Rothrock was supposed to be the *Armour*'s ultimate fighting guard, but after Jackie's injury, scheduling conflicts precluded her participation. She was replaced by four African actresses in black leather and painful high heels. They were doubled by mortifyingly-disguised Jackie stunt team members, but this final fight, before the literally explosive finale, was still exceedingly entertaining. Ironically, because the audience wondered how Jackie would bounce back from such an injury, *Armour of God* became his most financially successful movie ever.

Still, it is safe, and sad, to say that Jackie was never the same. Although he had suffered many a broken bone even before *Armour*, this closer brush with mortality made him twice shy. Much as the direction of the James Bond series veered into farce as a result of Sean Connery's retirement, and George Lazenby's foolish resignation, Chan's injury caused him to reexamine his future — to the detriment of his films. Rather than continue to break new ground, Chan embarked on a series of sequels and "culmination" productions. It seemed as if the kung fu film clown prince wanted to get in as much sure-fire action as he still could.

Project A II (1987), the follow-up to *Pirate Patrol,* didn't lack ambition. It was Jackie's most obvious homage to Buster Keaton, and his last great attempt at a sophisticated story. Playing the same intrepid Coast Guard/police officer as he had in the original, Jackie is seconded to a corrupt police troop in a small city, where he must fight his own bribe-taking comrades as well as crime bosses, revolutionaries, sadistic mainland Chinese agents, and even the ax-wielding remnants of the pirates he defeated in the prequel.

Jackie took the opportunity to streamline and perfect the French-farce touches he had attempted in previous films, as well as mount a series of comic confrontations that take place in an exotic nightclub, a soy-milk factory, a fish hatchery, a chicken-plucking establishment, and, finally, throughout an entire town he had specially built on the back lot of the Shaw Brothers Studio. His accident also seemed to effect his approach to the fight scenes. When, before, he would clearly defeat his adversary, in *Project A II,* he went to obvious lengths to just dump them, or have them chased, off screen. It was as if, having experienced the pain of nearly dying, he couldn't bear to do it to his beloved creations.

He didn't seem to mind still doing it to himself, however. One of the climax's most memorable moments is when he stuffs his mouth full of hot peppers so he could spit the chewed mulch on his hands to blind his opponents with it. "They were real," Jackie told me. "I, for one, will never forget that scene, that's for sure." Nor will his fans, many of whom declare *Project A II* Jackie's finest directorial effort.

Next came *Police Story 2* (1988), which continued the traditions of villain-dumping established on the prior production, while adding a new wrinkle. This sequel was really two one-hour films: the first being a continuation of the original (where a dying Chu Yuan attempts to make the hero's life miserable), and the second seeing

Jackie take on a team of, literally and figuratively, explosive extortionists. Although not as cohesive as his previous films, the stunt team was at the height of its powers, mounting one amazing fight scene after another — fight scenes of such complexity and speed that they needed to be reviewed repeatedly to capture all the nuances.

The now de rigueur end credit outtakes give witness to the price: both Jackie and co-star Maggie Cheung received head wounds during the production (thankfully neither as dire as *Armour of God*'s accident). Chan's old friend Sammo Hung's professional situation was far more dire. At the same time Jackie was flying high, Hung's filmography had hit a rough patch. In addition to decreasing box office returns for his work, Sammo had gone public with his contention that his films wouldn't have failed if Jackie had agreed to appear in them. While that may have been true, as far as it goes, it didn't exactly endear him to his Peking Opera School junior.

Even so, Jackie was now in his mid-thirties, and his internal alarm clock was ticking louder every day. The idea of a final "Three Brothers" film — one that would immortalize their kung fu skills at their optimum, was not anathema to him. So deciding, they shot the works with *Dragons Forever* (1988), a literally fight-filled extravaganza featuring almost every kung fu supporting player they could cram in (including Dick Tei Wei, Philip Kao Fei, Billy Chow, Yuen Wah, Chin Kar-lok, Fung Hak-on, Liu Chia-yung, and much of both Jackie's and Sammo's stunt teams).

Curiously, each of the stars played anti-heroes (Jackie an amoral lawyer, Sammo a gun runner, and Yuen Baio a benignly demented burglar) — two of whom are redeemed by true love with sisters who are being persecuted by an eccentric, sadistic drug lord. As the three struggle through the plot, the fights are fast, ample, and amazing. The trio fight each other and literally dozens of thugs in restaurants, nightclubs, parking lots, pleasure boats, and, finally, in a drug factory where each does some of his most impressive work.

The Clown Prince of Kung Fu

There Sammo stages a rematch between Jackie and Benny "the Jet" Urquidez, the villain's main cocaine taster. "This one took a little longer," Urquidez explained to me. "We worked for weeks on this fight, and, yes, they [i.e. the action director, choreographer, and stuntmen] do pretty much make it up as they go along." The humor in this fight is more facile than in *Wheels on Meals,* and the brutality lessened, but they still get their kicks in, although, for the first time ever, Jackie is clearly doubled by a stuntman (most likely Chin Kar-lok) for the fight's penultimate kick.

"Jackie was on another set," an insider who did not wish to be identified maintained. "Sammo works so fast that Jackie didn't have time to be both places at once ... and we needed that shot." It would not be the last time Sammo used stand-ins for Jackie in the midst of his frenetic fight sequences. But, despite an interesting story and many terrific fight scenes, it appeared as if the audience had not forgiven Sammo, or perhaps was a bit jaded by the trio.

For whatever reason, *Dragons Forever* had a surprisingly soft box-office take — even in Japan, which had traditionally been a Chan stronghold.

That, among other things, convinced Jackie to go his own way. "I've done everything three times," he told me. So he decided to stop trying to honor Buster Keaton, Bruce Lee and Gene Kelly, and start trying to honor his latest screen idol: Steven Spielberg. So, for the next year, Chan slaved on what was originally titled *Miracle,* but eventually became *Mr. Canton and Lady Rose* (1989). It was his combination of *Project A,* Francis Ford Coppola's *The Godfather* (1972), and, most especially, *Pocketful of Miracles* (1961).

It was also Jackie's favorite directing job, featuring his most complex camera work, elaborate musical montages, and highlighted by a sweeping crane shot that took seventeen hours to set up (and had to be done twice). Even so, this particular amalgam of a thirties' gangster movie, a romantic musical comedy, and a kung fu flick leaps from genre to genre over its two-hour running time — and not always elegantly. Wedged between more French-farce sequences and classic Cantonese comedy scenes were four brilliantly conceived fights, climaxed by one of Chan's finest.

Having completed the rest of the filming, Chan and his stuntmen, now numbering seventeen, started to plan the finale. They set the crew to work building the interior of a rope factory from the ground up, and designed an intricate series of amusing and amazing battles amongst the many floor levels, stairs, elevators, and gigantic spools of hemp. The resulting choreography of flying bodies, wrapping cord, and rolling barrels is awesome. Some say, however, that it was too much, too late. The fights were only punctuation for long patches of somewhat desperate comedy. Although more impressive each time it is watched, *Miracle* was not enough of a miracle, so all involved looked across the globe to the single biggest box office in the world.

"No American movie theater will play a movie with an all-Chinese cast," Golden Harvest producer David Chan was told. "But what about Bruce Lee?" was his inevitable reply. "Oh," came the equally inevitable answer. "He was the *exception*." So the seemingly unexceptional Jackie Chan, at least in American eyes, set about to create his most spectacular film: a world-hopping challenge to his skills as a director, producer, and star, featuring only two Asian actors in a large cast of Caucasians. This was *Armour of God II: Operation Condor* (1991). Taking an idea from famed Italian actor Aldo Sambrell (seen in every Clint Eastwood "Man With No Name" spaghetti Western) about Nazi gold buried beneath the Sahara, they developed an exciting script to be filmed on location.

But as soon as they left the comforts of Hong Kong, everything went wrong. "I think *Operation Condor* was Jackie's *Apocalypse Now*," said Vincent Lyn, the actor, model, composer, teacher, and kick-boxing champion who played Mark, the scarred villain. "Sets were being blown away and burned down. Equipment and film were actually melting in the Sahara heat. His entire crew was getting sick, and not just with the flu. The assistant director (seen in the opening sequence being supported by two native women) had a stroke. Jackie's production manager was arrested and kept in jail for months because extras were using the fake prop money in town."

Even Lyn's participation was as a result of a problem. He was brought in because one of the other Western actors accidentally kicked Jackie in the throat (the moment captured in the movie's end-credit outtakes). Originally, this actor and his on-screen partner were to fight Jackie in the film's "Nazi wind-tunnel" climax, but were replaced by Vincent and Jackie's long-time friend, bodyguard, and trainer Ken Lo after the accident.

"Even though I had been in eighteen Hong Kong kung fu movies, Jackie and his crew made me feel like I had two left feet," Lyn confessed. "They really were incredible, but Jackie had way too much to do. Even though they had moved the production back to Hong Kong by this time (bringing tons of Sahara sand with them for authenticity), Jackie was directing, starring, choreographing, producing, and rewriting as he went along."

Days became weeks, weeks became months, and months became years as Jackie struggled to finish *Operation Condor*. By the end of production, the characters had become unreasoning ciphers, and the three female co-stars — a Chinese (Do Do Cheng), a Japanese (Shoko Ikeda), and a white girl (Eva Cobo de Garcia) chosen to "please" the three movie markets Chan hoped to top — seemed to be sharing the same handicapped brain. Just about the only thing that was truly effective was that Chan used the film to display a compendium of ways to imaginatively disarm gun-toting opponents.

Needless to say, the final result failed to supply Jackie with the breakthrough he was hoping for. Instead it nearly broke him. After that nightmare, Chan was probably at his lowest point, physically and mentally. So, naturally, the wolves who then ran in the Hong Kong film business moved in. That's how *Island of Fire* (1991) — Jackie's weakest feature since the Lo Wei days — came about. Done as a favor to powerful mob "producers," and cobbled together by Jimmy Wang Yu from pieces of *The Wild Geese* (1978), *The Dirty Dozen* (1967), *Cool Hand Luke* (1967), and *The Longest Yard* (1974), the Philippine sci-fi prison break adventure (also featuring the kowtowing Sammo Hung and Andy Lau) had some decent fights, but was best forgotten by all involved.

Upon his return to Hong Kong, Jackie was at a loss. To save Chan's sanity, Golden Harvest hired stunt coordinator Stanley Tong to direct *Police Story 3: Supercop* (1992). Until this film, the women in Jackie movies were set decoration (or, as they called it in Asian cinema, "jade vases") at best. Although the marvelous Maggie Cheung was still playing Jackie's long-suffering girlfriend in this installment, she was always portrayed as having something short of a full intellectual deck. Reportedly, it was Tong's idea to hire the magnificent Michelle Yeoh to play Jackie's mainland equal, and she matches him kick for kick and stunt for stunt (so much so that Jackie reportedly kept upping the danger of his own stunts to keep pace with her). The film also has the distinction of being the very first Hong Kong film ever to be shot with live synchronized sound.

Supercop reinvigorated Jackie enough to float the idea of a straight-forward love story, but first he was pressed into service on a film created to benefit the Hong Kong Director's Guild (so they could build, buy, or rent a headquarters). Co-directed by Tsui Hark and Ringo Lam, *Twin Dragons* (1992) featured dozens of directors in bit parts (including Liu Chia-liang and Johnny Wang Lung-wei) and starred Jackie in the dual role of twins separated at birth. One grew up to be a tough, hard-living Hong Kong car mechanic who's in with the local mob, while the other became an orchestra leader in America. When the latter returns to Hong Kong for a concert, he finds that the two share nerves and reflexes, ala Alexander Dumas' classic novel *The Corsican Brothers*. A merry mix-up of identities ensues, often placing the two Jackies on-screen together. It was Chan's first foray into the world of special photographic effects, and was less than inspiring for him.

"In special effects, you can do anything, and the audience knows it," Jackie mused. "Where's the excitement in that?" Even so, it opened a door for Jackie, who entertained himself experimenting with how much he could mix kung fu with sfx (special effects). He dabbled a bit with it in his next film, which was also designed to put him back into the Japanese audience's good graces. *City Hunter* (1993) was the Hong Kong version of a popular Japanese comic book (manga) character, directed by schlockmeister supreme Wong Jing. As silly as most of Jing's work, it still boasts two classic sequences: one where Jackie takes lessons from an on-screen Bruce Lee in a movie theater fight scene, and another where, in a fantasy/dream sequence, Chan becomes several characters from the *Street Fighter* arcade videogame — including a dead-on impersonation of the female fighter Chun Li!

Coming off that giddily entertaining "anything goes" lampoon, Jackie wanted to sink his teeth into something a little more substantial. He found it in *Crime Story* (1993), which was supposed to be new wave director Kirk Wong's first film in a projected modern crime trilogy starring real-life wushu champion Jet Li. However, after Jet's manager was murdered in an underworld battle for control of the Hong Kong film industry, Li went to mainland China for awhile, and Jackie decided to take the role. After a much publicized tug-of-wills between the director and star, the movie became Chan's manifesto.

Although the script started as the tale of a conflicted cop trying to settle his psyche with the help of a sexy female psychiatrist while searching for a kidnapped millionaire, there's a telling moment early on. Jackie has tried desperately to prevent the businessman's abduction when a motorcycle cop is hurt in the ensuing chase. Jackie carries him to the emergency room, where his gorgeous shrink waits. He takes one look at her sympathetic, caring, beautiful face ... then purposefully steps around her to share his frustration with the hospital wall. He might as well have picked her up and tossed her off-screen, because from that moment on, *Crime Story* is for, by, and about Jackie Chan.

In fact, the climatic scenes might serve as autobiographical sequences. As the bad guy lies under rubble in an exploding apartment block, he tells Jackie that everyone thinks he's crazy, that he tries too hard, and that he never gives up. Jackie replies that he can't help it, and continues to manically save the dying villain as well as an innocent child trapped by the blaze. Aside from a confusing finale in which the kidnap victim is seemingly drowned, only to turn up fine in the next scene, *Crime Story* is as psychologically revealing as any Woody Allen film.

It certainly seemed to free Jackie up enough to make a long awaited return to his roots. Sixteen years after making his first Huang Fei-hong film, Jackie hired none other than Liu Chia-liang to direct *Drunken Master II* (aka *Legend of Drunken Master*, 1994). Remarkably, the then-forty year old Jackie is credible playing the mischievous "twenty-something" Huang, despite the fact that the majestic Ti Lung, only seven years older than Chan, is playing his father. The plot was a recognizable retread of Jackie's trademark "evil gang selling Chinese antiquities," but it didn't matter. The combination of Jackie's Spielbergian ideas with Liang's classic traditions made for a monumental achievement, which many consider Chan's best film.

"There can't be two tigers on the mountain," is an old Chinese proverb, and Chan quoted it often after firing Liang and taking over the film. Gutting a major supporting role by Andy Lau, Jackie brought back Ti Lung and Anita Mui to reshoot and design new sequences over a six-month period. He complained that Liang only wanted him to do drunken boxing during the final battle, then to wipe out nearly hundreds with it. Instead, Jackie set about establishing the drunken style earlier in the film, and creating a spectacular, albeit more intimate, climatic battle.

Meanwhile, Liang took Lau and went off to make *Drunken Master III* (1994), a weak attempt at payback. Even so, the master of the kung fu movie did manage to complete one more film prior to his retirement, *Drunken Monkey* (2003), for a temporarily resurrected Shaw Brother Studio film unit. Co-starring Jacky Wu Jing and Gordon Liu Chia-hui, it was a fitting kung fu-filled finale that also served as a metaphor for the director's triumph over adversity and illness (Liang beat cancer in addition to everything else).

Back at *Drunken Master II*, Chan was obviously inspired to live up to Liang's kung fu skills. The final fight, in an audaciously designed metal foundry set, is among the best things Chan has ever accomplished, mixing amazing martial arts and acrobatics with involving and emotional moments — culminating with Huang Feihong drinking industrial alcohol to achieve his ethereally unbeatable Drunken Master status. Rather than take on dozens as Liang had reportedly intended, Chan narrowed his focus to a few, culminating in a one-on-one tour de force with his friend, ex-bodyguard, training-mate, and super-kicker Ken Lo.

"In the last fight scene, I was going to fight someone else (Ho Sun-park)," Jackie revealed. "He's a very good marital artist, but he couldn't get the rhythm down — he keeps twisting his ankle, so I used Ken Lo. I had Ken train hard for three months even before we started filming it."

But even then, accidents happened. Adding to his list of on-set injuries (dislocated shoulder, dislocated sternum, broken fingers, broken eyebrow ridge, dislocated cheek bone, crushed legs) was a broken nose when the alcohol-powered Jackie charged his adversary.

"I've broken bones from head to toe," Jackie said. "But broken legs and fingers don't matter. I hurt for weeks and months, but my films give people memories that can keep for years." And many people think of *Drunken Master II* as Jackie's kung fu masterpiece.

The only discordant note in the finished film was the final scene where, in the original Hong Kong release, Huang is shown to have been rendered mentally incompetent by his ordeal — his performance enough to make even Jerry Lewis cringe (in fact, the scene was removed from the American version).

Drunken Master II was a critical and financial bonanza, and clearly the best movie Jackie Chan made since *Project A II*. And with it, he had accomplished something no other action star had ever done: he gained entry to the mainland. Only Jackie Chan films were allowed into Red China. Although ticket prices there were less than a dollar, the cinemas had a potential audience of billions. With voracious audiences in Japan and China, and a Hong Kong studio willing to give him all the time and money in the world, Chan was unique: clearly the most popular action star in the world, the only filmmaker with unquestioned authority, resources, and power, and the only man on the planet willing to die for his audience.

"I'd much rather die on a movie set than in a car or plane crash," he said. "I love making movies ... and I don't want to die for nothing." The writing on the marquee was clear. It was time for him to conquer the one mountain that had always eluded him. It was time to return to America.

Even though *Police Story* had been the hit of the New York Film Festival, Hollywood was slow to accept Chinese-style action, but the underground video world was quick to pick up the slack. Intrigued by a book on the subject, as well as television specials that were broadcast on the Arts and Entertainment and Discovery channels (hmmm…wonder who wrote and/or instigated those?), thrill-seekers sought out Chan's films in Chinatowns and through vaguely legal specialty mail-order houses.

By the time New Line Cinema made a deal to distribute Chan's new films in America, and Dimension Films arranged to screen some of his older movies, the audience that made *Star Trek*, *Star Wars*, *Superman*, and *Batman* famous were already well aware of Jackie's talents. Now all he had to do was create new films for the international market that lived up to his past classics. Easier said than done.

"American stuntmen try to teach me how to fight," Jackie recalled. "I ask them, 'How long have you been fighting?' Two years. I studied Northern Style ten years, Southern style five years, hapkido, six months, karate, four months, boxing three months…. 'How long have you been in the movie business?' Three years. I've been in the action movie business for more than forty years. Most people who choreograph martial arts films in the U.S. only know how to fight. They don't know about their audiences, and the effects needed to excite that audience."

Still, Double-Boy wasn't giving up on his American dream. First came *Rumble in the Bronx* (1995), fueled by an exceptional New Line promotional campaign. It made more than thirty million dollars, a respectable sum for a film where the kung fu finale had to be scrapped because Jackie broke his ankle. It was infuriating. While Chan was used to being injured on his sets in some spectacular way, now his ankle was snapping after a mere hop from a bridge to a hovercraft. Even so, he merely had a sock painted to look like a sneaker, put it over his cast, and reworked the ending so it could be a car stunt instead of an extended kung fu fight.

Then, much to his fans' dismay, Jackie discovered that he liked replacing his tiring, challenging, final, extended, fight scene with a car stunt. *Thunderbolt* (1995), a wild, aimless auto racing thriller that starred Jackie as an erstwhile *Speed Racer*, featured two great

Sammo-choreographed fight scenes but little else to recommend it. *First Strike* (1996) was a surprisingly tepid spy saga. *Mr. Nice Guy* (1997) and *Who Am I* (1998) — both set in Australia — had some fine fights as well, but that hardly made up for their amateurish acting and feeble plotting.

The year 1998 saw Jackie Chan's American hopes under siege. His U.S. box office had been hurt by the re-editing, re-scoring, re-dubbing, re-titling, and re-releasing of his older movies in America. Chan's movies kept making money, but not the kind of money they could have been making, and one American filmmaker was getting pretty fed up with it. So he took a script about a married couple of cops who bicker their way to find the abducted child of a Chinese diplomat, rewrote it to replace the married couple with a fast-talking, streetwise African-American cop and a straight-laced kung fu cop from China, recruited an actor from his previous film, *Money Talks* (1997), then went to Jackie with a promise: to make him as big in America as he was in the rest of the world.

Brett Ratner was as good as his word, despite the fact that *Rush Hour* (1998) was only his second major feature film. But although Ratner loved Jackie's Hong Kong films and was certain he could translate their joys into the "buddy cop" idiom, it seemed that Jackie didn't like being just an actor, nor being at the mercy of co-star Chris Tucker's quick improvisational wit — especially in a language he had always been uncomfortable with. At first his worries seemed justified. Studio execs who viewed the footage, and critics who attended the premiere, gave the picture only a middling chance of success. Even the director himself was reported to have thought that the movie would probably gross only thirty million, tops.

But those who went to the movie its opening weekend knew different. In hundreds of cinemas across the country, the seats were filled with young and old, male and female, black, white, and Asian — and all of them were smiling. Rarely had any movie attracted such a cross section of filmgoers, and rarely had any movie pleased every one of them. *Rush Hour* turned out to be the movie Jackie Chan had been promising for years — fast, funny, warm, action-filled entertainment with virtually no swearing and essentially no actual violence. Instead, viewers were treated to an effective synthesis of Jackie's trademarks: an inventive use of props as well as an amalgamation of kung fu, wushu, acrobatics, and imagination — all layered with Chan's anti-Bruce approach (humor, showing pain, etc.).

The stars' real-life distrust of one another and their own career ambitions blended perfectly with their characters' motivations, and their well-honed performing skills only inspired each other to greater heights. Tucker's mind and mouth aligned with Jackie's brain and body, resulting in a consummate crowd pleaser. *Rush Hour* went on to gross more than two hundred million dollars, and instigate a series of sequels ... each less effective than the last. And even though Jackie was happy to finally be king of the American hill, he far preferred it on his own terms. The British lease on Hong Kong had run out in 1997, so, as Hong Kong was returned to Chinese rule, Jackie Chan returned to China.

From then until now, he has bounced back and forth between America and Asia, making films in both countries that have ranged from uninspired, though well-meaning, to merely agreeable. In 1999, there was *Gorgeous*, his middling remake of Kevin Costner's romantic comedy *Message in a Bottle* (1999), with some good fight scenes. There he showcased another on-going technique: the imaginative use of putting on, and taking off, his jacket as a martial weapon.

In 2000, he was back to America for a "wushu Western" with Owen Wilson, *Shanghai Noon* (which begat the loosely limbed *Shanghai Knights* in 2003). In 2001, he had the anticlimactic, confusing *The Accidental Spy* in China and *Rush Hour 2* in the U.S. 2002 was a bleak year, indeed, giving rise to, arguably, Chan's worst films:

America's *The Tuxedo* and China's *The Medallion*. It was obvious that his fight scene prowess had reached a physical and mental crescendo. There was precious nothing new, even in the action.

Even Jackie realized he had scaled new lows, so he attempted a return to glory with the tough-minded (but weak-willed) *New Police Story* in 1994. But rather than find new ways of integrating kung fu, he merely ramped the emotional content up to eleven, seemingly crying every chance he got. The American weak-kneed *Around the World in 80 Days* remake during the same year didn't help matters. 2005 saw Jackie in India for *The Myth* — another ultimately unsuccessful attempt to meld his kung fu with special effects. He tried to do a Chinese take on *Three Men and a Baby* (1987) in 2006 with the awkwardly structured (and awkwardly titled) *Rob-B-Hood*. 2007 was marred by the indifferent *Rush Hour 3*.

2008 was the best of Jackie times and the worst of Jackie times. As an example of what American studios can do badly, Lionsgate and The Weinstein Company hired the three greatest kung fu film minds in the world — stars Jackie Chan, Jet Li, and choreographer Yuen Wo-ping — then apparently told them how to do what they did better than anyone else. *The Forbidden Kingdom* is supposedly a film created to honor kung fu, but it has virtually no kung fu in it. There's "martial arts," sure, but from all the balance-robbing-wires, and stiff-armed, stiff-legged, muscle-driven, hip-less action going on, it certainly appeared that someone told the trio to do "mixed martial arts … that's what all the kids are digging these days."

There's a joke in Jiang Hu: know what mixed martial arts is mixed with? Crap.

It's just a joke.

Anyway, the finished film is a mass of misplaced homages, messy battles, ham-fisted story development, and missed opportunities by the dozens. The nominal hero doesn't even learn to avoid a bully's kick, despite the fact that it is used in the exact same way repeatedly throughout the film. When he finally does counter it, it's with a ridiculously self-damaging defense that has as much to do with kung fu as a swan has to do with a dead cow.

Meanwhile, on the other side of town, DreamWorks Animation decided that their first cartoon that wasn't created to undercut or satirize Disney/Pixar would be about a *Kung Fu Panda*. More about that in a later chapter, but suffice to say that Jackie Chan did the voice of the Monkey, and the Chinese Government chided its own cinema industry for not coming up with something as excellent and accurate as it.

Jackie kept busy in 2009 with the well-intentioned *Shinjuku Incident*, a crime thriller devoid of all kung fu, the idolizing mock documentary *Looking for Jackie* (aka *Jackie Chan and the Kung Fu Kid* aka *Jackie Chan Kung Fu Master*), and *The Founding of a Republic*, the Chinese Government's sixtieth anniversary latter-day propaganda film. Chan started 2010 with *The Spy Next Door*, a demoralizing Disney-produced, agonizing American family comedy. But then came the summer and the Will Smith-produced remake of *The Karate Kid*, starring his son Jaden and Jackie in the "Mr. Miyagi" role.

Although the Smiths had lobbied for a title change (and, indeed, the film is known as *The Kung Fu Kid* elsewhere in the world), the studio marketing department demanded "brand recognition" — even though calling this remake *The Karate Kid* would be like calling the tale of a young baseball player *The Football Kid*. Nevertheless, the Harald Zwart-directed remake, although overlong and featuring another fairly ludicrous final defense, is honorable and enjoyable in the extreme, featuring one of Jackie's best performances and an extended central training travelogue sequence that's worth the price of admission.

It was also abundantly clear that, unlike certain aforementioned films I could rename, the kung fu on screen was left up to Jackie. Naturally his veteran fans got a little boost from seeing his "jacket-on, jacket-off" technique return as a fitting, effective, accurate replacement of the witty "wax on, wax off" of the original (although I'm sure the ludicrous final move would not have been Chan's first choice ... but what American would go for a subtle devastating technique when they can do a circus aerialist routine?). Happily, the film was a surprise box office hit, and a sequel was planned.

As of this writing Jackie Chan is still considered the reigning emperor of kung fu films, despite the fact that he is planning to slowly phase out his on-screen involvement in the genre — but not before two farewell productions: the prequel *Drunken Master 1945*, and his ultimate statement in kung fu films, *Chinese Zodiac*, which is about ... surprise, surprise ... the illegal selling of Chinese antiquities. Although he will always be mentioned immediately after Bruce Lee, he has secured his legacy as the anti-Bruce, remaining a vitally important pioneer, a welcome diplomat, a generous philanthropist (with a specialty for education), and an influential ambassador for all good things.

"Before, when I made a movie, it was for money," Jackie told me. "But now when I make a movie, it is my craft. Money comes second. These movies are my babies. To me, movies are my life."

CHAPTER FIVE
THE CLOWN'S COURT

Picture identifications (clockwise from upper left):
Sammo Hung in *Spooky Encounters*; Lam Ching-ying, Chung Fat, Li Hai-sheng, Fung Hak-on, and Yuen Mao in *The Magnificent Butcher*; Moon Lee, Yuen Baio, and Mang Hoi in *Zu Warriors of the Magic Mountain*; Sammo in *The Dead and the Deadly*, Yuen Baio and Jackie Chan in *My Lucky Stars*; *Warriors Two*.

The Clown Prince's Court

Jackie Chan's ascension to the top of the Hong Kong cinematic heap had no real precedent in terms of speed and strength. When Bruce Lee burst upon the scene, it came as a total surprise. No one had done the kind of kung fu he was displaying. But Jackie's way had been prepared for — by Bruce and, especially, Liu Chia-liang, who had conceived the kung fu comedy Jackie perfected. So, by the time Chan did his *Drunken Master* thing, it seemed a welcome, subconsciously anticipated, delight — as if even the audience was his appreciative collaborator.

Although some attributed the success of *Eagle's Shadow* and *Drunken Master* to novice director Yuen Wo-ping, it became rapidly apparent that these films' winning formula was more Chan than Yuen. Wo-ping, born in 1945, and an experienced stunt coordinator, performer, and kung fu choreographer since 1971, subsequently displayed a much rougher, more bizarre bent than Jackie.

Following the success of his first two, Jackie-starring, films, Yuen instituted The Wo Ping Film Company to make a series of increasingly crazier films. He started by cementing his father's fame with *Dance of the Drunken Mantis* (1979), a semi-sequel in which Simon Yuen Siu-tien's "Sam the Seed" (aka Beggar Su) discovers his son, Foggy, only to almost lose him to a vengeful drunken mantis fist fighter named Rubber Legs (Huang Jang-li).

Beyond the odd story, Yuen filled the crude-looking film with family, as well as truly weird comedy characters and situations. He also gave the "Jackie" role to his brother Sunny Yuen Shun-yi, who, although an exceptional martial artist, was hardly what anyone would call classically handsome. He also cast Sunny as the star of *The Buddhist Fist* (1980), another weird, cheap-looking, kung fu-filled effort that combined truly peculiar comedy with a nasty plot about a masked killer rapist (played by Tsui Siu-ming, a Sammo Hung look alike who has had an extensive, eclectic career).

Speaking of Sammo, he and Golden Harvest came calling on

Wo-ping to essentially say, "You know what you did for Jackie in *Drunken Master*? Could you do that for me, please?" The request was not unnatural. Fans had been waiting years for Sammo to play rotund Butcher Wing, one of Huang Fei-hong's favorite disciples (who, in real life, was sifu to Liu Chia-liang's father). So Wo-ping and his own father set to work on *The Magnificent Butcher* (1979), which promised to do Jackie's films one better by having Kwan Tak-hing play the "real" Huang Fei-hong in it. Then, tragically, midway through production, Simon Yuen passed away, requiring a hasty recasting of veteran character actor Fan Mei-sheng in the Sam Seed role.

Although Fan was famous for his many Shaw Studio performances (such as Black Whirlwind in *All Men Are Brothers*), he was hardly as venerated as Simon. Wo-ping attempted to compensate by creating some of the best, and most memorable, Huang Fei-hong scenes in history (including a calligraphy fight that ranks amongst the best ever conceived), but, as good as it was, *Magnificent Butcher* didn't do for Sammo what *Drunken Master* did for Jackie.

Even so, it did great, so naturally, it was Third Brother Yuen Baio's turn to say "please?" That resulted in *Dreadnaught* (1981), Kwan Tak-hing's final Huang Fei-hong performance, where-in a young launderer (Baio) runs afoul of a psychotic murderer (Yuen Shun-yi again) hiding out in a Peking Opera troupe. Wo-ping tries to do the calligraphy scene one better with a "mad tailor" sequence in which an assassin tries to kill Huang while measuring him for a suit, but it didn't cut it (all puns intended).

Those responsibilities to Jackie's classmates concluded, Yuen returned to his predilections, leading to two of the strangest kung fu films ever foisted by a major talent. *The Miracle Fighters* (1982) and *Taoism Drunkard* (directed by Wo-ping's brother Cheung-yan in 1984) have to be seen *not* to be believed. Featuring much of the family as always, it also portrayed such things as a "banana demon" — a black, Pac-Man-like, ball on legs with antennas and a watermelon-slice-shaped, chomping mouth lined with shark teeth.

Whether the film is wacky or wonderful, Wo-ping approached the kung fu choreography in the same way. "I know the plot from start to finish," he explained, "how it progresses and develops. I study how many action scenes, and work out which should be big ones and which should be small ones. Each scene should have its special theme, and they should progress and develop the way the rest of the film does." But within a year, he would find a new path amongst his peers via a developing appreciation of taichi. His directing *Drunken Tai Chi* in 1984 would announce his intentions, as well as introduce a new star to the world: Donnie Yen. But more on him later.

Ironically, Simon Yuen's final appearance as Sam Seed wasn't directed by Yuen. It was in *World of Drunken Master* (1979), which was directed by Joseph Kuo Nam-hung. Simon appeared only in the prologue — replaced for the bulk of the film by Li Yi-min as "young Beggar Su." Joseph Kuo (aka Kuo Qing-chi) is generally considered the monarch of Taiwan martial art moviemakers, which was a bit like being one-eyed amongst the blind. As mentioned earlier, Taiwan produced literally thousands of genre films, so any that even approached Hong Kong quality were considered genius. Kuo approached approaching genius throughout his (unsurprisingly) prolific career. He made dozens of films in a variety of genres, but his best known kung fu efforts include *The Blazing Temple* (1976), *The Seven Grandmasters* (1978), *The Mystery of Chess Boxing* (1979), and *The 36 Deadly Styles* (1979) — while his *Swordsman of all Swordsmen* (1968) and *The 18 Bronzemen* (1978) were landmarks in Taiwan cinema.

By that time, he had hit upon a winning kung fu formula. Using brothers Jack Long Sai-ga and Mark Long Kwan-wu (as well as Corey Yuen Kwai and Yuen Cheung-yan) as choreographers, he filmed fight after fight, and plotline after plotline, and then pieced them together until they filled ninety minutes. Anything left over was saved for the next ninety-minute slot. However disjointed his stories, there was always ample entertainment value in the fighting.

The same was true of Lee Tso-nam, another Taiwan moviemaker who rose to the top. He co-starred in Kuo's *Swordsman of All Swordsmen*, and was assistant director on *The Big Boss* — learning his mentors' lessons well. He became a full-fledged director in 1973, and quickly made his name with such fun, catch-all, kung fu films as *The Hot, The Cool and The Vicious* (1976), *Eagle's Claw* (1977), and *Fatal Needles vs. Fatal Fists* (1978). They were also elevated by the assured, pleasantly complex choreography by Tommy Lee Gamming, who learned his craft in a Taiwanese Opera School, and was exceptional at designing multi-group fight scenes of eight or more, so the camera could move seamlessly from one group of fighters to the next.

All these starred Delon Tan (aka Tan Tao-liang) and Don Wang Tao (who was once groomed as a "new Bruce Lee"). The Bruce connection was not lost on Tso-nam, since he also made some of the most enjoyable "Bruce Clone" films, such as *Exit the Dragon, Enter the Tiger* (1976, with Bruce Li), *Chinese Connection 2* (1977, with Bruce Li), *The Tattoo Connection* (1978, with Jim Kelly), and *Enter the Game of Death* (1978, with Bruce Le).

Both Kuo and Tso-nam benefited greatly by filling their films with the best acting and fighting talent they could find. Their cast lists are a who's who of superior supporting players, including Ku Feng, Bolo, Bruce Leung Siu-lung, Li Hai-sheng, Philip Kao Fei, Chen Kuan-tai, Shoji Kurata, Lo Lieh, and Chang Yi. If you watch kung fu movies at all, you'll see these guys again and again.

But beyond the relative quality of their work, Joseph Kuo and Lee Tso-nam assured their international fame through a stroke of luck. Both made deals with pioneering exporter Ocean Shores Limited to sell their flicks internationally for the home entertainment market,

The Clown Prince's Court

catching the first wave of American interest in the genre. While the rest of Hong Kong was belittling kung fu films, Ocean Shores and its farsighted boss Jackson Hung, was instituting a ground-breaking Los Angeles office (run by Matthew Tse), and selling its made-in-China videotapes to whoever would buy or rent them. They even instituted a then-revolutionary rent-by-mail program for the individual American kung fu movie fan.

Although they tried to follow fads (shoving the word "ninja" into any title they could) and swallowed a lot of producers' propaganda (that Americans didn't want widescreen or subtitles), many Asian filmmakers might never have been known on these shores without Ocean Shores. Following quickly into the fray was Tai Seng Entertainment — its American office run by general manager Helen Soo — who snapped up many VHS Ocean Shores videotapes to make the transition onto DVD. This included Sammo Hung's seminal *The Victim* (1980), not to mention the best independently-produced Liu Chia family films (such as 1977's *He Has Nothing But Kung Fu*, 1978's *Dirty Kung Fu*, 1980's *Fists and Guts*, and 1984's *Warrior from Shaolin*).

Back in the early 1980s, Jackie Chan's Peking Opera school senior, Sammo, was chafing a bit over his "younger brother's" mega-success. Born in 1950 and nicknamed after the famous Chinese cartoon character "Sam-mo" (meaning "three hairs"), Hung Kam-po enrolled at the Peking Opera School at the age of ten, started appearing in films at age eleven, then became a freelance stuntman at sixteen. Show business, it seemed, was in his blood.

"I was born into a movie family," he told me. "My father and mother both worked in the Hong Kong movie industry. I learned karate, judo, taekwondo and hapkido, which were the basic needs of my profession then. I worked for all the studios. Even though they didn't look real on screen, I had to spend a lot of time preparing for the fight scenes. It was old-fashioned, traditional kind of kung fu before the stardom of (Jimmy) Wang Yu.

"Actually, I like every kind of kung fu. I didn't think about which one was better than the other, I just learned everything I could. [Style] names were not important. The most important thing was how to defeat somebody. When I was young, things could get very violent. I had a lot of fights. That's how I got my facial scars. I was in a nightclub, and some drunk got so angry that I did a flip on the dance floor. When I got to my car, there were three people waiting to ambush me. One comes up behind me and swings a broken bottle into my face. I'm actually very lucky. If it had gone into my eyes, that would have been it. Even so, it took twenty-three stitches."

Sammo didn't let the scar stop him. He didn't let anything stop him. He got his first kung fu choreographer job at the age of twenty, for *The Fast Sword* (1970), then worked both behind and in front of the camera for several King Hu films, including *A Touch of Zen*, *The Fate of Lee Khan* (1972), and *The Valiant Ones* (1974). He was twenty-three when he started working with Bruce Lee and only a few years older when he got his most prestigious assignment.

"My first major movie as star and director was called *Shaolin Monk* (1977), and the funny thing was I wasn't originally supposed to be in the movie. I wanted Jackie Chan to do it. He was nothing at that time, but I wanted him. But the producers say no. They decide that I'm not too bad, so they say 'Go, you do it.'"

That led to more directing assignments, from *Warriors Two* (1978) to his charming satire of a Bruce-fixated pig farmer, *Enter the Fat Dragon* (1978). All this new-found work necessitated that he finalize his own loyal team of collaborators. The three at the team's core were Yuen Baio, Lam Ching-ying, and Chan Wui-ngai — an eclectic trio culled from Sammo's life at the China Drama Academy, other Peking Opera School alums, and friends made on movie sets. Baio, born in 1957 (making him seven years younger than Sammo and three years younger than Jackie) grew up with his new boss. Ching-ying used to pal around with Sammo when they were both in different schools, and Wu-ngai was an old school sort, who had learned his craft from Han Ying-chieh. Between the three, Sammo got the best of all perspectives.

"From the very beginning I like to do things different," Sammo explained to me. "I like to combine comedy, tragedy, and a lot of action. I like unusual heroes. The audience has more sympathy toward them. Later on, I found out it was better to concentrate on comedy. The audience likes to laugh more than they like to cry, but still the hero has to go through changes."

So Sammo put himself, as well as Jackie Chan, through changes. "Jackie and I worked together often, but I didn't want to be compared with him, just as he didn't want to be compared to Bruce Lee all the time. Everybody has a different idea and approach to filming kung fu. For Jackie the camera hardly moves ... Jackie moves! I like to use the camera to get, and keep, the audience's attention. Same with the editing. Some other directors think that editing is not their job, but I do."

And it showed. Sammo established himself as one of the finest fight scene makers ever in what many consider his finest film: *The Prodigal Son* (1981). A beautiful, brilliant, powerful film about a young man who's fooled into thinking he is a great fighter, an asthmatic Peking Opera performer who teaches him wing chun, and another young man whose rich father kills his kung fu opponents, it cemented Sammo's team of co-stars and co-choreographers.

Yuen Baio, the youngest of the Seven Little Fortunes, was Sammo's go-to star and collaborator, while Lam Ching-ying, who worked closely with Bruce Lee on *The Big Boss* and *Enter the Dragon*, became a star in his own right via his performance as the asthmatic "wu dan" (Peking Opera female fighting star) in this film. Sammo's team also utilized such other Little Fortunes as Yuen Wah and Corey

Yuen Kwai — both of whom would also go on to become acting and choreography mainstays.

At the same time Sammo conceived *The Prodigal Son*, he also came up with the brainstorm of H.A.M. (Horror Action Movies). "Since I was a small boy I heard all kinds of ghost stories from my mother and my master in the Peking Opera School. All the old people told me all these great stories of the supernatural until I became afraid of the dark. I still am!" So Sammo created *Encounters of the Spooky Kind* (aka *Spooky Encounters*, 1980), as well as *The Dead and the Deadly* (1982), and, most notably, the *Mr. Vampire* series (1985-1992) — starring the personable Lam Ching-ying as the "one-eyebrowed priest," and featuring the fascinating Chinese hopping dead known as the "gyonshi."

By then, a Sammo Hung fight scene was as recognizable as a medicine ball on a golf course. In his own movies, Jackie Chan would toss an opponent off screen. In a Sammo Hung movie, he'd beat and kick them insensible — even plant a machete in their heads (as in *Heart of Dragon*). Sammo himself, despite spotlighting wing chun in *Warriors Two* and *Prodigal Son*, leaned toward the more externally powerful-looking hung gar to bounce his opponents all over the set.

Things proceeded smoothly, and profitably, through the landmark "Three Brothers" movies until, after *Twinkle Twinkle Lucky Stars*, Jackie didn't want to play anymore. Sammo responded by plunging into a plethora of productions as producer, choreographer, and director through his production companies Gar Bo, Bojou, and Bo Ho. It was at that moment that the Shaw Brothers closed its film units, and suddenly dozens of Hung's associates were out of work. Although he maintains that had nothing to do with it, suddenly Sammo mounted two of his most expensive, expansive movies ever, which called for a large cast of experienced kung fu talent.

Millionaire's Express (aka *Shanghai Express*, 1986) was a catch-as-catch-can action comedy with hunks of spaghetti Western thrown in, featuring an entire western-style town that the studio built in the middle of nowhere, filled with more than three dozen action and comedy stars (including Yuen Baio, Shih Kien, Jimmy Wang Yu, Dick Tei Wei, Eric Tsang, Cynthia Rothrock, Richard Norton, Johnny Wang Lung-wei, Hsaio Ho, Philip Kao Fei, and Liu Chia-yung). Although it featured a full-scale kung fu free-for-all finale with the entire cast, the rest was an exercise in time-filling.

"It took three months to prepare and five months to shoot," Sammo recalled. "It was a lot of work, but it wasn't difficult." But it was expensive and didn't exactly set box office records. Then came *Eastern Condors* (1986), which many Westerners consider Sammo's masterpiece (being just about the only film where Sammo's weight is never even mentioned), but others consider a camp classic. Combining *The Dirty Dozen* and *The Deer Hunter* (1978) with a James Bondian climax, it featured another large cast crammed with renowned kung fu stars, as well as Oscar-winner Haing S. Ngor, directors Yuen Wo-ping and Corey Yuen Kwai, and Yuen Wah in a career-making performance as a supremely creepy, cunning, and capable Vietcong villain. It also showcased Sammo's future wife: the statuesque green-eyed ex-Miss Hong Kong, Joyce Mina Godenzi (aka Kao Lai-hung).

"Pre-production started in July 1987," Sammo explained. "We started shooting in November 1987 in Canada. We shoot for a month, then go to Hong Kong to film a basketball scene. That took a month, and we wound up editing it out! Then we went to Bangkok for a month. In January 1988, we all go to the Philippines and spend five months there. Finally, we come back to Hong Kong and spend another month there. We finished in June, 1988. All together, almost a year." Although it had plenty of entertainment value, Sammo's Asian audience, and studio, began to think he was taking advantage of them.

The final straw was *Lucky Stars Go Places* (1986), a flick co-written, co-starring, and co-produced by Sammo, that combined two of the colony's most popular action-comedy film series — *Aces Go Places* and *The Lucky Stars* — into one sloppy, condescending, mess. Suddenly the masses turned on Sammo, giving everything he threw at them, including *Dragons Forever*, the cold shoulder. After that, Sammo tried to get back into the industry's good graces by playing his own Peking Opera school teacher in the lyrical, heart-felt *Painted Faces* (1988) — the story of the Seven Little Fortunes' school days — but it seemed too little too late.

So began Sammo's "Look Back in Anger" era — full of his greatest fight scenes, but also his most outrageous bouts of racism, sexism, and homophobia. Whenever anyone wonders why Sammo is not vaunted alongside his more popular peers, some explain that it is because Hung is overweight and facially scarred. Part of the whole truth, however, is evident in the title of one of his last personal films: *Don't Give a Damn* (1994). Although largely responsible for some of the greatest action movies, the most influential horror films, and simply the best individual kung-fu fights of all time, Sammo is consistently undermined by his own seething apathy — a bad attitude that sinks too many of his movies under the weight of scenes that go way beyond political incorrectness.

A perfect, and painful, example is in the aforementioned *Don't Give a Damn*, when two Chinese cops vie for the opportunity to blacken their faces and put on "nappy" wigs (to unconvincingly impersonate the African-American villain's brother), while detailing how the black man has ruined society. The following scene, where the ridiculously disguised Chinese actor pretends to be black, makes *Amos and Andy* (1928-1966) look like *Roots* (1977). It was embarrassing and shameful, but despite the protestations of the actors, Sammo went ahead with it anyway.

The closest thing anyone could get to an explanation was that

The Clown Prince's Court

he was paying back Westerners for years of similar racism toward Asians. That explanation, while possible, doesn't make up for his misjudgments that have kept him from the pantheon of movie success. It certainly hasn't crimped his output, however. Having been involved with at least eighty movies by the time of *Dragons Forever*, he went on to appear in, produce, and direct at least fifty more — ranging from his award-winning performance in *Eight Taels of Gold* (1989) to an even worse "Lucky Stars" film, the awful *Ghost Punting* (1992).

Thankfully, there was the Shaw Studio-flavored *Pedicab Driver* (1989), which even featured a show-stopping fight scene with Liu Chia-liang. Maintaining that aura, Sammo eventually produced *Operation Scorpio* (1994), starring Chin Kar-lok as an aspiring comic book artist who runs afoul of a Scorpion-style killer, but is saved by the "Wok-fu" taught to him by a chef played by Liang. Then came *Encounters of the Spooky Kind II* (1989), an honorable sequel to Hung's groundbreaking H.A.M. of 1980. He then tried to recapture the pre-*Lucky Stars Go Places* magic of 1978's *Dirty Tiger, Crazy Frog* with *Skinny Tiger and Fatty Dragon* (1990), which featured the same co-star — comic actor Karl Maka — while borrowing the plot of the 1986 Billy Crystal vehicle *Running Scared* ... but it wasn't exactly welcomed (not helping matters were scenes of Maka beating up girls).

Sammo reacted to that rejection by really sticking it to the audience with *Pantyhose Hero* (1990), a variation on the unfortunate Ryan O'Neal/John Hurt movie, *Partners* (1982), in which a cop has to pretend he's gay to find a serial killer of homosexuals. Seemingly daring the viewer to call him on his outrageous stereotypes, Sammo filled the film with some of his most savage fights and unbelievable stunts (such as actually being hit by a car in slow motion).

"My fighting got more savage in these because I was in an increasingly worse mood," he explained. "Everything was the same in these movies. I was getting in a rut. So I got more serious and savage in my fighting."

Wanting to share the love, he tried to do for his wife's career what he was doing to his own. Teaming with Corey Yuen Kwai, they made her the star of *She Shoots Straight* (aka *Lethal Lady*, 1990), an overwrought martial melodrama that featured a climatic wedding scene slaughter. Audiences and distributors reacted in kind: *Pedicab Driver*, *Pantyhose Hero*, *Spooky Encounters II*, and *Don't Give a Damn* have never legally appeared on DVD. But, eventually, even they learned the same Sammo lesson that everyone in the film industry ultimately accepts. The guy is just too great a talent not to eventually rehire.

Although he has not been given his own film since those heady days, he has contributed exceptional performances, choreography and direction for dozens more, including *Moon Warriors* (the 1993 movie that inspired the kung fu of the *Star Wars* "prequels"), Wong Kar-wai's seminal *Ashes of Time* (1994), and *The Stunt Woman* (1996). Then came *Martial Law* (1998-2000).

It was with the knowledge of Sammo's incredible talents, not his lapses in judgment, that Stanley Tong approached successful television producer Carlton Cuse — then best known for the successful cop show *Nash Bridges* (1996-2001). Cuse knew that CBS television desperately wanted to attract young male viewers to its Saturday night lineup, and Tong had a proposal for a series based on *Supercop*, the movie he directed for Jackie Chan. When Jackie declined to play the role for American television, Tong turned to Sammo. Anxious to fill a 9:00 pm time slot, CBS-TV gave the team a green light, and within record time, production on the series started.

Sammo Hung played Sammo Law, a top Chinese police detective who comes to Los Angeles to track an Asian crime lord and then stays, thanks to a convenient cop exchange program. Within six episodes, the network knew it had a hit, and according to unnamed

The Clown Prince's Court

sources, the production knew it had trouble. Sammo was used to the kind of control he had back in Hong Kong, and, like Jackie, wasn't comfortable with English. He also wasn't enthusiastic with the kind of early mornings and late nights American TV production required. The rumored tensions behind the scenes started showing in unusual ways.

First, actress Tammy Lauren, billed as a full co-star, mysteriously left the show after six episodes. Law's partner, played by Louis Mandylor, and his L.A.P.D. boss, played by Tom Wright, were marginalized. Then *Rush Hour* premiered, and, during the ninth episode, Arsenio Hall was introduced as a wisecracking African-American press liaison. The stories and dialog began to degenerate to a noticeable degree.

New producers were brought in for the second season because of "runaway production costs." Mandylor and Wright were gone. Hall and co-star Kelly Hu were reduced to static stake-outs in such exotic locations as a nondescript building's hallway. On the last episode of the year, Law returns to China. Within two seasons, *Martial Law* went from being CBS' most successful new drama (with Sammo winning the first *TV Guide* Award as Most Promising Newcomer) to being quietly and ignominiously cancelled. The Sammo Syndrome had struck again: snatching defeat from the jaws of victory.

On the one hand, he had nimbly avoided the growing pains of Hong Kong's return to Chinese rule by being in America. On the other: "When I got back to Hong Kong, everything had changed. It was getting harder to find good actors anymore. Also, people do movies with many guns. You have guns, there is no fighting. But there is still television, and I still had good friends. Soon I was back to work."

And he is still working, despite having stents put in his heart during 2010 (after which he only rested for a few weeks before being back on set). I asked him if he ever thought about slowing down.

"If I come across a rewarding role," he promised, "I will still be fighting."

CHAPTER SIX
WOMEN WUSHU WARRIORS

Picture identifications (clockwise from upper left):
Michelle Yeoh in *Wing Chun*; Brigitte Lin in *The Bride With White Hair*; Anita Mui, Michelle Yeoh, and Maggie Cheung in *The Heroic Trio*; Brigitte Lin in *Swordsman 2*; Early Swords(wo)man; Michelle Yeoh in *Project S: Once a Cop*.

Women Wushu Warriors

Back when action films began to captivate Chinese audiences, the aforementioned accepted adage was that movies were, literally, just for women. Men were too busy bringing home the barbeque pork to waste their time watching films, so only housewives went to theaters. And since no wage-earner wanted his pregnant, barefoot cook swooning over handsome heroes, every major hero on screen was played by a woman.

Some of the pioneers included Chin Tsi-ang, whose unique skills (including trick horse riding) were well utilized in 1920s movies. Her first starring role was in *The Lady Swordfighter of Jiangnan* (1925), made in mainland China, but she went on to establish herself in Hong Kong — becoming so respected that she instituted her own studio.

Suet Nei was responsible for creating some of the most lasting images of him/her heroes, including the "cool, unbending hero" of *The Deadly Dragon Sword* (1968) and the "Mad Diva" of *The One-Armed Magic Nun* (1969)! "I was a girl then and didn't know fear," she was quoted. She did trampoline jumps, leaps from rooftops, and wire work. She drew the line, however, at somersaults for some reason. For that, in came stuntmen, such as Tsui Chung-hok, who was known as the "king of the doubles for female leads."

An even more popular kung fu contemporary was Connie Chan Po-chu, who became so skilled in playing men that, when she played a woman, she didn't recognize herself. "My movements were hard and rough," she said. "I was like a man playing a woman." Although never quite credible to Western eyes, she more than sufficed for her Asian audience in such films as *The Six-Fingered Lord of the Lute* (1965), *Paragon of Sword and Knife*, and *The Virgin Sword* (1969), among others.

But for kung fu fans, she was best loved as on-screen partner to the iconic Josephine Siao. Born in China, but moved to Hong Kong at the age of two, she first appeared in movies at the age of six. Like

Connie, she was a teen idol, but unlike Connie, she got to play a woman most often. In fact, in several of the films they made together, Josephine played Connie's lady love. Always a pioneer, Siao co-directed a ground-breaking independent kung fu film, *Jumping Ash*, in 1976.

Her contemporary, Hsu (aka Xu) Feng was notable for starring in many of legendary director King Hu's films, including *The Valiant Ones* (1974) and *Raining in the Mountains* (1979), even though, as she put it; "I am a martial arts star who hardly knows any martial arts." It helped when she had people like Sammo Hung to instruct her, but she also had a valuable point of view. "Whenever I'm making a movie, I think of it as my last, so I really try my best."

But all bowed before the power and talent of Cheng Pei-pei. Born in 1946, she became famous in King Hu's lyrical, exciting, artful 1966 Shaw Brothers Studio film *Come Drink with Me* (which was only her fifth film), in which she played knightess errant "Golden Swallow," who takes on a group of kidnapping bandits. She immediately became a sought-after heroine, who such directors as Lo Wei, Ho Meng-hua, and even musical master Inoue Umetsugu vied for. Then Chang Cheh got her for his nominal sequel, *Golden Swallow* (1968).

Not surprisingly, the creator of "yang gang" used it as a showcase for co-star Jimmy Wang Yu, but Cheng quickly locked horns with the chauvinist director. "I threatened to walk off the picture if he didn't [treat me equally]," she has said. "I love to do fight scenes!" Pei-pei made many popular action films, including *The Golden Sword* (1969), *Lady of Steel* (1970), and *The Shadow Whip* (1971) until she was declared the "Queen of Swords." But then she went to America to marry. Not to worry, however. She'll be seen again.

That era's "Queen of Kung Fu," however, was undoubtedly Angela Mao. There had been kung fu heroines and slashing swordswomen before her, but never had a female action star taken center stage in world cinema, and held it, the way Angela Mao did. To many martial arts movie fans, she is, and will always be, "The" woman. Mao, like the Venoms, was a graduate of a Taiwanese Opera school. Luckily for her, and her legion of fans, she was born late enough in the century (1952) when women were finally allowed to play the female roles in these fascinating Chinese mixes of grand opera and martial ballet.

In fact, she became one of the most popular and famous wu dan (female martial leads) of her time — known for being able to deflect twelve spears in succession with one foot (tantamount to Pavarotti hitting a high C three times in a row). She never failed to bring down the house, but the then prevalent Shaw Brothers Studio didn't really recognize the value of a main woman action star. They, after all, had Lily Li, who seemed satisfied with supporting roles. Besides, to directors like Chang Cheh, women were window dressing, and fighting women might as well be boys. They felt that in the eyes of the public, a fighting girl lost her femininity.

"To tell you the truth, they don't look at me the same way they look at purely dramatic actresses," fellow Shaw Studio actress, Kara Hui Ying-hung told me. "They don't want to fool around with me because they know I can fight."

Upstart studio Golden Harvest, however, didn't hold as much sexism. Studio head Raymond Chow would do whatever he needed to get attention, and films starring an accomplished kicker might just do the trick. Angela co-starred in a few ensemble pieces, but it was in 1972, with her first major leading role, *Lady Whirlwind,* that she caught the populace by surprise. Director Huang Feng understood her allure and showcased her in a series of increasingly frenetic and exciting films: *The Angry River* (1971), *Hapkido* (aka *Lady Kung Fu,* 1972), *When Taekwondo Strikes* (choreographed by Sammo Hung, 1973), and *The Opium Trail* (aka *Deadly China Doll,* 1973), among others.

She was so well established, in fact, that when it came time for King Hu to find a suitable female co-star for Hsu Feng in *The Fate of Lee Khan*, he signed Angela. And, of course, when it came time to find the actress to play Bruce Lee's sister in *Enter the Dragon*, it was Angela. From there, sadly, there was no place to go but down. As if you hadn't figured it out by now, China is a paternalistic culture, and the desire to present Mao as more "ladylike" never died, despite the fact that she was a third-dan hapkido black belt in real life.

She was dressed as a boy through most of *Stoner* (his name, not his vice, 1974), a fairly sad attempt to milk the then nearly nonexistent fame of George Lazenby, who, as I have obsessively repeated, would be forever pitied as the man who turned his back on James Bond after barely completing *On Her Majesty's Secret Service*. Angela even tried to kick-start her comparatively stalled career by re-teaming with Huang Feng for *The Himalayan* (1976), which remains one of Korean kicker Tan Tao-liang's best films. Finally, after such forgettable Taiwanese fare as *Snake Deadly Act* (1979), she married ... and in her male-dominated society, that meant she had to stop working — a fate which befell many great Hong Kong screen sirens, even as late as the 1990s.

Other filmmakers used talented female kung fu stars, like Sharon Yang Pan-pan in *Story of Drunken Master* (aka *Drunken Fist Boxing*, 1979) and Hsia Kuang-li in *The Leg Fighters* (aka *The Invincible Kung fu Legs* aka *The Incredible Kung Fu Legs* 1980), but even Kara Hui Ying-hung didn't graduate to full-fledged superstar status in Angela's wake. The only person who really came close to filling the gap was the previously lionized Lily Li (aka Lee Li-li). Born in 1950, she entered the Shaw's actors training course at the tender age of fourteen. With her attractive, yet assured and even maternal, good looks, she quickly became one of the Studio's most valued players. She had already been featured in ten films, for a variety of directors, when she achieved public prominence in *The Wandering Swordsman*

Women Wushu Warriors

(1969), starring David Chiang and directed by Chang Cheh.

In addition to credible performances in romances and Cantonese comedies, a good female action star is rare, so Chang Cheh and Liu Chia-liang constantly put her to work. Even with excellent performances in *The Heroic Ones* (1970), *Challenge of the Masters*, and *Shaolin Mantis*, she never got the kind of starring roles that Angela Mao essayed. The only time she got close was in *Executioners from Shaolin*, highlighted by the wedding-night battles between her crane style and Chen Kuan-tai's tiger style. But even that didn't do the trick. Soon Li became a free agent, continuing to give exceptional performances in more than a hundred films and TV series, working with everyone from Jackie Chan to Yuen Wo-ping.

Meanwhile, the kung fu film industry continued the way it had always been: a boy's club. Most actresses got movie roles via beauty pageants, and few (outside of Jackie, Sammo, and Karl Maka) were going to risk those faces and forms by putting them too close to flying fists and feet. Possibly the greatest exception was the remarkable Brigitte Lin Ching-hsia. Discovered at fourteen, she's had four distinct eras in her career, starting with a beloved series of romantic melodramas which seemed to take over her personal life from 1973 to 1981. Wanting to leave all that behind, she threw herself into a series of campy, crazy, action films with titles like *Pink Force Commando* (1982), *Seven Black Heroines* (1982), and the aforementioned *Fantasy Mission Force* — all directed by hackmeister Kevin Chu Yen-ping.

Finally, Tsui Hark cast her as a demigod in his landmark extravaganza *Zu Warriors of the Magic Mountain* (1982) — which introduced *Star Wars*-style special effects to Hong Kong cinema. That led her back into better filmmakers' good graces. Jackie cast her in *Police Story* before Tsui showcased her in his remarkable feminist-romantic-action-comedy-drama *Peking Opera Blues* (1986) alongside co-stars Sally Yeh Tse-man and Cherie Chung Chor-hung (not to mention such Shaw Studio stalwarts as Ku Feng, Wu Ma, and Li Hai-sheng). The latter film set her on an entirely new road. As beautiful as she was, she played an obviously heterosexual woman who preferred dressing as a man in the film — as a statement of political power and inequality.

That statement became an intriguing shout when she then played a man who became a woman via a particularly powerful but emasculating kung fu style in *Swordsman 2* (1992). She played variations on the role for years afterwards — most notably in *Dragon Inn* (1992), the amply symbolic *Swordsman 3: The East is Red* (1993), and *Deadful Melody* (1994). But arguably, her most memorable contribution to the kung fu genre was the mesmerizing romantic wuxia tragedy *The Bride With White Hair* (1993). Directed by Ronny Yu, who is now known for his elevated slasher movies (2001's *Bride of Chucky* and 2003's *Freddy vs. Jason*), it told a particularly powerful and poetic *Romeo and Juliet*-like Jiang Hu tale involving sword sects as well as a villain who is/are a pair of male/female Siamese twins joined at the spine(!).

Finally, Brigitte found her happy cinematic ending by way of Wong Kar-wai, who featured her in his famous art films *Chungking Express* (1994) and *Ashes of Time* (1994). Then Lin gracefully retired from acting. Even in the worst of her one hundred and six films, she was never less than a class act.

Meanwhile, the boys' club that was the 1980s kung fu film industry rolled on. That is, until the pendulum swung again, and mogul/producer Dickson Poon got a really bad idea: Why not launch his fledgling D&B production company with a film about two butt-kicking beauties? Why not, indeed. The resulting film, *Yes Madam* (1985, but made years earlier) — named for what police subordinates say when replying to a superior female officer — was deemed unreleasable when director Corey Yuen Kwai finished it ... possibly out of standard operating sexism.

Women Wushu Warriors

Kwai (aka Ying Gang-ming), another Peking Opera school "Little Fortune," was already well-established as an actor, stuntman, and choreographer. But his directing career had just begun, having helmed the surprise hit *Ninja in the Dragon's Den* (one of the first non-Liu Chia-liang films to show Japanese — in this case Hiroyuki Sanada — in a positive light) in 1982. Having lost face by his new film being shelved, off he went to direct, action direct, and write Jean-Claude Van Damme's breakthrough film *No Retreat No Surrender* (1985).

But producer Dickson was attracted to one of the starring actresses of *Yes Madam*, and decided to give her another chance. He showcased her in a new Japanese/Hong Kong co-production called *Royal Warriors* (1986), directed by noted cinematographer David Chung. This action-packed, over-emotional tale of a female Hong Kong cop and a male Japanese detective running afoul of a killer's brother after spectacularly foiling a jet hijacking, caught the public's fancy. But the audience, like Dickson, was especially impressed by the lead actress. She was as beautiful as she was charming and capable, and they wanted to know more about the budding superstar that Poon had dubbed Michelle Khan.

Michelle was born to a lawyer's family in Ipoh, Malaysia, on August 6, 1962 with the name Yeoh Choo-kheng. Growing up in a tropical, tin-mining, town, young Michelle represented Malaysia in national swimming, diving, and squash competitions. But her real passion was dance (her mom went on record, saying that her daughter started to dance before she could even walk). She eventually attended the London Royal Academy of Dance, but her dreams of ballet stardom were cut short by a rotated disk in her spine.

When Michelle returned to Malaysia in 1983, she discovered that her mother had entered her into a national beauty contest, and she was crowned Miss Malaysia at the age of twenty-one. Taking advantage of the travel that came with the contest, she met Dickson

Poon, who was looking for someone to do a TV commercial with Jackie Chan. Michelle wound up doing two charming spots with both Chan and Chow Yun-fat. The public reaction was so positive that the producer quickly offered her a film contract. But that, with *Yes Madam*, seemed over before it began.

But *Royal Warriors* did what she, Rothrock, Corey Yuen, and sanity could not — its success freed *Yes Madam* from the vaults and into theaters, where, of course, it became a huge hit. Looking at it now, it's hard to figure out what anyone could consider unreleasable about it (outside of standard operating sexism). The tale of a female Hong Kong cop and a female Interpol agent running afoul of three petty thieves (played by comic actor John Shum, stuntman/choreographer Mang Hoi, and director Tsui Hark) while trying to bring down a crime lord had snap, crackle and pop to spare. It also had a future action star to whom ignorance was bliss.

"In the beginning, I substituted my lack of experience with guts and bravado," Michelle told me. On the first day of filming the climatic fight in the villain's palatial home, Michelle was supposed to do what the action choreographer referred to as an "easy" stunt … which, unbeknownst to Michelle, had already sent one stuntman to the hospital. All she had to do was sit on a balcony railing, fall back, curl the back of her knees on the railing, swing head-first through a pane of glass beneath the railing, grab the legs of two villains, and then pull them back the other way so they could crash to the ground below.

"What did I know?" Michelle remembered. "I had dancing training. I just got up there and did it." And, by so doing, won the admiration of the entire crew. But she wasn't alone in this admiration society.

"I think the crew was impressed," blonde American martial artist Cynthia Rothrock told me, "because here I was, a little foreign woman who they thought would be afraid to get hurt. But I did everything they asked" — including such terrific stunts as doing a split on the wall while fighting off thugs with a bamboo pole. It was all in a day's work for the real-life martial artist, who was the number-one female kung fu stylist in the world two years running.

Corey Yuen put the two through their paces, making the kung fu movie fan yearn for a director's cut that would include a no-holds-barred battle at a temple and the scene in which the two fight off the ferocious Dick Tei Wei — both of which were left on the cutting room floor. But what remains is the seminal Hong Kong woman-warrior epic.

While Michelle went on to *Royal Warriors,* Rothrock moved on to an even more impressive follow-up. *Righting Wrongs* (aka *Above the Law,* 1986, not to be confused with Steven Seagal's 1988 film of the same name) is also considered one of Yuen Baio's best movies — an insane melange of *Death Wish* (1974) and *The Untouchables* (1987), produced by Baio and directed by Corey Yuen Kwai. Baio plays a law student whose professor is gunned down in front of him. After annihilating his prof's killers in a sizzling car chase and fight scene, Baio decides to go outside the law for justice. Rothrock plays the well-meaning Interpol agent who tries to stop him, not realizing how deep police corruption goes.

Briskly brutal, with some amazing moments of kung fu black comedy (as when Cynthia and Yuen do an acrobatic martial arts dance all over a seated murder victim), *Righting Wrongs* is not a happy movie, but it is consistently exciting with some great kung fu (choreographed by the star, the director, Sammo Hung, Mang Hoi, and even Hsu Hsia). Not only does Rothrock fight Baio, but also fellow Caucasian Karen Sheperd, who played a martial arts hit woman who murdered a teenage witness to the villain's homicidal politics. In the original version, everybody dies, but when that reality hurt the box office in certain countries, new scenes were shot that allowed either Yuen and Cynthia, or both, to live. There are literally four versions of *Righting Wrongs* floating around: one in which they both live, one in which they both die, and two in which only one lives.

Meanwhile, Michelle "Khan" was balancing her film work with a budding romance with the powerful Dickson. She completed a nominal follow-up to *Royal Warriors* called *Magnificent Warriors* (1988), but it did not premiere until two years afterward. Although entertaining in its own right, it had nothing to do with its predecessor. Taking place during World War II, Michelle makes like a vengeful cross between Bruce Lee and Indiana Jones to save a small town from Japanese invaders. Marred by a tone that fluctuated between honest emotion, insane action, and inopportune slapstick comedy, *Magnificent Warriors* didn't slow Khan down, but marriage, by dint of Chinese tradition, did.

Once she became Mrs. Dickson Poon, her movie career was all but over. Cynthia Rothrock, however, carried on. The only thing that slowed her down, ironically enough, was the color of her skin, not to mention hair. Just as American filmmakers had been slow to accept Asian action stars, Hong Kong looked upon the blonde, round-eyed Rothrock with skepticism, curiosity, and, in some rare cases, downright hostility. It wasn't that the film industry was racist (oh, no!) but the audience ... would the *audience* accept her?! Of course they would, but the game played out in its usual pattern. There was hemming and hawing about what kind of role they could give her. Hong Kong was not exactly a melting pot, and a blonde white woman stood out like a marshmallow in butterscotch pudding.

Sammo Hung, who had given Michelle her first, non-fighting, role in his weak comedy *Owl vs. Dumbo* (1984) eliminated the problem by making Cynthia just one in a mob of interracial robbers for *Millionaire's Express*. But Sammo's no fool: she got extra attention, because, first, she was the only white woman villain, and second, she was the one who fought director and co-star Sammo. While Yuen Baio fought Dick Tei Wei and Japanese action actress Yukari

Women Wushu Warriors

Oshima beat off a gang of co-stars, Rothrock faced off against Hung in a memorable, nicely structured one-on-one in a hotel lobby. She gives him far worse than she gets until Sammo is forced to take her seriously. He does his patented Bruce Lee impersonation to get in the proper mood, and then makes her spine sorry it was ever thrown onto the marble floor.

Although the film did poorly at the box office, both Rothrock and Oshima were the talk of the industry. Sammo's friends, Jackie Chan and Frankie Chan (no relation), took advantage of their skills. Although Jackie's *Armour of God* injury prevented an on-screen face-to-face with Cynthia, he tried to make it up to her by having her cast in *The Inspector Wears Skirts* (aka *Top Squad,* 1988), a slapstick comedy he produced, inspired by the American *Police Academy* movies. As successful as that was (sprouting a fistful of increasingly inferior sequels sans Cynthia), it was Yukari who was one step away from attaining Angela Mao status when Frankie cast her as his co-star in his clever *Outlaw Brothers* (1987).

Frankie played one of two sibling, high-end, car thieves who accidentally steals a female drug lord's latest shipment. Statuesque Michiko Nishiwaki is the villain, while Yukari is the cop assigned to bring down both the thieves and druggies. Frankie, a Southern Shaolin Long Fist fan, cleverly plays out their romantic comedy in both banter and fight scenes (choreographed by Fung Hak-on and Yuen Shun-yi). This is clearly Frankie's best film, and apex of his directing career, which began promisingly, but faltered shortly after this. Don't feel sorry for him, though — he was the second unit director for *Operation Condor,* still reigns as one of Hong Kong's most prominent and sought-after soundtrack composers, and, twenty-three years later, was chosen by producer Jackie Chan to direct *Lady Warriors of the Yang Family* (2011).

Still, this movie is enough. It has several excellent kung fu sequences, culminating in a warehouse battle royal filled with snakes, chickens, cigarettes, rice, and gweilo bad guys who wield blade-encrusted fans and ringed swords as well as guns. It would have made a great series except for the sour fadeout, where Oshima reveals that she was playing Frankie for a sucker all along (the film ends on a freeze-frame of a handcuffed Frankie kicking her across the screen). Instead, Oshima guided her unlikely career through a fairly unique set of roadblocks. First, she was a woman in chauvinist Asia. Second, she was Japanese in Nippon-hating Hong Kong. Third, she shifted her skills between Japan, Taiwan, and the Philippines, as well as Hong Kong.

Following *Outlaw Brothers*, she made a memorable appearance in the Chinese live action adaptation of the hyper-violent *Story of Ricky* (aka *Ricky O*, 1991), based on a ridiculously graphic Japanese manga (comic book). But the rest of her career, numbering more than fifty movies, was in cheap exploitation films (save for a glorified cameo at the beginning of *Project S*, the sequel to *Supercop*). But for woman wushu warrior fans, these B movies were catnip. In 1992 alone she made fourteen, including *Kickboxer's Tears*, *Fatal Chase*, and *Beauty Investigator* (many released in America by Tai Seng). She was also a mainstay in the *Angel* series — a bunch of flicks made by a variety of companies based on the *Charlie's Angels* TV show (1976-1981). It all began with *Angel* (aka *Iron Angels*) in 1986, which launched the "Girls with Guns" subgenre, and wound its way for years, giving new life to the career of one of the industry's best-liked ingénues.

Moon Lee Choi-fong (named for her cute, expressive round face) went right from graduating school to appearing on Hong Kong television. Coming to the attention of Sammo Hung, he featured her in *Winners and Sinners*, his kung fu soccer film *The Champions* (1983, years before *Shaolin Soccer*), *Twinkle Twinkle Lucky Stars*, *Mr. Vampire*, and *Mr. Vampire 2*. Many of Sammo's peers liked what they saw, so Tsui Hark cast her opposite Yuen Baio and Mang Hoi in *Zu Warriors of the Magic Mountain* (1983) while Jackie Chan used her in his version of *The Protector*.

Then she made the mistake of appearing as the heroine in *Angel*, and her fate was sealed. Gone were the roles in major studio movies, and in flooded offers to be in *Angels 2* (1989), *Angel 3* (1989), *Killer Angels* (1989), and *The Revenge of Angel* (1990). Delightful in demeanor, demonic in her fighting, she impressed fans across the world, but her fame in English-speaking territories did nothing to endear her to home-grown producers. She made it into the Sammo-produced *Bury Me High* (1991) and the Jackie-produced *The Inspector Wears Skirts 4* (1992), but otherwise it was one nasty, cheap, sizzling little film (like 1990s *Fatal Termination*, 1991's *Angel Force*, and 1993's *Angel Terminators 2*) after another.

Although Moon was always a joy to behold, she deserved better, and wisely walked away in the late 1990s. In the meantime, Cynthia Rothrock fought on, finding that getting good parts in decent movies was almost as difficult as it was to defeat her on-screen foes. *Magic Crystal* (1988) was up next — an enjoyable kung fu/sci-fi hybrid dreamed up by the extravagant schlockmeister Wong Jing. It had a strong supporting cast, which included Richard Norton and Andy Lau, and some great action (as well as some truly silly slapstick). Rothrock is back in Interpol, trying to save a kid from an alien assassin out to claim the title rock: a big magical gem that turns out to be a sentient being.

Then came *Blonde Fury* (aka *Lady Reporter,* 1989), the last time Rothrock took center stage in Hong Kong. At first, it was directed by her friend Mang Hoi, but when rumors of a Rothrock film with Sylvester Stallone reached the producers (a movie that never materialized), Corey Yuen Kwai was brought in to upgrade the effort. Kwai, in turn, brought in sixth-degree black sash Vincent Lyn.

"That was a tough shoot, but Cynthia was a real trooper," Lyn told me. "She did everything they asked with no fuss. I was the problem on that set. I couldn't get the timing right! Corey Yuen got so fed up that he bounced a peanut shell off my head in frustration. Eventually, however, it all came together for a pretty exciting fight scene."

But it seemed to be enough for Cynthia. Hong Kong was hurtful to say the least, and, no matter how low the budget got on American films, she would still be paid more and be better protected from injury. Rothrock hopped back and forth from Asia to America for awhile, showing up in stuff like *Angel the Kickboxer* (1993) until she stayed stateside for good.

Her timing was excellent, because Asian producers were soon asking actresses to thrust more than their arms and legs at the camera. With the release of *Robotrix* (1991), Hong Kong action cinema had unleashed its libido. "Now that was one wild shoot," co-star Vincent Lyn told me. "The cast and crew were all over the place, and you were lucky to find out what you were doing before the cameras rolled. I spent more time laughing on the set than anything else."

With the ample assistance of voluptuous Amy Yip and the kung fu prowess of Billy Chow, this tale of sex machines fighting a raping robot was laughed off the screen … by millions of fans who paid again and again to keep laughing. In America, these movies are known as erotic R-rated thrillers. In Hong Kong, they are called Category 3 films, and the floodgate was now officially open. Thankfully (or unfortunately, depending upon your point of view) martial arts and mammaries rarely mixed, but there were a few that snuck through. *Black Cat* (1991) was actually the Asian version of *La Femme Nikita* (1990), the French film that begat *Point of No Return* (1993) and two TV series.

The pouty Jade Leung starred as the street slime recruited as a top secret killer, and while she was able, she was far from experienced. The real star, aside from Leung's looks, was director Stephen Shin, whose stylish action made *Point of No Return* seem truly pointless. Unfortunately, he was not so lucky with the 1992 sequel, subtitled *The Assassination of President Yeltsin*. Since there wasn't a *Femme*

Women Wushu Warriors

Nikita sequel to rip-off, this edition relied heavily on unbelievable intrigue and espionage nonsense. Jade, too, ran into some bad luck herself — literally — in the form of an on-set fire accident that left her permanently marked. Even so, she's still working in both Chinese film and television.

Wong Jing was fiddling while the *Black Cat* set burned. Seeing the audience grow slavish for exploitation, the producer-writer's fervid mind was more than up to the task. *Naked Killer* exploded into theaters in 1992, making jaded viewers' jaws drop heavily onto sticky cinema floors. The sexy, seemingly lascivious Chingmy Yau opened everyone's eyes to pure screen perversion.

Okay now, pay attention: Chingmy kills her father's killer, which brings her to the attention of a nun/hit-woman who throws her into her basement with a rapist. Passing that test with flying internal organs, Chingmy then runs afoul of her new teacher's former student, a lesbian assassin who has stopped trying to kill rapists and started trying to kill her mentor, while Chingmy is protected by a traumatized cop who vomits every time he holds a gun. Got that? Who cares. *Naked Killer* was stylishly directed by Clarence Ford, cleverly written by Wong Jing, and nicely choreographed by Lau Shing-fung. It was the first major movie for feminists *and* perverts, and, although many slick, sick films would follow (led by a kung fu-less sequel, memorably titled *Raped by an Angel* in 1993), *Naked Killer* was the best of its kind.

The same year *Naked Killer* appeared, someone else reappeared. Her marriage over, the once Michelle Khan returned to acting — only this time proudly bearing her own name: Michelle Yeoh. Poon, in the meantime, passed a pseudonym onto a personable, but limited, Taiwanese actress named Yang Li-tsing, by mixing parts of Michelle and Rothrock's names to create "Cynthia Khan" — the newly anointed star of D&B's *In the Line of Duty* series (the sequels to *Yes Madam*). While no Michelle nor Rothrock, the new Khan was cute and capable enough, especially during *In the Line of Duty 4* and *In the Line of Duty 5: Middle Man* — the best of the lot because they were directed by a somewhat down-on-his-luck Yuen Wo-ping (and featured both Donnie Yen and Vincent Lyn).

Li-tsing did nine films in 1992 alone, but once Michelle returned, the fabricated Khan kept sinking in cheaper and cheaper flicks while her namesake kept rising. *Police Story 3: Supercop* was Yeoh's comeback film, and, not for the last time, she was rescued by filmmakers hitherto fore-not-known for their kindnesses toward actresses. It was a mark of Yeoh's talent and personality that such world-class superstars were willing to take a step aside to make room for her — not as pretty window dressing or a damsel-in-distress, but as a full-fledged co-star of equal rank. And once Jackie Chan gave his approval, the line grew outside her offices.

Yeoh followed *Supercop* with the greatest superheroine movie Marvel Comics *never* made: *The Heroic Trio* (1992). Co-directed by the great Johnny To and actor/choreographer turned director Tony Ching Siu-tung, this was the movie that comic book fans had been waiting for. Three of the world's most beautiful actresses slipping into second-skin spandex to take on a superpowered eunuch who wants to plunge an alternate universe film noir world back to the dynasty system. His method: kidnap babies until he finds the reincarnation of the emperor.

The only thing between him and total domination is "Wonder Woman" (no, not *that* Wonder Woman) — a deeply maternal acrobat who can hurl kung fu darts faster than bullets and runs across telephone wires — Thief Catcher — a money-grubbing mercenary in leather short-shorts who packs a mean sawed-off shotgun — and, eventually, Invisible Girl (no, *not* the one from the *Fantastic Four),* who starts the film working with the bad guys because they are holding her dying scientist boyfriend hostage. The movie's very absurdity works in its favor, as the rarely invisible Michelle, amazing Anita Mui, and magnificent Maggie Cheung leap all over the screen, supported by splendid visuals and an Oscar-worthy silent supporting performance by Anthony Wong as a monstrous henchman not averse to eating his own hacked-off fingers.

The ending borrows heavily from the original *Terminator* (1984), but, as usual, who cares? The movie is so shamelessly entertaining, it more than makes up for its inspirations with original, uniquely Chinese action. The pure exhilaration of *The Heroic Trio* raised expectations for the sequel, but no one expected the bleak, brutal, post-apocalyptic world of *Executioners* (1993), wherein the trio returned, but now deeply changed and essentially suicidal. In their attempt to find unpolluted water and survive a clash between a religious deity and power-mad politicians, much blood is spilled and much audience goodwill is squandered.

Happily, Yeoh didn't make it a point to trade in misery. Her happiness to be back in movies permeated her performances. *Butterfly Sword* (aka *Butterfly and Sword* aka *Comet, Butterfly, and Sword*, 1993), is a far more enjoyable costume epic, with Michelle flying around with Donnie Yen, among others. By this time, however, honest kung fu had given way to wire-enhanced fantasy. While Chinese "swordplay" fiction had always had flying blade-masters, the line between these wuxia films and kung fu movies had become increasingly blurred as more Westerners discovered them.

Much more recognizable was *Project S* (aka *Once a Cop*, 1993), the semi-sequel to *Supercop*, directed and choreographed by Stanley Tong. In it, Michelle plays the same mainland police officer, but Jackie Chan only appears in a jarringly silly cameo scene in which he has gone undercover, disguised as a woman, to crack a jewelry store robbery ring — complete with a snub-nosed revolver between his pantyhosed legs. Once that out-of-place sequence is over, the story remains serious as Michelle tracks a corrupt cop who leads high-tech bank robbers all over, and under, Hong Kong.

With that out of her system, Michelle returned to mainland China for a pair of pure kung fu productions directed by the venerable Yuen Wo-ping. Both announced to the industry the director's intent to continue moving away from action cinema's hung gar roots. First was *The Tai Chi Master* (1993) starring Jet Li, which we will get to in good time. But next was a title role of her very own: *Wing Chun* (1994), in which she plays the woman who shared, and developed the kung fu style of, the same name. Although reportedly inspired by the Haka (wanderers) style of ling gar kung fu, wing chun had a long and storied history of trial and triumph — none of which this light-headed romantic action comedy really touched upon.

"Although the film had many light moments and was even silly sometimes," Michelle admitted to me, "Yuen Wo-ping was very particular about the martial arts. Since I was playing Wing Chun and the movie was called *Wing Chun,* the movements had to be wing chun." All involved managed to make it so, despite obvious wire-enhanced leaping and spinning. Serious kung fu fans wished for a less loopy story, and were aghast that the powerful Donnie Yen was reduced to a comic supporting role, but even they enjoyed Michelle's repeated, climatic confrontations with a sexist bandit lord (played by *Bastard Swordsman* Norman Chu Siu-keung).

Her second movie of 1994 signaled another change in direction. *Wonder Seven* was done as a favor to director Ching Siu-tung, who was using the knock-off of *The Magnificent Seven* (which was, in turn, a knockoff of *Seven Samurai*) to showcase an Olympic-medal-winning Chinese gymnast. Not surprisingly, the result was a mixed bag, to say the least, with Yeoh as a lovelorn villainess won over by the honest affection of a gymnast turned secret agent. After that, Michelle knew she would have to find more serious roles if she wasn't to suffer the fate of Yukari Oshima, Moon Lee, Cynthia Khan, and even Cynthia Rothrock — namely, to toil in increasingly cheap, unimaginative, exploitation movies for the rest of her career.

Michelle knew it could happen: after all, Yukari Oshima had been in *Project S*, but only as one of many unnamed villains in the pre-credit sequence. So she put her extraordinary managers Terence Chang and Chris Godsick to work, and then waited for better scripts to come her way. In 1996 she appeared in two films — only one of which was even nominally an action film. The other, *The Soong Sisters*, was an important, heartfelt drama that proved that Yeoh was more than a pretty face, a dancer's body, and fast limbs. But she was also that, so her final, pre-handover Hong Kong film was especially disappointing.

Stuntwoman: The Story of Ah Kam seemed made for Michelle. It was directed by the illustrious Ann Hui, who was known for such powerful dramas as *Boat People* (1983). It also featured Sammo Hung, playing an action choreographer. What could go wrong? Two things. First, the action was awful. Like so many movies about stuntpeople made by people who don't use them much, the director seemed loathe to show the audience the way stunts are actually done — creating absurd continuous, multi-angle, multi-cut action sequences instead.

Second, and in a more personal vein, although Yeoh had suffered many bumps and bruises along the way, *Stuntwoman* was the only movie up until then in which she got seriously hurt ... which was all the more unfortunate since the movie's action is so ridiculous. After a completely unnecessary shot where she jumps from a bridge, Michelle landed badly, tearing ligaments, fracturing a rib, and nearly breaking her back.

"I felt my spine bend," she told me. "I was afraid I had broken it in two." It would have been terribly ironic, since she was just months away from one of the greatest coups in movie history. Only once before in action movies had an established action superstar allowed a veritable unknown to step in and share the spotlight. That was Jackie Chan in *Supercop*. But lightning struck again for Michelle when the only action icon in the world greater than Jackie invited her to become "Double Yeoh Seven."

That would be James Bond, of course, in the person of Pierce Brosnan, and the film was *Tomorrow Never Dies* (1997) — the eighteenth movie in the series. Reportedly, the movie was set to be called *Tomorrow Never Lies,* and the wife of a megalomaniacal media mogul was supposed to be sharing Bond's bed at the fadeout. But the "Die" was cast because the filmmakers decided it sounded better and, for whatever reason, the media mogul's wife was dead within fifteen minutes of her introduction on-screen.

The day before Michelle was to report to the set, she was at a party in New York celebrating her films. There, the rumor spread that the 007 producers were discussing cutting her action scenes, so as to not upstage their Bond and his then Bond girl. "Why hire me if they aren't going to use me?" she was overheard as saying. But once Michelle arrived on set that story, true or not, changed. Roger Spottiswoode, the director, and Pierce Brosnan were both charmed and impressed by their new co-star, and the producers saw a prescription for a revitalized series. If many considered 007 out of fashion, then what about a woman who could believably match him kiss for kiss, kill for kill? No one had really been convincing in that role since Honor Blackman's Pussy Galore in *Goldfinger* (1964).

Thus the set was staged for one of the greatest introductions in the annals of action films, because, just years before, this sort of thing couldn't happen to a white Anglo-Saxon, let alone a "woman of color." And it wasn't just the film world that accepted Yeoh with open arms; it was Madison Avenue as well. It was Michelle's face, alongside Brosnan's, in the cosmetic ads. It was Michelle who was standing next to Pierce in the supermarket beer standees. It was her character who was made into an action figure along with Commander Bond.

Women Wushu Warriors

Rumors of an extremely difficult production were rampant, yet Michelle insisted that her fight scenes be choreographed by a kung fu pro, so they let her bring in ex-Venom Philip Kwok Choy, and even used him as a walk-on villain. If only the filmmakers had trusted him with Pierce Brosnan's action scenes as well. But veteran stunt arranger Vic Armstrong, of *Indiana Jones* fame, worked on Brosnan's battles instead. As a result, James looks old-fashioned, especially after the fine martial arts moves 007 showed in his first Bond outing, *GoldenEye* (1995). Sadly, the hoped-for finale in which 007 and the dully-named Wai Lin trade styles and skills, never materialized.

Even though director Spottiswoode chose to have the villain (ably played by exceptional actor Jonathan Pryce) make fun of Yeoh's kung fu skill without giving her a chance for an audience-satisfying response in the climatic battle, all could be forgiven (I suppose), since the crew was purportedly making up the film as they went along, and Michelle was so lovingly showcased otherwise. Then, to add monetary success to critical success, the movie was the largest grossing film in the series thus far, making more than $300 million worldwide. There was even talk of giving Michelle a parallel series to Bond, allowing a new 007-produced action movie to come out every year in a "boy, girl, boy, girl" sequence, but that was not to be (even when they tried it again years later for Halle Berry's character, Jinx, from 2002's *Die Another Day*).

Rumors abounded that Yeoh had turned down roles in the *Charlie's Angels* film series, a live action adaptation of the *Danger Girl* comic books, and even *The Matrix* movies, to concentrate on a long-term goal. Like her mentor Jackie Chan, Michelle apparently wanted full control of her creative destiny. So deciding, she instituted Mythical Films, and set to work on movies that she could run completely. It wasn't easy. She labored for years on just the right stories. And while she labored, so did another humble, unassuming, Taiwanese filmmaker named Ang Lee.

While Michelle was reviving her career in *Supercop*, he was starting his career with the thoughtful, effecting *Pushing Hands* (1992), about a Chinese taichi teacher who unavoidably disrupts his family by moving in with his son and daughter-in-law in New York state. Already the director was showing the depth of his artistry by melding external taichi practice with internal taichi healing, as the teacher attempts to create a balance between his son's responsibility and daughter-in-law's resentment. As such, the director created one of the best "pure" kung fu films ever, although there is apparently no obvious kung fu in it.

When Michelle was starring in Wong Jing's forgettable *Holy Weapon* in 1993, this Taiwanese filmmaker created his first hit, *The Wedding Banquet*, a comedy of manners about a gay Asian man pleasing his parents with a sham heterosexual marriage. While Michelle was *Wing Chun*, he continued his career with the heartwarming (and mouth watering) romantic dramedy *Eat Drink Man Woman* (1994). As Michelle waited for better scripts, he pressed his advantage by making a sparkling, very English, adaptation of Jane Austen's *Sense and Sensibility* (1995). And, while Michelle was cavorting with 007, this modest moviemaker stunned critics by making a powerful evocation of a lost American generation in *The Ice Storm* (1997).

Finally, after an underappreciated western (1999's *Ride with the Devil*), this eclectic, extremely talented director finally decided to return to his cultural and cinematic roots by taking on both the wuxia genre, and every inaccurate American film industry preconception about what the audience will accept. Bruce Lee, Jackie Chan, and now Ang Lee (no relation) had been told: one, that Americans would never accept an all-Asian cast. Two, that U.S. audiences would never accept a subtitled film. And three, that Western filmgoers would never accept a film with women as the main action heroes.

The tragic romantic action film, *Crouching Tiger Hidden Dragon* (2000), made lies of all these standard operating racisms, went on to make more than a hundred and twenty-five million dollars in America alone, and won four Oscars — as well as four British Academy Awards, two Golden Globes, five Hong Kong Film Awards, three Independent Spirit Awards, and many others. It was a suitable reward for a film that seemingly came out of nowhere, but was, in fact, the result of a long, arduous production that was fraught with setbacks — including the exit of its original male star, Jet Li, due to a scheduling conflict.

Li's loss was the film's gain. Chow Yun-fat replaced him, and, because he was so unskilled in kung fu, Ang and his choreographer, Yuen Wo-ping, only really had time to teach him the bare necessities. That not only served to enhance the fight scenes of his female co-stars, but set him apart from them, since one sign of true kung fu masters is that they only move as much as they absolutely have to, rather than show off with elaborate displays of physical pyrotechnics. Or, as one world champion put it to me: "You ever notice that the louder they are, the less skilled they are?"

Further complicating matters was that both Chow, and his co-star Michelle Yeoh, didn't know the source material's original language, Mandarin, which Ang insisted be spoken. They learned their scripts phonetically. Sets burned down and blew away. Cast and crew froze, sweated, and got lost in the desert. Each shot was an agonizing trial of multiple languages and cross-purposes. Not a frame was created with computerized digital effects. Instead, the actors were outfitted with thick cables, and hoisted from construction cranes. Like human yo-yos. they were lifted and thrown across ceilings, lakes, and trees — often to heights greater than sixty feet. Finally, Michelle got a serious injury during her first fight scene with co-star Zhang Ziyi.

"I was doing a forward jump kick that I've done thousands of times," she told *USA Today*, "but I had a mishap landing. My knee just gave out."

Ang shot around her as she went for an operation and intense rehabilitation. And when it was all over, after more than two years of intense work, they had only spent a bit more than fifteen million dollars, launched the career of the ethereal Zhang Ziyi, and created a fitting culmination to the career of a woman who had never before played the villain: Cheng Pei-pei.

"I'm the good girl!" she laughed. "But the film was very good, very important, so I did it."

Very important, indeed. Not only did it introduce Western audiences to a genre the Eastern audience had come to take for granted, but did it with an artistry never before communicated. Despite the talents of King Hu, Chu Yuan, and all the others who made the genre famous, only Ang Lee made that small, seemingly obvious, connection that explained why these seemingly normal swordspeople could soar across the tops of trees and even fly: their bodies were doing what their hearts could not.

American, European, and Canadian audiences were invigorated by the soaring images that embodied the powerful passions of the exotic (yet somehow powerfully normal) swordswomen, desert bandits, perverse villains, and heartsick martial arts masters who filled the film. It was the first fully realized, universally understood kung fu "art film" — a great wuxia movie, a wonderful tragic romance, and simply a remarkable film made by an exceptionally courageous and dedicated filmmaker.

Naturally, the American film industry rallied to make it "the exception," rather than the norm. Hundreds of kung fu and wuxia films were bought by American distributors — the bulk of which were then shelved, with only a precious few edited, dubbed, re-scored, and/or sporadically released with misleading, or flatly inaccurate promotion. Even the dean of film critics, Roger Ebert admitted that, when asked by a novice fan what they should watch next, his reply was *Seven Samurai*. With all due respect, that's like answering a query for another great football movie with *Pride of the Yankees*.

But that really didn't matter to Michelle Yeoh. She had her production company and finally set about creating her own films. Sadly, both the misbegotten *The Touch* (2002) and the misconceived superhero film *Silver Hawk* (2004) were panned by critics and rejected by audiences. Then came the arrogantly woe-begotten American adaptation of the best-selling book *Memoirs of a Geisha* (2005). This supremely Japanese tale was bone-headedly handled by a condescending, blissfully tone-deaf crew who chose to cast three Chinese (Michelle, Zhang Ziyi, and Gong Li) in the leading roles, then "improved" the strictly-designed, meaningful geisha wardrobe with blinkingly ignorant Hollywood costuming changes.

Nevertheless, Michelle slowly worked her way back into the audiences' good graces with a series of honorable supporting roles, including Danny Boyle's science-fiction epic *Sunshine* (2007), Yuen Wo-ping's elaborate retelling of the Beggar Su story, *True Legend* (2009), and John Woo's critically acclaimed romantic fantasy wuxia, *Reign of Assassins* (2010).

"Each time I make a movie," Michelle has said, "I put my heart and soul into it." It showed.

CHAPTER SEVEN
JET POWERED

Picture identifications (clockwise from upper left):
Jet Li in *Fist of Legend*; Jet Li in *Swordsman 2*; Jet Li in *Fong Sai-yuk*; Jet Li in *Fong Sai-yuk 2*; Jet Li vs. Vincent Zhao in *Last Hero in China*; Jet Li vs. Billy Chow in *Fist of Legend*.

Jet Powered

His name is Li Lin-jei and he was a mainland Chinese wushu champion at the age of eleven. Shortly after Bruce Lee died, Li was performing at the White House for Richard Nixon and Henry Kissinger. After being all-around winner of the National Martial Arts Championships five times, Li even received a backstage bouquet for his performance from Jackie Chan. Little did either man know that, in a few years, they would be vying for the championship of the Asian action film box office.

It all started in 1981, when Li was eighteen, and already considered a wushu superstar in his homeland. "Kung fu" was a form of self-improvement that Jet would later define on-screen as "concerted effort toward a specific goal." Wushu is translated as "martial arts," but is actually more along the lines of a national sport. It's kung fu with its more powerful internal and external elements removed, making it more comfortable for government officials worried that it might be too effective for them to control — a state of affairs that had been repeated throughout Chinese history. Li, however, excelled at both kung fu and wushu.

After the death of Mao Tse-tung, filmmakers' freedoms were enormously extended. Greatly influenced by the work of Liu Chia-liang, the Hong Kong Cheung Yuen Film Production Company conceived *The Shaolin Temple* (1981), a realistic kung fu epic featuring an all-champions cast, to be filmed on actual locations. Despite having every Chinese kung fu artist at their disposal, the filmmakers only thought of Li to play the leading role of Shiu Hwu, a young revolutionary who is out for revenge against the emperor's evil nephew.

The inexperienced actor threw himself into the production with the same energy he had brought to his martial arts. After three years of production, and ten million dollars in expenditure, the movie exploded onto the international scene with the newly renamed Jet Li in front (although the Bruce-baiters tried to graft "Jet Lee" onto him in English-speaking territories). The film was a magnificent showcase for authentic kung fu, and is, in effect, a distillation of all the ingredients that made Hong Kong movies work for decades. In fact, it even used Shaw Brothers Studio space and Liu Chia-liang's expertise in a four-seasons training sequence.

Director Chang Hsin-yen was also able to utilize the country's best equipment — resulting in a splendidly visual film, with impressive attention to detail, sumptuous cinematography, and truly great kung fu. Although advertised as an "all-gravity" kung fu film with no special effects, there are hints of such old-school tricks as reversing the film, and maybe a wire or two. Otherwise, *The Shaolin Temple* tells the tale of the conflict that ended the Sui dynasty and started the T'ang with wit and imagination — through the eyes of a boy seeking vengeance for the murder of his father. The boy is rescued from his father's killer and then taught a wide range of kung fu styles by an unusual group of monks — outsiders who are not averse to drinking wine, eating meat, and even killing when they have to. And as far as they are concerned, when it comes to Sui soldiers, they have to.

Yu Cheng-wei, the creator and master of the real-life "Shark Fin Broadswordplay," portrayed the villain, while mantis fist champion Yu Hai played Li's sifu, and National All-Around Champion Hu Chien-chiang played Li's temple "brother." The lovely Ding Lan played the sifu's niece and Li's love interest, who just barely loses him to the temple when the newly crowned T'ang emperor arrives a moment too late to prevent Li from taking the monk's "Thou Shalt Not Sex" oath. The monks celebrate as he eliminates the "Thou Shalt Not Drink" rule by royal decree, leaving the niece to tearfully sneak away.

The movie was a greater success than anyone anticipated. It was so popular in its home country that the government had to issue a request that students not leave school in order to go searching for the

Shaolin Temple. Meanwhile, Jet Li was now a movie superstar in addition to being a martial arts champion. In fact, one of the billboards greeting President Ronald Reagan when he visited China showed Jet hawking "Shaolin Wine." Such popularity was a double-edged sword, however, especially in the topsy-turvy Chinese world where success elicited government scrutiny.

The sequel, *Shaolin Temple II: Kids from Shaolin* (1983), displayed some of mainland China's political habit of responding to "one step forward" with "two steps back." Although the main cast and crew were the same, the moviemaking prowess of all concerned seemed to retreat to classic propaganda film techniques — including a crudely animated title sequence, an old-fashioned Peking Opera-esque soundtrack, and even wildly out-of-place musical numbers. That probably wasn't surprising since the story was reminiscent of *Seven Brides for Seven Brothers* (1954).

Taking place after the destruction of the Shaolin Temple, the new film told of the Lung family of seven men, who lived across the Likiang River from the Pao family of seven girls (plus one tired mother and one frustrated, son-obsessed father played by the villain of the last film, Yu Cheng-wei). The dragons (boys) knew Shaolin kung fu. The phoenixes (girls) knew Wu Tang swordsmanship. The father wanted a male heir, but rich husbands for his daughters: he forbade them from fraternizing with the family on the wrong side of the river. Little did he know that his eldest daughters were already in love with the eldest Lungs, or that he was getting set up for the kill by his main adviser, who was, in reality, the leader of a marauding (but in this case, unrealistically patient) band of murdering, raping brigands.

Upon this tenuous plot, the crew lavished heaps of eye-filling spectacle, highlighted by fun family comparisons between empty-handed and sword styles along the riverbanks, as well as astounding swordfights inside gem-encrusted caves. It all comes together in the bandits' massive attack. By this time, the Lungs have been framed, exiled, and their house burned, while the Pao patriarch struggles mightily to protect his newborn male child (who was introduced to the audience with a massive close-up of his newborn baby penis). Naturally, the Lungs come leaping, chopping, and kicking back just in the nick of time.

The final fray, with all fourteen members of the family strutting their stuff, is a fierce piece of fight choreography, with Jet leading the way with fists, feet, a sword, rope darts, and three-sectional staff. Then, just to make sure the whole shebang wasn't too internationally friendly, the final cut is deep between the villain's legs. But the fade-out finds true love conquering all — with a little help from killer kung fu.

The Asian audience was delighted, and the floodgates of cheap imitations opened. Even Li was a bit stymied by the rush of stuff that followed from both Hong Kong and mainland studios. There were almost as many Shaolin Temple movies as there had been Bruce Lee rip-offs (the best of which being 1981's *Shaolin and Wu Tang*, co-starring and directed by Gordon Liu Chia-hui).

What was good for Lee was good for Li as well. Now proclaimed the biggest star in China, Jet used his fame to secure control of his next movie. At the tender age of twenty, he ambitiously decided to direct and star in the awkwardly titled *Born to Defense* (1985). But he was to discover that, like Gordon, directing was not to his liking. The plot was not at fault: Li played a young soldier coming back from World War II, who is stunned to discover that his own village was proclaiming the Americans heroes while ignoring their own warriors.

"Forget the atom bomb!" Li cries out in anguish at one point. "What about my fists?!"

Naturally, the Americans start beating up old rickshaw drivers and raping the women with seeming impunity. Repeatedly maligned by his own people, Li is finally given the chance to fight back when the Americans arrange boxing matches at the local bar. Unmercifully pummeled as he slowly learns this new fighting form, Li finally explodes in a match that literally brings the house down (during a typhoon). Once that scene is over, however, the film also goes to pieces, just barely holding together long enough for Li to kill the most corrupt American oppressors using a combination of boxing and kung fu. A good idea gone really wrong, *Born to Defense* made Jet realize that he had a lot to learn about filmmaking, not to mention American grammar.

It was lucky, therefore, that the great Liu Chia-liang had just been given the chance to complete a lifelong dream. He was signed to direct *Shaolin Temple III* (1986). Not surprisingly, the man now known as "Kung Fu" Liang subtitled it *Martial Arts of Shaolin*, then set about to make his martial art magnum opus. Having spent his career training actors to look decent doing kung fu, he now had at his disposal literally hundreds of great kung fu athletes, whom he could train to be decent actors. If Busby Berkeley had learned kung fu instead of dancing, this is what his great 1930s musicals might have looked like. Liang crammed dozens of Shaolin monks and evil Manchu warriors into every shot he could — having them all do the same intricate moves in unison.

Freed as he had never been before, Liang designed fight scenes of such subtlety and complexity that they are occasionally eye-splitting. And he filmed them on locations never before used, including the Forbidden City and the Great Wall of China. The plot, as almost always, was simplicity itself. A myriad bunch of young revolutionaries want to assassinate a sadistic Manchu general (Yu Cheng-wei, back in place as a knee-slapping, constantly sadistically laughing bad guy). Sure, there are some complicating factors, like a fairly superfluous love triangle between Jet, his Shaolin brother, and the lead female revolutionary, but that mushy stuff takes a back seat to the color pageantry of Liang's kung fu tour de force.

The director saves the best for last — a no-holds-barred battle on a Yangtze River war-boat, featuring some of the most dexterous swordplay ever captured on film. It culminates in a guava field, showcasing the finest mantis fist yet pictured. All's well that ends well, with the two lovers getting together as Li heads back to the Shaolin Temple with his wise sifu. The actor was not as lucky as his on-screen character. Following this final Shaolin Temple movie, he discovered that the rest of the film industry was just churning out product.

Yu Cheng-wei went on to star in the strangely sadistic, but beautifully filmed, *Yellow River* (aka *The Yellow River Fighter,* 1987), playing a grief-stricken, blinded, poisoned warrior whose six-year-old daughter was delivered to him by an enemy at the end of a spear. But Jet was grounded, unable to find a quality project. When he finally returned to the screen, it was in a strange pair of movies set in America: *Dragon Fight* (1988) and *The Master* (1989). The former was set in San Francisco and featured Jet as a recent immigrant who had to fight racism as well as Chinatown gangs. Its one distinction was Jet's co-star, Stephen Chiao Sing-chi, who was soon to become Stephen Chow — the king of HK comedy in a string of delightful, hugely-successful, madcap comedies which satirized kung fu as often as they depicted it.

Meanwhile, Jet was left with the role of the student in *The Master* (the title character played by the great Yuen Wah, who had been raised in that brutal Peking Opera school along with Jackie Chan, Sammo Hung, and Yuen Baio). Here, both he and Jet were at sea in a hoary modern miasma about evil Americans inexplicably wanting to take over Yuen's California kung fu school. These, of course, were *Born to Defense*-type Americans: boorish, seemingly mentally-handicapped, hyper-violent bullies who are constantly trotted out in Asian movies to this very day. The single most important thing

Jet Powered

about this failure, however, is that it was directed by Tsui Hark.

Hark, often called the Hong Kong's father of special effects, was the country's most politically daring filmmaker. Having graduated from film school in Texas, Hark returned to Hong Kong in 1977, where he embarked on a series of challenging films in many genres (including 1979's landmark *The Butterfly Murders* and 1980's controversial *Dangerous Encounters of the First Kind*). He even made an unforgettable kung fu zombie film called *We're Going to Eat You* (1980). He gained his greatest fame, however, with the phantasmagorical action film *Zu Warriors of the Magic Mountain* (1983) — an eye-popping fantasy adventure featuring Yuen Baio, Mang Hoi, Moon Lee, and Adam Cheung battling demons and demigods for the fate of the world.

He followed that with *Peking Opera Blues* (1986), a wonderful comedy action romance starring three of Hong Kong's most beautiful and talented women (Brigitte Lin, Sally Yeh, and Cherie Chung) as reluctant revolutionaries and eager acting hopefuls who run afoul of sadistic sheriffs and mad military men. Eager to push filmmaking technology further, Hark produced two groundbreaking classics: Ching Siu-tung's *A Chinese Ghost Story* (1987) and John Woo's *A Better Tomorrow* (1987), both of which revitalized and revolutionized their respective genres. But with the new decade came cinematic confusion. The press reported Hark's seeming habit of creatively intruding upon his filmmakers to the point of dissolving partnerships, so it seemed he had little choice but to keep exploring new ground.

Rooting around for another genre to resurrect, he took a look at *The Master* and realized that there was one man Jet Li seemed born to play — Huang Fei-hong ... only now the translators were spelling it Wong Fei-hung. Go figure. In any case, who better to embody the young, serious, honorable man than the man whose name was once translated as Jet Lee? Inspired by this thought, and Liu Chia-liang's *Legendary Weapons of China*, Tsui turned his attention to the Chinese pugilist's vain attempts to defeat the gun with kung fu ... but added layers of relevance by having Hong Kong harbor filled with heavily armed ships from Britain, the United States, and Germany.

As the foreigners vied for political clout in the emperor's palace, Wong would rescue his lady love, Aunt Yee (Rosamund Kwan) from the clutches of evil English-speaking white slavers, as well as a homicidally jealous tiger claw kung fu master. The climatic battle takes place on a series of precariously balanced ladders and was an influential landmark of martial arts and special effects (during which Jet broke his shin).

Once Upon a Time in China (1991, named in honor of Sergio Leone's ground-breaking *Once Upon a Time in the West* [1968] and *Once Upon a Time in America* [1984]) was a huge hit — revitalizing both the Wong Fei-hung series and Jet Li's career. He played Fei-hung with an assurance and command hitherto fore unseen in his filmography. Not surprisingly, *Once Upon a Time in China II* appeared in 1992. Surprisingly, however, it was even better than the original — beautifully balancing action, romance, comedy, emotion, and politics in this tale of Wong meeting real-life revolutionary Dr. Sun Yat-sen while fighting the gweilo-hating White Lotus sect.

Veteran star David Chiang and relative newcomer Donnie Yen are standouts in this terrifically entertaining, exceptionally well-directed piece. Chiang plays Sun's assistant, who gives up his life for the cause, while Yen plays the violent, corrupt, arrogant "sheriff," who is a little too anxious to test his kung fu skills against Wong. The action is plentiful and impressive throughout (choreographed, as in the original film, by Yuen Wo-ping), but it is the three-part climax that stays in the memory. Wong decimates the White Lotus headquarters, then battles Yen in a soybean factory before taking it outside into an alley.

From that dizzying height, there was no place to go but down, and *Once Upon a Time in China III* (1993) showed signs of strain.

Jet Powered

Seemingly an attempt to combine the first two films, while climaxing the action with the most elaborate (and essentially ridiculous) lion-dance competition of all, the third time was not the charm. In fact, it sounded the death knell of Jet's partnership with Tsui Hark … but not before another side of Li's talent and career was broadened by his starring in Hark's *Swordsman 2* (1992) — the nominal sequel to the troubled *Swordsman* (1990, a "King Hu Film" that had to be completed by at least three other directors — Hark, Ching Siu-tung, and Raymond Lee — when Hu became ill). There he displayed a charm missing since the Shaolin Temple days.

But charm alone wasn't enough for him to avoid the "Tsui Curse." According to press reports, Li felt he was as important to the Wong Fei-hung movies as Hark, but the director-producer apparently felt differently. Allegedly, Hark's parting words were along the lines of "without me, you're nothing," and the disjointed, overblown story line of *Once Upon a Time in China III* reflected the backstage conflict. With that, Jet turned his back on Tsui, but not on Wong Fei-hung. With the director's harsh words ringing in his ears, he had a lot to prove, and he wanted to prove it fast.

Jet Li made five movies in 1993, the first being the aptly titled *Last Hero in China* (one that Jet intended to be his last Wong Fei-hung movie). Adding insult to injury, he worked with the madman of Hong Kong cinema, Wong Jing, to put Wong and Tsui in their places. Although Jet played his martial arts straight, the plot was the goofy tale of Wong being forced to move his kung fu school and healing hospital next to a brothel. As is Jing's wont, there is even a musical number as the kung fu students drool over the semi-clothed girls next door.

The climax also mixes straight kung fu with satire as Wong defeats the villain using chicken style. Maybe not so coincidentally, the man Jet defeats is played by Zhao Wen-zhou, the actor Tsui Hark chose to replace Li in 1993's inferior *Once Upon a Time in*

China IV and 1994's *Once Upon a Time in China V*. By soundly vanquishing Zhou in this (and a subsequent film), Jet clearly (although perhaps unintentionally) signaled his fans that Wen-zhou was no competition.

Although younger, and a quite capable martial artist, the actor who was to take on the name Vincent Zhao did not have Jet's looks or charisma, and, despite the fact that Hark used him in several subsequent Wong Fei-hung television shows, the *Once Upon a Time in China* series was considered over the moment Li left it. Jet, in the meantime, continued to leave Wong and Tsui in his dust. He enrolled the help of the popular kung fu film director/choreographer Yuen Kwai, and traveled to mainland China to take on the role of firebrand *Fong Sai Yuk* (1993) — the famous, hot-headed Shaolin Temple survivor whose love for his mother is only exceeded by his kung fu power. Former superstar Josephine Siao's career was revived by this film, which also rematched Li against Zhao Wen-zhou as Fong fights against the evil Qing dynasty.

This turned out to be one of Li's biggest hits, so out came *Fong Sai Yuk II* (1993), which is even more entertaining — at least from a kung fu standpoint. Here, Li is reunited with Ji Chun-hua, who played villains in all three *Shaolin Temple* movies. His performance adds weight to the quickly-produced film, in that he plays an insanely envious member of the initially chivalrous Red Lotus sect, who frames Fong and ultimately murders the sect's true leader, played by the charismatic Adam Cheung.

The climax has a blindfolded Fong chopping his once faithful sect brothers to bits (so he wouldn't have to see their betrayal) before rescuing his mother, who the bad guy has put in a hangman's noose atop a tall series of wooden workshop horses. It was another triumph for Li, Siao, and, especially, Yuen Kwai, who proved again what a fast and imaginative director he was. Yuen took the American name Corey (an asexual moniker which never failed to amuse his friend and "big brother," Sammo Hung) once he had directed a lion's share of successful kung fu flicks.

Even after those successes, Li's year was not over. He continued to have fun with martial arts traditions with *Kung Fu Cult Master* (1993), another Wong Jing extravaganza that was supposed to be the first part of a series based on a famous martial arts novel. Perhaps Jing went a bit too far kidding the audience. They seemed to want to see Jet Li do kung fu, not make fun of it. And little wonder. Classically trained, Li had a chi-driven energy that seemed to spark his every move. There was an elegance, balance and power to his screen kung fu that exceeded actors and dancers who were just quickly instructed how to fight. Viewers can instinctively identify the real deal, and Jet was clearly the real deal.

So, despite some amusing scenes (highlighted by one in which, coincidentally and ironically, Jet learns a new martial art in just a few minutes) and the fact that it was choreographed by co-star Sammo Hung, *Kung Fu Cult Master* was Li's weakest film of 1993. One of his strongest, however, was the aforementioned *The Tai Chi Master*, which marked a new direction in both Jet's and director Yuen Wo-ping's on-screen kung fu career.

As remarked upon before, taichi is one of the most misunderstood kung fu styles. Most westerners seem to think that it is "merely" a nice little dance that helps the elderly and has no fighting application at all. In fact, it is one of the most powerful styles … it's just that its strengths as a martial art aren't apparent on the surface. Which is odd, since it's very name is translated into English as "balance," and its symbol, the yin-yang sign, represents that balance. Yet, in a majority of American classes, only one half of it is ever taught.

Stephen Watson, the world heavyweight taichi push hands champion, displays its full power by starting the "dance" — i.e., the form — then invites anyone in the class to attack him at any time. Then he will repulse each attack, no matter when, no matter how, without changing the form in any way. Unbeknownst to most students, not to mention teachers, each move of that "dance" has a devastatingly effective martial application. The internal healing properties of taichi fuel the external martial properties.

Yuen Wo-ping discovered that to his joy. Now he had only one problem: how to translate that entertainingly and acceptably on film. *The Tai Chi Master* was his first try. It also starred Michelle Yeoh, who was working with Li for the first time. "Everyone had told me that Jet was so serious," Michelle said. "But I found that far from the truth. We had a wonderful time on the set. In fact, we used to drive the director crazy with all our cutting up. Of course he was a better martial artist than me, but he never tried to show off. In fact, he always made sure that I was okay, and was always very supportive and helpful — both as an actor and as a martial artist."

Wo-ping compensated for taichi's mystique with some labored comedy and too much time dwelling on inconsequentials, but the film ends in an effective flurry of activity, as Jet learns to harness nature's energy. The film is best in the self-learning sequences, not the battles. Standing in a windy clearing, Jet creates a spinning ball of fallen leaves without touching them, simply by a supreme movement of his arms. He then uses his new skill to defeat a power-mad eunuch as well as an insanely corrupt betrayer. The film ends on a satisfying note, but Wo-ping was not satisfied by his visualization of taichi's delights. He would return to it again and again.

Meanwhile, by any criteria, 1993 was an important year for Jet Li. On the plus side, it was clear to the entire film industry that he was still very much somebody, even without Tsui. But on the minus side, this was also the year when Jet's manager was gunned down in an underworld battle for control of the film industry. According to the Hong Kong press, Jet hastily returned to mainland China, ostensibly to seek a divorce from his wife. According to insiders, however, he was waiting for the smoke to clear in Hong Kong. Be-

Jet Powered

cause of that, his output in 1994 was reduced to "only" three movies — but one of them remains a kung fu classic while the other two were the result of his newfound producing powers.

One of the two was innocuously titled *New Legend of Shaolin,* in which Jet played Hung Hsi-Kwan, another legendary kung fu character who took the road of vengeance after the Shaolin Temple was betrayed and destroyed. This new movie version, however, also showcased the pubescent martial arts prodigy Xie Miao, who played Jet's son. Given that this effort was also directed by Wong Jing, things don't stay sane for long. Soon the Shaolin betrayer becomes super-powered, able to spit poison, and rides all over ancient China in a silver-spiked deathmobile. Besides that, Hung is eventually saddled with a whole bunch of Shaolin kids, all of whom must unite in the very confusing and, ultimately very silly, final battle.

Of a little more interest was *The Bodyguard From Beijing,* director Corey Yuen Kwai's Chinese take on the Kevin Costner-Whitney Houston *Bodyguard* (1992). This Asian variation features the sultry Christy Cheung as a rich man's wife who witnessed a horrible murder and now must be protected from a brutal kung fu killer (powerfully played by Ngai Sing). The beginning of the film is taken up with the staunch mainland bodyguard getting used to Westernized Hong Kong ways. The middle is given over to silly comedy and gunplay, but the last half-hour is solid action, as Jet and Ngai go at it in Christy's darkened, gas-filled apartment.

Jet's audience was impressed by his ability to segue from classic kung fu to modern gun play, but no one seemed pleased when it was announced that he planned to remake what was arguably Bruce Lee's best film, *Fist of Fury.* The media was in an uproar: sacrilege! And, indeed, when Jet's more politically correct, revisionist version first came out, the HK box-office returns were weak. But it was immediately embraced by fans in the rest of the world as Jet's martial art magnum opus. Like Liang's *Legendary Weapons of China,* Sammo's

Dragons Forever, and Jackie's *Drunken Master 2*, Jet, with the help of director Gordon Chan, immortalized his kung fu at its height.

Jet maintained that his new *Fist of Fury*, now called *Fist of Legend* (1994), was more faithful to the source material and more relevant to the times. The differences between the two films were certainly telling. Unlike Bruce, Jet did not have to convince his audience that the Chinese were not the weaklings of Asia. Nor did he think it wise to maintain the rampant hatred of the Japanese that drove the original. Instead, they created both good and evil Japanese, as well as good and evil Chinese. They even added an interracial love story: the hero, Chen Zhen, is in love with a Japanese girl — the niece of a great Japanese sensei (played by the great Shoji Kurata).

But it was the martial arts, choreographed once again by Yuen Wo-ping, which really made *Fist of Legend* a classic. The film is filled with great fights, each one better than the last. It starts with Chen studying in Japan when a bunch of karate toughs try to force him out of school. He mops the classroom with them, sometimes literally, in a bracingly brutal scene that shows him dislocating jaws and breaking limbs. When Zhen learns that his sifu has been killed in a martial arts duel, he confronts the winner's students and mops the place with them (at one point flipping a student by his mouth ... then slowly wiping the student's saliva from his fingers). He then tests the man who "defeated" his sifu in a lovely battle in which Chen repeatedly "gets in his face" — showing again and again that the "victor" is not skilled enough to even keep the sifu's student away.

By personally digging out his buried master's liver to test for poison, Jet runs afoul of both the enemy students and the racism of his own school's "brothers." He must confront his dead sifu's son, who is murderously envious of Li's skills. At first he goes easy on him, but Jet soon unleashes a new skill called "boxing" (shades of *Born to Defense*). Emerging victorious, he is still exiled by his racist superiors in the company of his Japanese lady love. Jet must then face

Jet Powered

her uncle in a terrific scene that compares and contrasts Asian styles. It ends with the film's most important dialogue.

After Shoji has called the confrontation a draw in the original Chinese version of the film, Jet asks: "But isn't the whole idea to win?"

To which Kurata replies: "If you want to win a fight, bring a gun. Martial arts is about balance and inner energy."

With that, Jet had struck the first blow for a new direction in the Hong Kong Kung Fu Cinema New Wave. But *Fist of Legend* was not over yet. Jet must still face his sifu's most virulent enemy (and the real killer): the man known as the General of Death — powerfully portrayed by Billy Chow (aka Chow Bey-lai). Chow also beautifully fought Sammo in *Eastern Condors,* Yuen in *Dragons Forever,* and Jackie in *Miracle.* Now it's Jet's turn, and, for fifteen marvelously orchestrated minutes, they go at it with brutal hung gar, taichi-flavored wushu, and even kick-boxing... until Billy grabs a samurai sword, forcing Jet to use his belt the way Bruce used his nunchaku.

Although they can't bring themselves to kill Jet at the end, ala Bruce (a loophole Donnie Yen would eventually leap through), *Fist of Legend* ranks with Li's *Shaolin Temple* and *Once Upon a Time in China II* as among the very best of the best. After that, Jet took time to slow down. He had been through monumental changes, and his early wushu teaching was grating uncomfortably against the dog eat dog world of kung fu cinema. Wo-ping had shown him a new way to synthesize fighting — something that didn't require muscle against muscle, anger against hated, and vengeance against vendetta. But while he considered this, he managed to make two more movies in 1995 — and they were odd, to say the least.

My Father Is a Hero (1995) is Jet and Corey Yuen Kwai's low-rent version of James Cameron and Arnold Schwarzenegger's *True Lies* (1994, which, in turn, was based on a 1991 French film called *La Totale).* This film reunites Jet with Xie Miao, the pubescent kung fu prodigy from *New Legend of Shaolin,* and uses the boy to wring pathos from its increasingly out-of-control plot. To push the audiences' buttons, they bring the kid back from the dead not once, but twice during the frenetic proceedings, and finish up the final fight with Jet using him as a living yo-yo — hurling him back and forth at the villains with a rope!

Also disappointing, but for entirely different reasons, was *High Risk* (1995) which was reportedly Wong Jing's attempt to co-star Jet Li and Jackie Chan. But when Jackie dropped out, the film became a vicious satire (read: attack) on Chan, featuring the talented Jackie Cheung as an action star who wears Bruce Lee's black-striped yellow outfit from *Game of Death,* has a father and manager who look just like Jackie's and, to top it off, is a drunk, skirt chaser, and total fraud.

Responding to rumors that it was director Stanley Tong, not Jackie, who did the jump between buildings in *Rumble in the Bronx,* Jing sets up a similar stunt in *High Risk,* and then shows how Cheung's character fakes it — but takes credit for it anyway. From there, the movie piles on — painting Cheung's character as a sniveling coward to boot — an attribute that even the most negative of Jackie Chan critics can't ascribe to the superstar. Even so, Jing continues to mercilessly lampoon Willie Chan, Jackie's manager, and even go so far as to cruelly kill Jackie's cinematic father. This cruelty really makes *High Risk* hit a sour note, despite Li's strong performance as a bodyguard who must save the star, *Die Hard*-style, from terrorists in a high rise. Despite its title, this mean-spirited effort marks a low point in Jet's filmography.

By then, however, it was clear even to Jet's most ardent fans that he was basically just making money in case things went south after Britain's lease on Hong Kong ran out in 1997. *Black Mask* (1996) was a stylish, entertaining action picture, directed by Daniel Lee, that allowed Jet to dress up like Kato. Touted as the most expensive

Jet Powered

non-Jackie Chan Hong Kong movie ($HK65,000,000), this tale of a top secret government plan to create super-soldiers has plenty of style, kinkiness (the heroine and villainess spend a notable amount of time in bondage), and deja vu (when our masked hero and super-powered super-soldier-supreme adversary slug it out in a gas-filled catacomb).

Jet coasted the remainder of the year in the very odd *Dr. Wai in the Scripture With No Words* (1996), a troubled movie within a movie. Li plays both a frustrated author, as well as the lead character in the writer's unraveling story. Although directed by Ching Siu-tung, neither the fantasy nor the reality portions of the effort were particularly riveting. So, with the end of an era fast approaching, Jet had to make a decision about his future. He may have realized that he needed cinematic closure, or they made him an offer he couldn't refuse. Whatever the reason, in 1997, Hong Kong's changeover year, Jet returned to the role of Wong Fei-hung.

"Okay, okay," Tsui Hark seemingly admitted by producing *Black Mask*, "Without me, you're something." Therefore Jet agreed to star in *Once Upon a Time in China VI: The Lion Goes West*, aka *Once Upon a Time in China and America* (1997). It was a cause for celebration for Jet's fans and a cause for resentment for Jackie's fans. Not only had Li starred in the insulting *High Risk*, but *The Lion Goes West* was a title and concept that Chan had publicly suggested as a project with Francis Ford Coppola. Then, to add injury to insult, Tsui signed Sammo Hung, fresh off helming *Mr. Nice Guy*, to direct and choreograph.

Apparently, Chan had the last laugh, as word has it that this was an extremely arduous and disorganized production. Jet, Sammo, Rosamund Kwan, and company reportedly tromped all over Texas, filming whatever they could think of as they went along. The finished film reflects the production chaos. Foreshadowed conflicts come to nothing. Main villains are changed midstream. Wong Fei-hung jerks back and forth between fighting bloodthirsty Indians and protecting Native Americans. Characters and subplots are introduced, only to be summarily eliminated.

There is some exciting kung fu, but it is essentially over by the film's midpoint. Running out of time and money, Sammo and crew hastily patched together a painfully anti-climatic final battle that relies far more on photography than fighting. *Once Upon a Time in China and America* was only successful if Jet's purpose was to disentangle himself from the character of Wong Fei-hung. Like *Diamonds Are Forever* (1971), which Sean Connery used to similarly detach himself from James Bond, *Once Upon a Time in China VI* made money at the box office, but not much else. Jet Li wrapped up his initial Hong Kong tenure with *Hitman* (1998), a minor, but enjoyable, action comedy in which a down-on-his-luck martial artist enters an assassination contest.

But then Mel Gibson, Danny Glover, and director Richard Donner came calling. They wanted a powerful Chinese villain for *Lethal Weapon 4* (1998), the latest in their series of landmark "buddy cop" films. Supposedly, they first offered the role to Jackie Chan, but he understandably didn't want to play the bad guy. Instead, he decided to do a riskier little film with no major stars instead ... *Rush Hour*.

When all was said and done, a reporter asked co-star Chris Rock if *Lethal Weapon 4* was Rock's breakthrough role. The talented comedian's reply was: "I don't know about that, but I do know it's Jet Li's breakthrough role."

Rock was right. After the original classic's serious undertones about a grieving cop's suicidal desire to take greater and greater risks, *Lethal Weapon 2* (1989) was that rare animal: a sequel as good as the original. *Lethal Weapon 3* (1992), however, was beginning to show signs of wear. Although not as effective as the first two, it held its own through the stars' charisma and chemistry. But then, sadly, the crew chose to play the fourth installment like one big joke, imbuing every scene, even violent ones, with an off-putting and self-conscious "we're only kidding" approach.

Every scene, that is, except when the camera was on Jet Li. His intensity and refusal to take his role lightly made every eye in the theater focus on him. Despite the usual ham-fisted editing of his kung fu skills, and the inclusion of a superfluous garrote wire secreted in prayer beads (which disappears midway through the film without explanation), Jet stole the show simply by refusing to belittle his part. While everyone else was cutting up and wise cracking, Li played it straight, even when asked to lose the final fight to Gibson and Glover — a misconceived mess where the two previously smart cops just flail around until they win for no apparent reason. Thankfully, director Donner's desire just to have fun served as the best possible introduction of America to Jet Li.

Then it was up to the rest of Hollywood to fumble the ball. *Lethal Weapon* producer Joel Silver tried his luck first, making the same short-sighted, blinkered, standard-operating-racism decision tinseltown always seemed to make. Just as Americans had taken great Chinese cuisine and reduced it to chop suey, the American film industry took great kung fu films, lumped them in with karate and samurai films, and dubbed them all by the patronizing term of chop-socky. And urban audiences liked "chop-socky" movies, so that's who all "chop-socky" movies would be made for. *Romeo Must Die* (2000) was Silver's first foray in Jet power, followed by *Cradle 2 the Grave* (2003).

Next, the inventive James Wong, best known for his contributions to *The X Files* TV, and the *Final Destination* movie, series, tried his luck with the sci-fi-flavored *The One* (2001), in which Jet got to play both hero and villain. Finally Jet teamed with French film mogul Luc Besson to make *Kiss of the Dragon* (2001) and *Unleashed* (aka *Danny the Dog*, 2005). Each of these increasingly okay films served its purpose — making Jet more assured in both his performing and producing prowess. It helped that he had brought Corey Yuen Kwai along to serve as choreographer and partner.

"If you want to do a more modern-day movie like *Romeo Must Die*, *Kiss of the Dragon*, or *Lethal Weapon 4*, choose Corey Yuen," Jet told me. "He takes modern style and ancient style and mixes them together."

But even Corey couldn't help when Jet turned down the lead role in *Crouching Tiger Hidden Dragon*. The official story was that he gave up the role to tend to his new wife, the beautiful Nina Li, during a particularly difficult pregnancy. Unofficial stories ranged from a soothsayer warning him off the picture, to his being too insecure in his acting skills to take on such an important and prestigious role.

Whatever the reason, when renowned Chinese director Zhang Yimou (who also made 1991's *Raise the Red Lantern*, 1994's *To Live*, and 1999's *The Road Home*, among other classics) came to him with the script for *Hero* (2002), Jet did not turn it down. *Hero* is not only one of film history's best kung fu films, it is one of the great works of cinema, period. Zhang uses this chronicle of China's first emperor to illuminate the nature of kung fu, as well as the art of movies.

Since it is a series of stories — each identified with a predominant on-screen color — told by an "assassin-killing hero" named "Nameless," to the Chinese Emperor he supposedly saved, it's a shame the title *Once Upon a Time in China* was already taken. Featuring a phenomenal cast including Tony Leung, Maggie Cheung, Donnie Yen, and Zhang Ziyi, kung fu is rapturously compared to music, calligraphy, literature, and nature, while romance, betrayal, love, passion, compassion, effort, and emotion are wrapped in brilliant mise en scene. And there's tremendous kung fu too.

"Given that everyone was talking about the fights between Michelle Yeoh and Zhang Ziyi in *Crouching Tiger*," Donnie told me, "Jet and I wanted to do even better. I mean, after all, we're the ones who actually know kung fu." Indeed, their confrontation in a rainy

Jet Powered

"chess inn" is a stunning fight scene between a sword and a spear, with special effects used to strengthen the symbolism, rather than cut corners.

For the rest of the gloriously beautiful film, Tony Ching Siu-tung served as choreographer. "If we talk about a sci-fi, comic book, or wuxia movie that's more romantic and where people can fly in the air," Jet told me, "I choose Tony. He's the best."

It's only right, since all the kung fu in *Hero* is not only great kung fu, but always symbolic of the fighter's state of mind or inner turmoil. It is also completely suitable in that the plot hinges on the more than a dozen ways to define the Chinese calligraphy of "sword," ending, as the film does, with a new definition that declares that the most powerful blade is the one that isn't used.

With that martial art monument making almost two hundred million dollars around the world (despite the delayed, fumbled, misleading American release), Zhang moved on to the season-based, kung fu allegory, *House of Flying Daggers* (2004), the color-crazed Chinese version of *Lion in Winter*, *Curse of the Golden Flower* (2006), and the Beijing Summer Olympics Opening and Closing Ceremonies — while Jet was ready to take his rightful place in the movie world.

"I think martial arts has many steps, like a building," Jet told me. "You must climb to get where you want to go. Becoming a good martial artist and becoming a good actor is two different things. I started learning martial arts when I was eight years old, eight hours a day, six days a week, for ten years. Now, twenty-nine years later, I think the top level is 'no action.'"

So, naturally, he wanted a "no action" action movie. He wanted a film to talk about what he called "martial arts in the heart. What is martial arts and what learning martial arts is really about," he continued. "Not just the physical but also the philosophy. What martial arts can do to help you understand life. Many think that martial arts is only for use against someone else, for revenge. If you use martial arts only for the physical, you're afraid a lot. You're afraid you'll lose your power, lose your name, lose what makes you feel special. So your biggest enemy is not from outside. It's from deep inside your own heart. Who's the enemy? The biggest enemy is yourself."

To find his inspiration, Jet looked back on his career. There he recognized a character who had been there all along. Not Wong Fei-hung or even Chen Zhen. It was the man Chen Zhen had been fighting for. In Asia, the resulting film was named for that poisoned sifu: *Huo Yuan-jia*. In the English-speaking world, it was called *Fearless* (2006).

"This character," said Li. "He fights a lot of people, and never loses. But he loses against himself. He figures out that he needs to fight and win against himself to understand life. That's basically what I believe. You can use violence to control other people, but you will not change their minds. The most powerful thing is that, by caring about them, you can turn your enemy into a friend. That's why I made *Hero* and *Danny the Dog*. Sure, if you're powerful, you can knock down twenty people in three minutes, but if you don't care about others and can't control yourself, you're no better than a mad dog. Physically you're very strong, but mentally you're very weak. So in my past three movies I tried to show a different angle, to show the audience a different view of martial art violence."

To supplement his vision, he called upon the choreographer who had opened his eyes to the self-improvement powers of kung fu. "I think Yuen Wo-ping is one of the greatest martial art directors in the world. He has a unique style by himself. He's a real martial artist. He just loves making traditional Chinese martial art movies. Like *Fearless*. We had ninety working days, and out of that, he and I had sixty days working together. He loves it! We're very close friends. For each movie we do together, we try to create something new. In the '90s, we tried to do it very fast for the camera. But now, for this film, we wanted to show the powerful physical side, but also we wanted to show what each character believed through how he fights. Wo-ping loves using martial arts to tell the story. Through the fighting, you can see the fighter's spirit without talking. That's his specialty.

"Huo tells his students, I don't want to see revenge any more. Martial arts is not just about training your body, it's about training your mind. That's the goal. To show that kind of choreography is very challenging for Wo-ping and I. We used a lot of energy to let the audience see the action, keep it interesting, and show the power, but also, at the same time, show the motivation and character behind the action. To show the inner peace. That was the difficult part."

Difficult, but not impossible. To find their way, Li, who also served as the film's producer, signed Ronny Yu to direct. Yu was best known in Asia for his lush romantic melodramas like *The Bride With White Hair* and *The Phantom Lover* (1995), while he's best known in America for his horror films. Li wanted a bit of both styles for his masterwork.

"The whole intention of making this movie is that it could touch everyone, even if you don't practice, study, or even understand martial arts," Yu told me. "Before this, I was crazy about kung fu films. But they were all about revenge and winning at any cost. I don't know if I should blame Bruce Lee or the Shaw Brothers who introduced us to the vengeance-filled martial art world. When I was growing up, I was a fanatic, but the only message I got was: somebody punch you? You learn martial arts and get even.

"So this is the one movie I threw in everything I learned, liked, and disliked from all the kung fu movies I've ever seen — from the old black and white Huang Fei-hong movies with Kwan Tak-hing to all the bloody Chang Cheh films ... everything! When I was starting to prepare this movie, I had long talks with Jet and Wo-ping and said, 'Why don't we go back to the basics? Because we have an actor who's actually a master in Chinese wushu, why don't we forget about the wire-fu, the quick cuts, and all that? Why don't we go back to long takes?' That meant we only used wires when we absolutely had to, for safety's sake."

With *Fearless*, Jet, Yuen, and Ronny set the stage for the next generation of kung fu films. They also set the stage for both Li's and Yu's exit from that very stage. "After making this movie I realized that the better at wushu you are, the better peacekeeper you are," Yu concluded. "The higher your level and ability, the more enlightened you are, the more you understand, and the more peaceful you become. So I don't think I'll ever do another wushu movie. What I wanted to say and convey to people on the subject is all in this movie. With *Fearless*, it's all been said."

Jet apparently felt the same way. During the American marketing campaign for the film, advertising announced that this would be Jet Li's final kung fu film. When I asked him about this, Jet smiled, and shrugged. "If that's what it says, that's what it says."

Since then, however, Li deservedly won his first Asian acting award for *The Warlords* (a 2007 remake of Chang Cheh's milestone *Blood Brothers* which featured some sweet "battlefield-fu"), reunited with Jason Statham for the shredder-edited potboiler *War* (2007), was yanked around on balance-robbing wires in both the misconceived *Forbidden Kingdom* (2008) and overblown *Mummy 3: Tomb of the Dragon Emperor* (2008), then got bounced around with Jason Statham and Dolph Lundgren in Sylvester Stallone's 1980s-style machismo mash-up *The Expendables* (2010).

Also in 2010, Jet starred in his first straight drama, *Ocean Heaven*, without a scrap of action. And, as of this writing, he's signed on for two new Tsui Hark wuxia films, one in 3D. But he spends a lot more time working with the charitable organization he created after he and his family survived the devastating "Great Southern Asian Tsunami" in 2004. Now, his "One Foundation" raises money for a

Jet Powered

multitude of worthy causes. In fact, he spent an entire year developing the charity rather than making films.

So is Jet Li truly done with kung fu movies? Happily, you'll get to decide for yourself. But for him, doing kung fu is now more than just a way to defeat villains.

"I saw a lot of movies, and I made a lot of movies," Jet told me, "and usually we only talked about violence against violence. A lot of old Hong Kong action films, they only talk about revenge. Whenever the good guy and bad guy use their physical strength to hurt the other, it's to show, to prove, that they are right. I think that's not good enough anymore. So, now I talk a lot about martial arts in the heart. What is martial arts and what learning martial arts is really about. Not just the physical but also the philosophy. What martial arts can do to help you understand life. Who's the enemy? The biggest enemy is yourself. So your biggest enemy is not from outside. It's from deep inside your own heart. You need to fight that. That's the highest meaning of martial art."

CHAPTER EIGHT
GUN FU

Picture identifications (clockwise from upper left):
Tony Leung vs. Philip Kwok Choy (Kuo Chui) in *Hard Boiled*; Chow Yun-fat in *Hard Boiled*; Chow Yun-fat in *Full Contact*; John Woo; Tony Leung, Jacky Cheung, and Waise Lee in *Bullet in the Head*; Chow Yun-fat in *God of Gamblers*.

Gun Fu

At the end of *The Warlords*, director Peter Chan's award-winning, 2007 remake of Chang Cheh's classic *Blood Brothers*, something very telling happens. After betraying his friends and spending his life acquiring power, Jet Li's character, General Pang, gets shot in the back by government assassins. Not confronted by a small army of blade-wielding soldiers, like Chow Yun-fat in *Curse of the Golden Flower*, nor by eighteen armaments and three styles of pugalism, like Liu Chia-liang in *Legendary Weapons of China*. Not even by a mob of shadow warriors brandishing nearly a half-dozen kinds of trickery, like Cheng Tien-chi in *Five Element Ninja*.

No, they just get a sniper's rifle and shoot him in the back from a great distance away. Where's your kung fu now, mister-wushu-champion-at-the-age-of-eleven? Of course this, again, brings into the focus the nature of kung fu (and people's reaction to it). Although designed as a system of self-improvement, its self-defense side effect became the main attraction to millions who sought a short cut to gaining some control over their mortality and/or power over others. But once the gun was invented and introduced throughout the world, all that training seemingly became moot.

No, now all you had to do was point and contract your index finger. As Shoji Kurata said in *Fist of Legend*; "if you want to win, bring a gun." Why seek self-improvement when you could just point and shoot? Turns out that not only worked on the streets, but inside studio walls as well. Why search for someone who could actually do kung fu beautifully when you could just overwhelm scripts, cameras, actors, and audiences with firepower?

After all, the Shaw Brothers kung fu training course was no more. The Peking Opera schools were mostly closed. Fewer and fewer students filled the mainland wushu academies every year. The rise of "Gun Fu" was inevitable once Hong Kong films became internationally famous. The main reason it hadn't happened before was that the Chinese were proud of their kung fu and sword-slingers. It was part of their culture. Although gunpowder had been invented in China, guns were seen as a foreign encroachment. Both China and Japan did what they could to ban them. In fact, Japanese law forced home-grown filmmakers to build prop guns for their movies — leading to many an action film where it looked as if criminals were pointing smoke-blowing toys at their enemies.

No one really took guns seriously in kung fu films for more than a half-century ... until a soft-spoken, innocuous Hong Kong immigrant named John Woo arrived. Born in Canton in 1946 to a tubercular ex-teacher father and doting, itinerant worker mother, Wu Yu-sen grew up in abject poverty — his only sanctuary being the Church ... and movie theaters. Back then, not only were movies considered fit only for women, but those women could bring their children along for free, and the Wu Yu family took copious advantage of that.

"I loved the musicals," the man who became John Woo told me. "I was fascinated by them."

By then his family had fled religious persecution and settled in Hong Kong, but problems still plagued them. Even though they survived in a slum, even that was destroyed by an infamous 1953 fire. Hope came in the form of a Christian education at a charitable Lutheran school, but a wise old priest saw more than religious fervor in the boy. He knew he was destined for an artistic life. Sure enough, by the time he was a teenager, Woo was making personal films with borrowed equipment. In his late teens, he was trying his hand at acting while learning film technique from books he stole from the library. Finally he secured a job at the Cathay Studios as a script supervisor.

"I was inspired by the French New Wave," he said. "The concept of the director as auteur was revolutionary and really intrigued me. Small budgets, small crews, a single camera ... I became determined to be a film director."

He got his chance in 1971, when Chang Cheh took Woo under his wing at the Shaw Brothers Studio. He became first assistant director on such classics as *The Water Margin* (1971), *Boxer from Shantung* (1972), and even the milestone *Blood Brothers*.

"I learned many things from Chang Cheh," he recalled. "The importance of brotherhood, filmmaking technique, editing ... it was a very important time for me."

Important, yes, but just like Liu Chia-liang before him, Cheh knew a good thing when he hired it, and was seemingly reluctant for Woo to move forward in his own career. So when Woo got his first directing assignment, it wasn't at Shaw Brothers. It was at Golden Harvest, on a little kung fu film called *The Young Dragons* (1973).

It was not an auspicious start. *Young Dragons*, like *Yes Madam*, was deemed unreleaseable, but *Young Dragons*, unlike *Yes Madam*, didn't set box office records when it was finally shown years later. Woo would retreat to serving as production manager for comedy king Michael Hui on several of the landmark Hui Brothers' comedies: *Games Gamblers Play* (1974), *The Private Eyes* (1977) and *The Contract* (1978). In between, he kept honing his craft by directing cheap martial art potboilers, including *The Hand of Death* (1976, aka *Countdown in Kung Fu*), co-starring and reportedly choreographed by the then "Jacky" Chan.

Apparently that was not a happy set. Chan supposedly suffered his first notable injury on that production; knocked unconscious for a full half-hour by a mistimed kick. The finished product was nothing to write home about either. Woo was more successful, critically, at least, with *Last Hurrah for Chivalry* (1978), a Chang Cheh-flavored swordplay epic featuring such stunting stalwarts as Li Hai-sheng and Mars. After that didn't find much in the way of financial favor either, Woo tried his hands at several genres, under several names.

He was most sought after for his kooky comedies, including *Money Crazy* (1977, where he was first listed as John Y.C. Woo),

From Riches to Rags (1979, his name finally shortened to John Woo), and *Laughing Times* (1981, as Wu Shang-fei). Finally, he teamed with Ricky Hui, the "Shemp" of the Hui Brothers, to make *To Hell with the Devil* (1982), a truly loony "religious horror comedy" that played like a demented "*Exorcist* meets *Airplane*." He gained further traction with 1982's *Plain Jane to the Rescue*, but betrayed his growing audience's trust with *Heroes Shed No Tears* (1983), a nasty tale of a mercenary tracking Vietnam drug lords. This was truly an unremitting, mean piece of work that seemed completely out of character (until years later).

In any case, by the time the middle 1980s rolled around, Woo was in personal, financial, and creative trouble. He had a vision for what he wanted, but no one else seemed inclined to let him do it. Except Tsui Hark. Hark had left the Golden Harvest confines to find his own artistic Shangri-la and invited Woo to join him at Cinema City. There they teamed the supposedly washed up director with a pair of supposedly washed up stars to create a film supposedly no one wanted: *A Better Tomorrow* (1986).

The posters for the film were up all over Hong Kong — plastered on construction site walls and movie theater hallways. They were stylish images, but looked to all the world like a drama about schoolteachers. Top-billed actor Ti Lung had floundered since the Shaw Brothers Studio film units had been shuttered. Co-star Leslie Cheung was best known for his singing career and lightweight romantic musical comedies. Third-billed supporting actor Chow Yun-fat was slowly being declared box office poison after a promising start as a nighttime TV soap star. Woo himself was hoping for the best, but planning for the worst.

Coincidentally, I met the director for the first time the night before the film premiered, and even after a long talk, I was not prepared for what I saw the following night. But the people of Hong Kong certainly seemed to be. Every showing of the film was sold out that day and that evening, causing us to drive to a remote cinema on the outskirts of town to find seats. And the reaction to the film was unlike any our group had experienced in the British colony. Hong Kong audiences were polite and undemonstrative for the many kung fu and wuxia films I viewed with them. Only occasionally had the older women in the audience repeatedly "tsked" when a hero was ignobly killed by a heinous villain ... a habit evidently left over from Peking Opera performances.

But it was as if the entire city had shared the same propulsive, convulsive response to *A Better Tomorrow*. This stylish, inventive, exhilaratingly violent tale of a nobly-suffering, honorable triad (mafia) gangster (Lung), his angry, resentful cop brother (Cheung), and the clever, cool underling (Chow) who tries to bridge them while an odious betraying gangster targets them all, elicited cheers, stomps, and fist-pumping. Hong Kong film fans maintain that they had not seen a reaction like this since Bruce Lee kicked the "No Dogs or Chinese" sign in *Fist of Fury*.

There had hardly been a hint of this consummately assured visual storytelling in any of Woo's previous work. His command of the action and emotion was unprecedented. He had clearly perfected Chang Cheh's themes of yang gang, taken to heart his mentor's love of *Bonnie and Clyde* as well as *Rebel Without a Cause*, eliminated all Cheh's affectation and stolid camerawork, then transferred the martial arts seamlessly into the gun age.

Woo's love of French gangster films was obvious here — especially in the character of Chow Yun-fat, who instantly joined Alain Delon (star of such classics as 1967's *Le Samourai*) as the world's greatest screen gunman. Both understood what Bruce Willis would borrow only temporarily in *Die Hard* (1988) and *Die Hard II* (1990) — that pulling the trigger of a gun was not easy. It requires effort along with the communication of both power and fear. It also calls for strength (of muscles, will, and mind), open eyes, and straight arms.

John Woo and Chow Yun-fat were superstars, literally overnight. Everybody wanted a sequel as soon as possible. Only one problem. John Woo didn't want to give it to them. While Chow reveled in his new-found fame, making twenty other movies in the next two years, Woo took a "been there, done that" attitude against ever-increasing pressure. Finally, taking a reverse psychology tact, he decided that if gun fu was what they wanted, he would give it to them in abundance. He would shove gun fu right in their faces. He would overwhelm them with gun fu. He would drown them in gun fu. He would make them sick with gun fu.

He should have known better. *A Better Tomorrow II* (1987) was full of outrageous moments — Chow Yun-fat sliding backwards down a stairway with his guns blazing, reams of white-suited gunsels falling out a doorway like slaughtered clowns at a circus, and Chow being engulfed, then knocked off-camera, by an on-screen explosion — but its very outrageousness worked in its favor because Woo had become too good a screen stylist. Even the plot was ridiculous — with Chow's character killed at the end of the previous film, they fall back on the hoariest of gambits: a twin brother.

Woo amped up everything: the emotional angst, the bloody slaughter, the sheer physical and mental bedlam ... but the power of the film cannot be denied. By trying to overdose his audience, Woo had not only effectively satirized himself, but painted himself into a blood-red corner. Now he would have to top himself with each subsequent production. But Woo was up to the challenge. It would take him two years, but he was up to it.

The Killer appeared in 1989, and Woo cemented his reputation with it. Chow Yun-fat stars as an expert assassin, whose conscience is resurrected by his accidentally blinding a beautiful bystander (Sally Yeh). To finance an operation to restore her sight, he takes the infamous "one last job" from exactly the wrong client ... the kind who likes to leave no witnesses to his misdeeds.

Gun Fu

Around this somewhat stereotypical story, Woo lavishes wit, invention, and style in addition to his customary flair for gunfire. An honest cop (Danny Lee) is hot on the title character's trail, but the film really takes off when he corners the killer in the blind girl's apartment. Unaware that the men have their guns in each other's faces, she makes tea and the two pretend to be friends for her benefit. This was a stunning, refreshing dance of death deftly designed by Woo, and it immediately separated the film and filmmaker from the pack.

Ultimately, the two antagonists team up against the greater evil, and Woo stages a final blowout in and around a church ... before capping the invigorating film with the bleakest of black comedy jokes that, again, delighted his attentive audience. Here Woo firmly establishes his cinematic trademarks: the "Cantonese Stand-off" of multiple antagonists pointing guns in each other's faces in various combinations, flocks of doves flying hither/yon, and an artful use of slow-mo. Movie lovers could see echoes of this in previous works by director Sam Peckinpah, but Woo brought it to new, nearly ludicrous levels. Woo created fever-dreams of violence on the nature of brotherhood, betrayal, moral villains, and immoral heroes, all delivered with a filmmaking prowess that echoed the best of Francis Ford Coppola, Martin Scorcese, Jean-Pierre Melville, and Sergio Leone.

Once up to such rarefied heights, Woo seemed unsure where to go in the down-and-dirty world of Hong Kong Cinema, which explains his name on the credits of *Just Heroes* (1989) — a fun, frenetic, but overly familiar film that could be considered *A Better Tomorrow*-lite. According to modern sources, Woo collaborated on the direction of this derivative film as a favor to his ex-mentor Chang Cheh, who was struggling to survive. So Woo teamed with another ex-Cheh-assistant director, Wu Ma, as well as actors Danny Lee, David Chiang, and even Stephen Chow, to finish this film.

It was just as well that Woo had this distraction because, elsewhere, the infamous "Tsui Hark Syndrome" was kicking in. Woo wanted to go his own way. Tsui Hark wanted Woo to go his way. There's some question as to what happened next, but what is unarguable is that Woo directed *Bullet in the Head* (1990) while Tsui Hark directed *A Better Tomorrow III* (1989), which had some "interesting" similarities to Woo's work. There's no question, however, that Hark worked round the clock to beat *Bullet in the Head* into Hong Kong theaters. There's also little question that *Bullet in the Head* is the better film, despite contractual alliances that locked Chow Yun-fat into Hark's prequel/sequel.

A Better Tomorrow III pictures Chow's character from the first film in Saigon of 1974 — showing viewers how he became the man he was. *Bullet in the Head* is a completely different animal — an epic saga of three Hong Kong friends who seek their fortune in Vietnam at the worst possible time. Tony Leung Chiu-wai took over for Chow in Woo's work (which would not be the last time he does that). Although smaller in stature, Leung's acting talent is large, and he suffers better than anyone in cinema. And that skill comes in handy in this bruising classic, as friendships dissolve into betrayal and brutality.

The title refers to the film's central betrayal, as a greedy friend ("All I want is this box of gold … is that so much to ask?" is the actual line in the film) shoots a wounded friend to keep him quiet as they hide during an attack. But instead of killing him, the lead lodged in his skull makes him a pain-wracked killing machine. Jacky Cheung (aka Jackie Cheung), once known as "little Jacky" because of Jackie Chan's support in his early career, had developed into an extraordinary composer, singer, and actor, and his performance here, as the one with the title affliction, is beautifully realized. And, of course, Tony suffers brilliantly as he's compelled to put his friend out of his misery — building to a final confrontation with the betrayer (Waise Lee, who played much the same role in the original *A Better Tomorrow*).

In the original release, the film ends with the screen going dark and a shot being heard. But in subsequent home entertainment releases, a different, longer finale was seen: the confrontation extends to the docks where the two ex-friends have an extended, exhausting, ferocious joust with smashing cars and blazing guns. Once again, the connections to Chang Cheh or Lu Chin-ku's bloody, battering wuxia films can be clearly seen. This is truly gun fu, with automatic weapons replacing swords.

Now a fan can hunt down the many versions of the film available in various incarnations all over the world. Woo's original cut was around three hours long. The studio's cut was about two hours. Film Festivals show, and certain DVDs contain, a two hour and fifteen minute version that Woo generally approves.

Following that exhausting effort, however, Woo needed to regroup and rethink. The grouping is obvious in his next film, *Once a Thief* (1991), but not necessarily the thinking. Although it marks a reunion with Chow Yun-fat and Leslie Cheung, the film seems forced and unnatural. Although it starts well, as a Hitchcockian romp about three art thieves, it eventually seques into an odd payback tale, with a wheelchair-bound Chow supposedly seeking revenge, before degenerating into an unwelcome slapstick slaughter that has more in common with *To Hell with the Devil* than *A Better Tomorrow*.

The writing was on the wall. With rumors spreading that Woo was tough to work with, and the 1997 changeover looming, the director started searching for safer shores. But, before he left, he wanted to leave his homeland with one last blast of concentrated Woo-ness. And, after glorifying criminals in most of his work, he wanted to do the same for cops. *Hard Boiled* (1992) was a cunning combination of Woo's best work, from the elegant to the overblown. Chow Yun-fat was back in the lead as this film's version of "Dirty Harry Bullitt," with Tony Leung alongside as a cop deeply undercover in the gun-running trade.

Woo fills the film with bravura sequences, from the opening gun battle in a tea house, through a blow-out in a garage, to the final, elongated, elaborate war in a hospital (which includes an extended sequence through halls, into elevators, and down stairs without a single cut). For pure, high-powered fun, *Hard Boiled* more than lives up to its name, and works well as Woo's suitable so-long to Hong Kong … for now.

But just because Woo was packing his bags didn't mean that Hong Kong was through with guns. Remember, this is an industry that created the Bruce Lee clones — and weapons were far easier to replicate than the king of kung fu. Even noted schlockmeister Wong Jing was able to till this fertile ground with what many consider his best film, *God of Gamblers* (1989). Chow Yun-fat starred as the title character, who, when egregiously betrayed by his brother, becomes a child-like amnesiac, who is convinced to impersonate the God of Gamblers by a con man (Andy Lau). Obviously inspired by *Rain Man* (1988) as well as *A Better Tomorrow*, the film's ramifications will be explored in a later chapter.

Meanwhile, predominantly filling the Woo void were Ringo Lam Ling-tung, Andrew Lau Wai-keung, and, perhaps most importantly, Johnnie To Kei-fung. Beatles-loving Lam was born in 1955 and studied cinema in Toronto before returning to Hong Kong. There he tried a few romances before teaming with Chow Yun-fat on the influential cop thriller *City on Fire* (1987) which deeply and sincerely influenced Quentin Tarantino. The director and star followed up that hit with *Prison on Fire* (1987), *School on Fire* (1988), and *Prison on Fire II* (1991) before creating *Full Contact* (1993), which was the closest thing to a Woo film without Woo.

Lau, meanwhile, had started as an award-winning cinematographer, filming *Legendary Weapons of China*, *Millionaire's Express*, and *City on Fire*, among others, before he made a jump into the director's

Gun Fu

chair in 1990. There he would again flounder in a variety of genres until he hit pay dirt with the *Young and Dangerous* series (1996-1998), which was basically *A Better Tomorrow: The Teen Years*.

He peppered his resume with some great wuxia fantasies like *The Storm Riders* (1998) before teaming with Alan Mak Siu-fai on the influential *Infernal Affairs* trilogy (2002-2003). This saga of a cop infiltrating the mob while a mobster infiltrates the cops was turned into *The Departed*, Martin Scorcese's Oscar-winning 2006 film. Many feel the Hong Kong version was superior — especially since the American adaptation goes head-shot-crazy as soon as it deviates from the original's plot.

But it was Johnnie To who took John Woo's inspiration and made gun fu something uniquely his own. Starting, like so many other Hong Kong directors, by trying a mix of genres, he found that he loved them all, and was able to excel in each. He was great at comedies (1990s *The Fun the Luck and the Tycoon*), dramas (1989's *All About Ah-long*), satires (1992's *Justice My Foot*), superheroes (*The Heroic Trio*), and even kung fu (1993's *The Bare-Footed Kid*). But even though it would be more than ten years between his first (1988's *The Big Heat*) and second gun fu film (1999's *The Mission*), it was in this genre that he would elicit international acclaim.

He followed those memorable thrillers with such blockbusters as *Running Out of Time* (1999), *Fulltime Killer* (2001), and *PTU: Police Tactical Unit* (2003) — all while also creating a wealth of such other comedy and martial art classics as *Love on a Diet* (2001), *Running on Karma* (2003), and *Throw Down* (2004) — often with his collaborator Wai Ka-fai. With *Election* (2005), *Election 2: Harmony is a Virtue* (2006), and *Exiled* (2006), he shows his Woo influence as well as his mastery.

With these three films essentially being his versions of *A Better Tomorrow* and *Bullet in the Head*, Johnnie To cultivates Woo soil with his own crops. Each of his successive films (2007's masterful

Mad Detective, and 2009's thought-provoking *Vengeance* being just two) have become a cause for celebration for film fans throughout the world.

And speaking of the world, that was John Woo's oyster when he left Asia. He was renowned as the greatest action filmmaker ever, with fans in every pocket of the globe. He was declared an artist and auteur ... even a genius. It seemed that nothing could stop him. What could possibly go wrong?

Read on ....

CHAPTER NINE
KUNG FU.S.A.

Picture identifications (clockwise from upper left):
Chuck Norris vs. Tadashi Yamashita in *The Octagon*; Chuck Norris vs. David Carradine in *Lone Wolf McQuade*; Teenage Mutant Ninja Turtles and Shredder; Steven Seagal; Tom Laughlin in *Billy Jack*; Mighty Morphin' Power Rangers.

Kung FU.S.A.

Let's face it. The American film industry doesn't like kung fu. One reason is that the American audience who loves it is not the same as the American audience that loves chop-socky. There's some overlap, sure, but mostly the ones who love true kung fu films are the ones who love musicals. Real kung fu films combine the emotions of opera with the movement of dance, even ballet.

This reality is totally lost on the producers who fashion and market their chop-socky to the urban audience. If they honestly looked at which American kung fu films succeeded beyond their wildest expectations, it was the ones that were fashioned and promoted to the *family* audience. *Rush Hour*, *Kung Fu Panda* (2008), The 2010 *"Karate" Kid*. Even *Crouching Tiger Hidden Dragon*.

The bulk of the American film industry denies this — relegating those films, and others, to the category of "exceptions." Or they take the likes of *Hero*, and, especially, *Shaolin Soccer* (2001), and package them as urban audience films, which they are, quite patently, not. It would be as if distributors had taken *Lawrence of Arabia* (1962) and *Blazing Saddles* (1974), stuck samurai swords in the characters' hands on the DVD covers, dressed them in t-shirts, swathed the foreign backgrounds in manila paper, and sold them as exploitation flicks. That is, if they released them at all.

Whether this is simply blinkered ignorance or standard operating racism, is for you to decide. What's quantifiable is that Hollywood is much more comfortable with Japanese martial arts: karate, aikido, judo, kick-boxing, even ninjitsu — the kind of straight-limbed, muscle-and-anger-driven fighting that has been tinseltown's stock-in-trade since the advent of the motion-picture camera.

In order to make the action clear in the earliest days of cinema, directors favored exaggerated, wide, movements like the classic round-house punch. This long, elaborate, telegraphed move found favor amongst producers and was cemented in the 1940s, when long fight scenes became common-place in Westerns and cliffhanger serials. There, subtlety was to be avoided at, literally, all costs. After all, training actors and filming elaborate fights took time, and time was money.

"In Hong Kong," Jet Li said, "a greater proportion of the audience are used to fight scenes that last five to ten minutes with unusual, esoteric wushu movements. But I think Americans may be more used to boxing — with all its straight strikes — that last maybe thirty seconds before someone falls down. But there really wasn't more time to do the martial arts in America than there was in Hong Kong. You see, in Hong Kong, if the shooting schedule is for three months, we work on the kung fu scenes for maybe two months, and the drama for one. In American films, maybe two months on the drama, one month on the fighting. So we still don't have enough time."

Studios may not have the time, but, in truth, they really don't have the inclination either. Because *Enter the Dragon* producer Fred Weintraub was right when he said that Americans think of kung fu as fantasy. First, it has been sold to them as a martial art, not as self-improvement, and second, what's the point of having a system that takes years to master when you can just pick up a gun? U.S. history is not about "excellence of self." It's about "excellence of *aim*." To put it bluntly, Americans have never been without the gun, and a majority of chop-socky filmgoers really can't understand why two people would engage in a dance of death with limbs or swords when a bullet could resolve matters much more easily.

Ironically, as more Asian kung fu films are bought for distribution in the English-speaking world, standard operating ignorance has come back to haunt the translators. Some of the best kung fu in John Woo's *Red Cliff* was edited out of the American version for being too unrealistic, when it most patently wasn't. It was merely unusual to American editors' eyes, who were accustomed to chi-wasting round-house punches. One of the best jokes in *Ip Man* (2008) was ruined by translators who didn't comprehend the kind of kung

Kung FU.S.A.

fu the hero was doing (changing "if you don't start fighting" to "if you start fighting" because they couldn't distinguish between defensive and offensive kung fu).

That originally started to change with the coming of Bruce Lee. Prior to him, martial arts in American movies were relegated to glimpses of exotic, esoteric fighting skills they called "judo" in *Blood on the Sun* (1945) starring Jimmy Cagney and *The Manchurian Candidate* (1962) starring Frank Sinatra. An argument can be made (and I often do) that the first real kung fu fight scene in English-speaking cinema was the train battle between Sean Connery and Robert Shaw in the second James Bond film, *From Russia with Love* (1963). There the characters only move as much as they have to, and shun round-house punches in favor of direct, effective techniques. They also involve their cramped environment Jackie Chan-style ... as much as two hulking, muscle-bound Englishmen can.

Also in there kicking was Tom Laughlin. Born in 1938, Laughlin became an actor in the 1950s, and was featured in several major Hollywood productions, including *Tea and Sympathy* (1956), *South Pacific* (1958), and the original *Gidget* (1959). His destiny, however, was in the exploitation genre. Giving up the tinseltown rat race, he decided to write, direct, produce, edit, and star in *The Young Sinner* (1965), establishing his ongoing theme of misunderstood youth. Two years later he hit the mother lode with *The Born Losers* (1967), which introduced his character of a heroic, laconic, karate-trained half-breed named Billy Jack.

The Born Losers made more than ten million dollars — an extraordinary amount of money for a mere exploitation film. He spent the next four years making, and then distributing, the movie he is most remembered for: *Billy Jack* (1971). This story of an ex-Green Beret who fights rednecks and a corrupt sheriff's office to protect a Freedom School for hippie runaways (located on an Indian reservation, yet!) featured real-life martial arts expert Bong Soo Han. The movie cost eight hundred thousand dollars to make, and made more than eighteen million. Laughlin followed that with heart-felt, but increasingly less effective, sequels, as well as *The Master Gunfighter* (1975) — his portentous remake of Hideo Gosha's great Japanese epic *Goyokin* (1969), transposed to the American West.

But, by then, *Enter the Dragon* had appeared. The Chinese kung fu cat was out of the bag, as it were, and once seen, could not be forgotten … but damned if Hollywood could figure out a way to exploit it. To their credit, producer Weintraub and director Robert Clouse tried to recapture lightning in a bottle. To their debit, they didn't do a very good job. Their big mistake: avoiding kung fu like the plague. In 1974, they featured *Enter* co-star Jim Kelly as *Black Belt Jones* (1974) — a fondly remembered blaxploitation effort with a serious credibility problem. Why would the white mob be so intent on taking over a martial arts school in the middle of Watts anyway?

Next the duo tried *Golden Needles* (1974). Brilliantly (sarcasm), they replaced the lithe Lee with the burly Joe Don Baker, who starred as a brutish mercenary out to find a fabled Asian statue that held the promise of eternal youth. When that didn't work in any way, Weintraub and Clouse finally decided to return to the source. If they had found a kung fu talent like Lee in Hong Kong before, maybe they could do it again. And here my memory runs into trouble.

After my formal interview with Fred Weintraub more than twenty-five years ago, I brought up the remarkable similarity between Yul Brynner in *The Ultimate Warrior* (1975) and Gordon Liu Chia-hui in *The 36th Chamber of Shaolin*, which appeared two years later. At the time of *The Ultimate Warrior*'s production, Liu was making the transition from a supporting actor and stuntman on Chang Cheh's films to Huang Fei-hong in Liu Chia-liang's *Challenge of the Masters* (1976). My contention was that if Gordon had starred in Weintraub and Clouse's post-apocalyptic action drama, they might

Kung FU.S.A.

have made America's second great kung fu discovery.

To the best of my recollection, Weintraub alluded to the fact that he had, indeed, scoured Hong Kong for a new star; that Gordon, although young, showed great promise; and, if not for Liu's Shaw Brothers contract and/or the American studio's desire for an established box office name, *The Ultimate Warrior* would have been a showcase for Liu Chia family fist the way *Enter the Dragon* was a showcase for jeet kune do. As it was, the well-intentioned, fight-filled film collapsed under the weight of its mediocre choreography and screenplay. Following that fiasco, Weintraub reteamed with Jim Kelly for *Hot Potato* (1976) — a dreadfully titled, painfully mediocre film with the actor demoted to playing one of three mercenaries hired to rescue a senator's daughter held captive in Thailand.

When that flick also died at the box office, Weintraub and Clouse decided to shoot the works. Taking the plots from *Enter the Dragon* and *Hot Potato,* they hired three of America's best real-life martial artists, then threw in a burly black, a beautiful blonde, and a heinous Asian villain. They called it *Force Five* (1981), and it was not good. Their hearts were in the right place, but their filmmaking skills were not. This painful waste squanders the abilities of World Heavyweight Karate Champion Joe Lewis, World Kickboxing Champion Benny "the Jet" Urquidez (who looked great fighting Jackie in *Wheels on Meals* and *Dragons Forever*), and Richard Norton (who looked great fighting Sammo in *Twinkle Twinkle Lucky Stars* and Jackie in *City Hunter*), not to mention Bong Soo Han, who played Reverend Rhee(!), an evil minister who lived on an island with his own "Maze of Death."

Sound familiar? Despite its obvious origins, had the script been half as clever and the fights half as good as in *Enter the Dragon,* the movie might have had a chance. It wasn't, they weren't, and it didn't. Weintraub and Clouse never gave up, bless them. They tried Jackie Chan in *The Big Brawl* and Cynthia Rothrock in the *China O'Brian* series (1990-1991), but the two stars, unlike Bruce, would not force superior kung fu on them. It seemed that without Lee, Weintraub, Clouse, and the American kung fu movie was in a maze of death without a map.

Things seemed about to change with the publication of *The Ninja* (1980), Eric von Lustbader's evocative espionage novel which introduced mainstream fiction readers to the ancient sects of Japanese assassin-spies thirteen years after 007 had showcased them in *You Only Live Twice* (1967). It took Lustbader's novel to inspire Richard Zanuck and David Brown, producers of *Jaws* (1975), to mount a multi-million-dollar, grade-A adaptation. And if that happened, maybe top producers would smile on Chinese kung fu as well. But it was not to be.

Instead of the exotic, long-suffering, tragic, anti-heroic spies with "no place on earth and none in heaven (which they historically were)," ninja were doomed to toil in cheap American exploitation films and lousy television shows as ludicrous superheroes and supervillains in black hooded pajamas who threw metal star-shaped darts like Frisbees. It was all because Cannon Films' Monachem Golan and Yoram Globus rushed out *Enter the Ninja* (1981), dooming the American martial arts movie to more years of schlocky, derisive, but profitable abuse.

"It was originally a script I wrote called *Dance of Death*," undefeated karate champion Mike Stone told me. Golan promised Stone the leading role, collected a crew, and sent everyone to the Philippines to start shooting. Three weeks later, according to Stone, he fired them all. "Golan brought in a completely new crew from Israel, save for the sound man. He brought in Franco Nero to star and then rehired me, for more money, to stay on as action choreographer and stunt double."

Golan's rationale may have been that he didn't like the way the film was coming out, but Stone had another point of view. "Appar-

Kung FU.S.A.

ently it's just the way they are," he explained, referring to Golan, who served as *Enter the Ninja*'s new director, and Yoram Globus, the producer. "From what I hear that's just their standard operating procedure."

The procedure continued through patently absurd sequel after patently absurd sequel, cementing ninja in the minds of non-Asian audiences as ludicrous, self-reverential tools. In fact, the concept of the ninja was such a joke by the end of the twentieth century, that the only major movies featuring them was a truncated series of bad kids films, *3 Ninjas* (1992-1998) and *Beverly Hills Ninja* (1997), one of the last movies starring *Saturday Night Live* alum Chris Farley.

Supposedly, that was all going to change (again) with *Ninja Assassin* (2009), a big budget, major studio release produced by the Wachowskis, who created *The Matrix* (1999) — which, itself, did much for the American kung fu genre. But the Wachowskis also created the disappointing *Matrix* sequels, as well as the honorable but ultimately ineffective *V for Vendetta* (2006) and *Speed Racer* (2008). Sadly *Ninja Assassin* fell in the latter category. Rather than illuminate the fascinating true character of the self-tormenting specialists, they were made veritable super-zombies in the special effects-burdened fantasia.

Ironically, the ninja movie as a viable genre disappeared almost as effectively and completely as the ancient assassin-spies themselves. But the insidious effect of Cannon Films on the development of American martial arts films was far from over. Just ask Chuck Norris. When producers couldn't get Bruce post-*Enter the Dragon*, some would take anything associated with him. And since Lee gave Norris such a great showcase in *Way of the Dragon* (and the two had reportedly worked together on *The Wrecking Crew*), Lo Wei (the prolific Chinese filmmaker who proclaimed to all who would listen that he launched Bruce as well as Jackie) cast Norris as the beating, raping, robbing, and laughing villain of *Yellow Faced Tiger* (aka *Slaughter in*

San Francisco, 1973) — the film designed to introduce Don Wong Tao as yet another "New Bruce Lee."

The film did little for Don, but served to inspire Chuck not to take the Hong Kong road. If he was going to be a movie star, he vowed to do it in his own country. Born in 1940 Oklahoma, he escaped a tough childhood by joining the Air Force. Once stationed in Korea, he discovered the joys of Tang Soo Do, another Korean martial art with roots in the Japanese occupation of the country, but also with a touch of Chinese flavor (the "tang" of the name supposedly referring to the Tang Dynasty). Once returning to the states, however, he excelled in karate tournaments and opened a chain of popular karate schools.

Leaving the San Fran slaughter behind, he worked diligently to create his own movie path. He got his next shot at stardom thanks to the short-lived mini-craze for truckers and the rustic "language" on their in-cab citizen's band (CB) radios — born of 1975's best-selling *Convoy* song (and subsequent 1978 film of the same name directed by Sam Peckinpah). He managed to get the lead role in *Breaker Breaker* (1977), an exploitation film written by a man best known as an editor (Terry Chambers) and directed by a man best known for composing soundtracks (Don Hulette). It was a mediocre movie, but was enough to get Chuck's spinning back kick in the door. In this movie, as in almost all of its successors, many stuntmen would wait around just to get his cowboy boot in their faces.

Although his first movie came and went like a passing truck, *Good Guys Wear Black* (1978) got more attention. Director Ted Post, who had helmed Clint Eastwood's *Hang 'Em High* (1968) and *Magnum Force* (1973), wisely decided to make Chuck the "poor man's Clint." The tale of a political science professor (a role that fit Norris like a sleeping bag) who is revealed to be the leader of the elite Black Tiger Unit, benefited from an exceptional marketing campaign, anchored by the moment when Chuck does a flying kick through the

Kung FU.S.A.

windshield of a moving car.

That film did well enough to ensure Chuck's next film, *A Force of One* (1979), which he also got to choreograph. It was a grateful flashback to his karate days, as he battles in a martial arts competition that serves as a front for drug pushers. In it, he fights Bill "Superfoot" Wallace, to much the same tepid response as when Jackie Chan fought Superfoot in *The Protector*. Although not as exciting as his previous film, *A Force of One* was superior to anything else that could have been termed an American martial arts movie at the time. Although limited as an actor, Norris cared about the movies he made, and he was intent on creating a breakthrough film — something that would bring him to the attention of the major studios.

The Octagon (1981) did it. With his wooden delivery and stolid screen presence, Norris seemed born to play a ninja (whose job was not to be noticed). Here, he plays a nearly somnambulistic fighter who resists taking on a present-day ninja camp despite the fact that all his loved ones are dropping like flies. The climatic assault on the octagon-shaped ninja camp is a good one, reminiscent of the opening Vietnam War sequence in *Good Guys Wear Black*. And, despite the fact that several protagonists die because Norris' character refuses to take action through most of the film's first half, *The Octagon* became his best-looking, and one of his best-loved, movies.

Following that, he reportedly wanted to do *The Destroyer*, the satiric, male-action, paperback book series about Remo Williams and Chiun, two masters of Sinanju — the Korean source of all the martial arts. But the authors, Warren Murphy and Richard Sapir, weren't selling to Norris. No, *Remo Williams: The Adventure Begins* began and ended in 1985, when Fred Ward and Joel Grey played the roles in the uninspired first film in an aborted series.

"You could have made *Rambo*, instead you made *Dumbo*," author Murphy told me he said to the film's producer after leaving a screening.

Chuck Norris made *The Destroyer*-esque *An Eye for an Eye* (1981), with Mako as Chan, an Asian mentor to a martial artist taking revenge for the killing of his policewoman girlfriend. Even with fights choreographed by Chuck and his brother Aaron, the result was tired. But, as uninspired as it was, the "Eyes" finally brought Norris to the attention of a major studio.

Columbia Pictures wanted him to star in seemingly the worst script they could find: *Silent Rage* (1982). Here Chuck plays a stiff but honorable small-town sheriff whose justifiable killing of an insane ax murderer is complicated when some scientists inexplicably bring the nutcase back to life as an unkillable monster.

While Chuck is breaking up a barroom brawl with his patented spin kick, the monster is running around town killing people in gruesome and gratuitous ways. Finally, Norris kicks the guy down a well and the film ends with a freeze frame of the monster struggling in the water, where he apparently is to this very day. Words cannot describe the pandering, moronic nature of this production. The only item of interest was that Chuck was playing a live man like a zombie while Brian Libby, who portrayed the killer, was playing a zombie like a live man.

So much for Columbia. Next on Chuck's studio tour was MGM/UA, which released *Forced Vengeance* in 1983. Originally titled *The Jade Jungle*, it was "Clint-lite" by any name, directed by James Fargo, whose main claim to fame was helming the third *Dirty Harry* movie, *The Enforcer* (1976). Chuck then moved on to Orion, who secured Norris' future with *Lone Wolf McQuade* (1984), which proclaimed to all the world that Norris actually *wanted* to be "Clint Lite." The plot, ostensibly based on the real-life exploits of Texas Ranger "Lone Wolf" Gonzales, was really a patchwork of Eastwood's *Dirty Harry* and "Man With No Name" spaghetti Westerns. Even the soundtrack was reminiscent of Ennio Morricone's brilliant music for Sergio Leone's trilogy (*A Fistful of Dollars*, *A Few Dollars More*, and *The*

Kung FU.S.A.

Good, the Bad, and the Ugly).

The final affront to martial arts movie fans was that David Carradine played the villain. However, Carradine, who had been given Bruce Lee's role in both the *Kung Fu* television series and the awful film version of *The Silent Flute* (1974), would only sign on if he was not seen beaten on-screen (so he was blown up off-screen instead). Norris was quoted as saying that Carradine was about as good a martial artist as he, Norris, was an actor. It was that self-deprecation/insecurity that would shape Norris' showbiz life. Still, he always tried his best and was a conscientious worker and an honorable professional.

It was his inherent promise that attracted producer Raymond Wagner. Wagner was working with a remarkable young man named Andy Davis, whose only directing credit up until that time was a minor movie called *Stony Island* (1977). But they had a workable script called *Code of Silence* (1985), which Davis knew he could make great if it was filmed in his favorite city, Chicago. Surrounding Norris with veteran "Windy City" actors (and playing to his star's monosyllabic strengths) Davis made Norris' best movie — a crackling good, emotionally involving cop thriller; low on martial arts but high on stunts and solid dialogue (probably the most memorable of which had Chuck growling, "If I need any advice from you, I'll beat it out of ya").

Finally, after more than a decade, Chuck Norris had made a good movie — one that he could have used as a foundation for a career that could've placed him alongside the action film greats. Ah, but there's the rub. In the annals of action-film history, there have been some notable turning points. George Lazenby quitting 007. Burt Reynolds deciding to concentrate on increasingly stupid car-chase movies despite great reviews in serious dramas and romantic comedies. And then there was Chuck Norris deciding to turn his back on *Code of Silence* to make down-and-dirty movies for Cannon Films.

Films of Fury

Coming from an impoverished childhood and still insecure about his acting, Norris chose to take money in the hand rather than pie in the sky. Golan/Globus apparently paid him one million dollars just for signing, and promised one million dollars for each of seven films. Besides, would major studios allow his brother, Aaron, to continue choreographing and directing his pictures?

Whatever the reason, it was a shame. While Andy Davis and Norris' action peers went on to bigger and/or better things, Chuck toiled in the slums of filmdom for the next ten years. The first few were okay. *Missing in Action* (1984), released prior to *Code of Silence*, but made afterward, was effective enough, as was its sequel, *Missing in Action 2: The Beginning* (1985) — both establishing Chuck now as "Rambo-lite." Now forty-five years old, Norris went the way of so many martial arts stars by downplaying karate for gunplay. He co-wrote his next Cannon loss leader, *Invasion U.S.A.* (1985), which had him taking on foreign terrorists in Florida.

The Delta Force (1986) was, arguably, his best Cannon Film, as well as one of Cannon's best. Monachem Golan returned to the director's chair for this combination of *The Dirty Dozen* and *Airport*, filling the cast with familiar but talented actors, ranging from *The Dirty Dozen's* Lee Marvin to *Airport's* George Kennedy to *The Poseidon Adventure's* Shelley Winters. In the mix was also the great Martin Balsam, Robert Forster, and even Joey Bishop. At two hours and ten minutes long, Golan was able to make two movies: one a fairly credible docudrama about the real skyjacking that the film was based on, and the other a patriotic revenge fantasy that had Lee and Chuck saving the day.

From there it was a slippery downhill slope. *Firewalker* (1986) had the right idea — teaming Chuck with Oscar-winning actor Louis Gossett Jr. to play wisecracking treasure hunters — but it had a script that did no one justice. Norris wrapped up his initial Cannon contract in 1988 with *Braddock: Missing in Action III* and *Hero*

Kung FU.S.A.

and the Terror, both which showed a creeping indifference on the part of cast and crew alike.

It only got worse. *Delta Force 2* arrived in 1990 after an on-location helicopter accident that killed a stuntman. *The Hitman* (1991) was an embarrassment, combining a greater violence and profanity quotient with the "heartfelt" tale of a boy looking for a father figure. But even it wasn't as bad as *Sidekicks* (1993) with Chuck training a kid to be a responsible martial artist. But neither of those efforts could compare to the nearly unknown U.S./Canada/Israel co-production *Hellbound,* which went directly to video in 1993 and had Chuck fighting a demonic spirit. Finally, there was *Top Dog* (1995) and *Forest Warrior* (1996), two sad attempts to sustain Chuck's career.

Thankfully, Chuck's saga has a happy ending. *Walker, Texas Ranger* went on the air in 1993, and was immediately decried as the most mindlessly violent show on television. Its millions of watchers didn't care. Recycling *Lone Wolf McQuade* into a teen-friendly action hour, the nearly sixty year-old karate champion found the success he had longed for in a medium that didn't intimidate him. Few expected greatness of Norris on television — his fans wanted good times and his bosses wanted good rating, and that's what he gave them for a full eight seasons. With a spinning back kick, of course.

Meanwhile, back in 1984, when Chuck was starring in *Missing in Action,* another film appeared that would have a lasting effect on American martial art movies. Ironically, it was one that Chuck was supposedly asked to co-star in, but turned down because of the script's negative view of American martial arts (a report Norris denies). In any case, the film's point of view might have been negative, but it was an accurate snapshot of American martial arts mentality.

The movie was, of course, *The Karate Kid* (1984), the canny original written by Robert Mark Kamen, directed by John Avildsen, and starring Ralph Macchio and Pat Noriyuki Morita as the venerable Mister Miyagi. Now this was a flick that made perfect sense to a short-cut-loving, anything-worth-having-can-be-paid-for society. Even so, it took a misshapen crane-style kung fu move to save the day during the finale. Nevertheless, it holds a deserved place in the hearts of many fans (including me).

The difficult reality of kung fu is that, while the pay-off is impressive, the set-up is strange to western eyes. Americans seem far more comfortable with angry emotion and muscular motion than calm, smooth defense. As I've said to my students, Japanese martial arts is like ice. Chinese kung fu is like water. Rarely was the difference more conspicuous than two years after *The Karate Kid*, when *Big Trouble in Little China* (1986) showed up. Original scripters Gary Goldman and David Weinstein wanted to create an American-friendly version of "manhua" (Chinese comic books) movies like Chu Yuan's *Heaven Sword and Dragon Saber*, Tsui Hark's *Zu Warriors of the Magic Mountain* and Lu Chin-ku's *Bastard Swordsman*, but set in the old west. Screenwriter W.D. Richter reportedly modernized it, then director John Carpenter further amended it to his liking.

The result was a major box office disappointment at the time, and remains an egregious missed opportunity. It's a classic example of what happens when an American film crew portrays an ethos they know little about. It didn't help matters when star Kurt Russell was inspired to play his leading role by doing an impersonation of John Wayne. It might have been interesting to see how Wayne's patented round-house punches stacked up against authentic kung fu, but *Big Trouble* had precious little of that.

Despite having Conan Lee (star of such outstanding kung fu films as Corey Yuen's 1982 *Ninja in the Dragon's Den* and Liu Chia-liang's 1988 *Tiger on Beat*) on set, stunt coordinator Kenny Endoso settled on more familiar pushing, punching, and kicking … when the stereotypical Fu Manchu-ish Chinese characters weren't ponderously floating or incongruously shooting lightning out of their

Kung FU.S.A.

fingers and/or eyes. Suffice to say, *Little China* didn't approach the power of the films that inspired it.

Elsewhere in 1986, when *The Delta Force* and *The Karate Kid Part II* hit theaters, a little movie called *No Retreat, No Surrender* also came out. It was a laughable effort, ripped off from *Rocky IV* (1985) with an American martial arts team fighting a seemingly unstoppable Russian bruiser. The filmmaking skill on display was barely above home-movie level (despite the fact that Corey Yuen Kwai directed it), but there was something about the intensity of the actor playing the Russian that stood out.

That was no accident. Twenty-five-year old Brussels, Belgium native Jean-Claude Van Varenberg (aka Van Damme) had been preparing for that moment almost all his life. "I'd been dreaming of working in show business since I was ten years old," he said. "I started to work in France, but I thought America was the best place in the world to succeed as an action film actor." The reason he felt that way could be summed up in one name: Arnold Schwarzenegger.

If Chuck Norris was the poor man's Clint Eastwood, Van Damme was certainly Arnold-lite. Like Schwarzenegger, he was a heavily muscled man with a heavily muscled accent. The comparison was not lost on Van Damme, who came to Hollywood with little money, no English, and the laughable Westernized name of "Frank Cujo."

"I tried to look as charming as I could and started knocking on every door. It took me three years to even begin making a name for myself. I was obliged to take a lot of odd jobs, including as a taxi driver and a bouncer." He also got work in *Missing in Action 2*, where he asked Chuck Norris to serve as his agent ("I was very naive at the time," he says) and in Schwarzenegger's *Predator* (1987), where he worked inside the alien suit.

"I was wearing the suit for three weeks before Kevin Peter Hall took my place," he explained, "because he's a lot taller than I am.

This experience was a big step in my career. I remember that they asked me to do a very dangerous stunt, and I was obliged to say no, because I had just been hired for *Bloodsport* and I was afraid I'd break my leg." Van Damme saved his leg for the Mark DiSalle production, which appeared in 1987.

The earnest, decent-looking variation on *Enter the Dragon,* which told of international martial artists competing in an illegal battle to the death, was silly and predictable, but enjoyable for all of that. And, of course, it had Van Damme giving it his all. Van Damme saw Chuck Norris' spinning back kick and raised him one: Jean-Claude could not only do a 180-degree flying front kick, ballerina-style, but he could do splits like nobody's business. Van Damme hoped *Bloodsport* would be his ticket to the major leagues, but he toiled in independent exploitation features for years more. Up next was *Black Eagle* (1988) in which he played villain to one of Sho Kosugi's last gasps as a ninja hero.

Cyborg (1989) treated Van Damme a little better, in that it was Albert Pyun's bargain basement variation on *Terminator* (1984). On the one hand, Van Damme found his new director even more inspiring than the man who made *Die Hard* and *Predator.* "John McTiernan is a wonderful, hardworking director," he said at the time. "But I'm more impressed by Albert Pyun's work because he gets wonderful results without a big budget. He's a very resourceful person." On the other hand, Pyun was not resourceful enough to avoid being second-guessed by his star. "I was very disappointed in *Cyborg* because I didn't like the editing," Van Damme also said at the time. "I had to go back and reedit it myself to make something coherent out of the film."

It would not be the last time Van Damme felt the need to do that to his director, nor would it be the last production Van Damme worked on where a stuntman was reported hurt. For the moment, however, he returned to work with Mark DiSalle, who directed

Kung FU.S.A.

his next picture, *Kickboxer* (1989). It worked along the same lines as *Bloodsport,* but to lessening returns. Even so, Van Damme's first five movies established him as an ambitious actor willing to do almost anything to get ahead.

Death Warrant (1990), coming from Canadian director Deran Serafian, was Van Damme's first movie with any real industry credibility. This was the old chestnut about a French-Canadian mountie being sent undercover into a prison to see who's killing convicts — but even aside from the clichéd plot, Van Damme's films were already of a recognizable type. He would glare, lose the first fight, do a split, do a slow-motion leaping front kick, and then win the second fight for no apparent reason other than the script said so. There was no training, no discovery of an enemy's weakness, no growth, and no change.

There also seemed to be no technique either. Although there were allusions to Van Damme's karate and kick-boxing career in Europe, there was no real evidence of martial art understanding or skill on screen — just glares, splits, slow-motion kicks, and inexplicable victory. Those were all in abundance in his next film, the seminal *Double Impact* (1991), his first major-studio film. Although a man named Sheldon Lettich directed it, Van Damme contributed the screenplay and was credited as fight choreographer in this two-headed Universal Pictures release. Two-headed because in it Van Damme played twins separated soon after birth who are then reunited years later in Hong Kong to avenge the death of their father. For reasons yet explained, Van Damme seems obsessed with playing twins.

Given his script credit, Van Damme was more than likely responsible for the totally gratuitous dream sequence in which he cavorts in the nude with beautiful co-star Alonna Shaw, as well as the scene where a bevy of leotarded beauties coo over his spandex-covered buttocks (while he does a split, naturally). Otherwise, it was business as usual, with Van Damme inexplicably losing his first fight with

Bolo Yang Sze-yeung, but just as inexplicably winning the second. As unfocused as *Double Impact* was, it had nothing on Van Damme's next movie, one which he reportedly concocted himself, which has been called *A.W.O.L., Wrong Bet*, and, finally, *Lionheart* (1991).

Sheldon Lettich was still in the director's chair for this tale of a foreign legion deserter who descends into the world of illegal street fighting. And it, like its predecessors, is full of loving close-ups, as well as repetitive fights that have no discernible dramatic structure. When the evil manageress bets against him in the final fight, Van Damme barks, "Wrong bet!" and trounces his opponent with, you guessed it, a slow-motion leaping front kick.

By the time of *Universal Soldier* (1992), he had become Universal Studio's good soldier, willing to appear in all manner of predictable, ultimately unsatisfying action fare. Here he shares the screen with Dolph Lundgren, whose *Rocky IV* role of the seemingly unbeatable Russian fighter Van Damme had borrowed for *No Retreat, No Surrender*. Their teaming did nothing to improve the uninventive tale of two super-soldiers, one who goes berserk and one who becomes heroic. Guess who played who.

But all of this is mere prelude to the real reason Van Damme is in this book. Following his Universal soldiering, Van Damme wanted singular credibility, and he thought the best way to get it was to become a one-man Ellis Island for Hong Kong's most kinetic and important action film directors.

"I know the new government won't allow me freedom of speech nor freedom of creation," said John Woo before Hong Kong was returned to mainland China in 1997. "I can't approve of totalitarianism, and I know people like myself will be crushed by the new regime." So, instead, Woo allowed himself to be pressed into service by Jean-Claude Van Damme, and Universal Pictures gave him a way out. But it came with a price. That price was *Hard Target* (1993), and the version which eventually made it to American screens could

Kung FU.S.A.

not honestly be called a John Woo film.

Reportedly, Woo delivered an over-two-hour first edit of this modern variation on *The Most Dangerous Game* (1932), i.e., people hunting people for sport. He was supposedly told that "We don't release Van Damme films that last over two hours." Mere weeks later he delivered an edit that was only about ten minutes shorter. Despite enthusiastic responses from test audiences, Van Damme was said not to like it (not enough close-ups of him, apparently). So the rumors started flying that Jean-Claude locked John Woo out of the editing suite to create a Van Damme-centric ninety-four minute version that had plenty of Jean-Claude close-ups, but much less of Lance Henriksen's charismatic turn as the villain.

Sadly, it was just the start of John Woo's Hollywood education. In ten years, Woo went from being declared the world's most important and best action filmmaker to being dismissed as a has-been hack. The powerful blend of emotion, effort, passion, and compassion that drove the complex heroes in Woo's Hong Kong films started to disappear in *Broken Arrow* (1996) and *Face/Off* (1997), became self-satirizing in *Mission Impossible 2* (2000), then was beaten to death in *Windtalkers* (2002) and *Paycheck* (2003).

Woo learned what so many other Hong Kong filmmakers discovered: the American film industry doesn't really like kung fu, no matter how much they glad hand or give it lip service. And Woo, like virtually all of the others who followed him, only returned to glory once he returned to China. He may have made some money in America, but he only makes great films in Asia. His latest, *Red Cliff* (2008) and *Reign of Assassins* (2010), has given him his best reviews and box office, since, well, *Hard Boiled*.

Hard Target, meanwhile, leveled out at about $30 million at the box office. The aptly named *Nowhere to Run* (1993) came next, after Van Damme made an ironic cameo appearance in Arnold Schwarzenegger's first major bomb, *The Last Action Hero* (1993).

Then Jean-Claude led the crew who completely fumbled *Street Fighter* (1994). Despite the fact that they had the kinetic videogame as inspiration and a great crew of martial artists ready to help, the live action adaptation was a dull dud.

Timecop (1994) was the last straw. Although the effort seemed to be promising, this tale of a time traveling policeman didn't have a clue. Jean-Claude had gone back in time to save his murdered wife, seemingly setting the stage for a clever, rousing climax in which he could counter every villainous ploy, since he knew what was going to happen, but, instead, the finale was an illogical, uninvolving mess where, just as in every other disappointing Jean-Claude vehicle, things occur simply because they do.

Before the critical and box-office drubbing *Timecop* took, however, Van Damme was already hard at work on their next film, a *Die Hard* knockoff titled *Sudden Death* (1995) in which Jean-Claude plays a fire inspector whose daughter is taken hostage by a quipping extortionist who threatens to blow up the Stanley Cup playoffs, as well as the attending U.S. vice president. When that, too, disappeared in the ocean of cinema without causing a ripple, Van Damme thought there was only one way to make a good movie ... direct it himself.

"Directing is my dearest wish," he proclaimed. "When I am the director, I'd love to hire unknown actors and make them stars. I think it's a wonderful thing to do, and I'm sure it's possible with a good script." Didn't happen. *The Quest* (1996) made no new stars, and the script was a warmed-over 1930s version of *Bloodsport*. Although the production proudly proclaimed the participation of fifteen of the world's greatest martial arts champions, you couldn't tell by the finished work. As usual, Van Damme merely swings his arms and legs the same way from the first fight to the last — the only difference being when his opponent falls down.

Something had to be done. Since John Woo wouldn't work with

Kung FU.S.A.

him again, back to the Hong Kong well Jean-Claude went. If he was the poor man's Schwarzenegger, then he would get the poor man's John Woo. Ringo Lam directed *Maximum Risk* (1996) and managed to invest what action scenes there were with some verve. Unfortunately, all too much of this middling thriller was taken up with boring intrigue as Van Damme fell back into his hoary *Double Impact* fixation of playing identical twin brothers.

By then Jean-Claude seemed to realize that all sorts of Hong Kong directors would love to get out of town on the eve of the 1997 Chinese takeover, so he next secured the participation of Tsui Hark, perhaps hoping that the revolutionary director could do for his career what he did for Jet Li's. But Van Damme was no Jet. *Double Team* (1997) and then *Knock Off* (1998) not only failed to restore Van Damme's reputation, but seemed to rob Tsui of all his filmmaking ability as well.

Even though Hark returned east a lot sooner than Woo, even his most exciting (2000's *Time and Tide*) and beautiful (2001's *Legend of Zu*) films were marred by an eroding story-telling sensibility, and his subsequent work ranged from awful (2002's *Black Mask: City of Masks*) to disappointing (2005's *Seven Swords*, 2006's *The Warrior*, and 2007's *All About Women*). Only in 2010 did he begin to regain his filmmaking footing with the well-reviewed *Detective Dee and the Mystery of the Phantom Flame*.

As for Van Damme, having squandered the opportunities that could have come from working with the world's best action film directors, he stumbled into the direct-to-DVD world of international co-productions. Although he's made more than fifteen other flicks since then, the only one that drew any real attention was *JCVD* (2008), a Mabrouk El Mechri film in which Van Damme plays himself during a post office robbery. Although promoted as a "mea culpa" film in which Jean-Claude supposedly addresses his shortcomings as an actor and person, it is actually a cunning defense of himself as a misunderstood victim... that, ultimately, fell on deaf ears and blind eyes.

In 1988, when Chuck Norris slummed in *The Hero and the Terror* and Van Damme excelled in *Bloodsport*, another story was taking shape in Hollywood. Rumors circulated that Michael Ovitz, agent extraordinaire — then considered one of the most powerful people in the film business — was holding up Warner Brothers on the *Lethal Weapon* deal unless they gave his aikido teacher a movie of his own. Whether or not this story is true, an entertaining movie called *Above the Law* premiered. It starred a thirty-six-year-old aikido teacher named Steven Seagal.

Again, aikido is a Japanese martial art, but one that is more water than ice. Seagal's aikido also served to prepare American audiences for the kung fu to come because it took the roundhouse punches that had been U.S. fight choreographers' stock-in-trade for more than fifty years and turned them back on themselves. It was the hand-to-hand equivalent of a wild-mouse roller coaster, spinning the antagonists in tight, fast, vicious circles. Unlike some other so-called American martial arts movie stars, it was instantly apparent to audiences that Seagal knew what he was doing.

According to his official studio bio, Seagal had been learning karate and aikido since he was seven years old. By the time he was thirty-one, he had opened an aikido dojo in Sherman Oaks, California, and whether he was teaching or, as others said, body-guarding Michael Ovitz, by 1987 he was working with Andrew Davis on a story that would become the script for his first starring role. That wasn't all. Not only would he help write the story, he would also be the producer and martial arts choreographer. It was more than possible that the studio didn't expect much from this collaboration. After all, what had the two done before?

Reportedly, Seagal had been the martial arts coordinator on the samurai sword picture *The Challenge* (1974), while Davis had merely

Kung FU.S.A.

managed to make Chuck Norris look great in *Code of Silence*. But other than that, what? Davis had been the director of photography on some minor independent exploitation movies like *Cool Breeze* (1972), *Hitman* (1972, not to be confused with the Jet Li film of the same name), and the gangster thriller *Lepke* (1975). Since the Norris picture in 1985, he'd no major credits to speak of in three long years. The odds were that *Above the Law* would make some lean, mean money and disappear.

The odds were wrong. From a final screenplay penned by himself, Steven Pressfield, and Ronald Shusett, the director once again spun gold. Set in his beloved Chicago, Davis weaved an entire life around Seagal, whose career-long concerns were already evident. More than just a well-trained, no-bull cop, his character was also a caring and religious husband/father. Long before Quentin Tarantino worshiped actress Pam Grier in *Jackie Brown* (1997), Davis cast her as Seagal's partner in this tale of an obsessed cop trying to take down an FBI-protected drug lord. And long before she hit gold in such films as *Total Recall* (1990) and *Basic Instinct* (1992), Davis cast Sharon Stone as Seagal's understanding wife. The rest was up to Seagal, and he delivered.

Whether blasting away with an automatic, or clothes-lining some thugs, the aikido ace made all the other Hollywood action stars look like pretenders. Outside of a rushed, perfunctory climax, and an odd finale where Seagal lectured the press on corruption, *Above the Law* was a complete success. Critics and fans alike sat up and took notice, while Seagal moved quickly to show that he needed neither Ovitz nor Davis. Warner Brothers, however, seemed less than enthusiastic about their new star.

For the aptly named *Hard to Kill* (1990), the basically unknown Bruce Malmuth was in the director's chair, while the star took the additional credits of screenwriter and martial arts choreographer. Both the script and action were in good hands. Its martial arts highlight was an engaging scene set in a liquor store where Seagal taunts a punk into attacking him, because aikido, like taichi, works best when channeling an attacker's energy back at them. Playing another pragmatic, prepared cop, Seagal is blasted into a coma by a corrupt politician who he had been investigating. When he awakens seven years later, his muscles haven't atrophied, but his family has been slaughtered. The remainder of the film's ninety-five minutes was a very satisfying hunt for revenge.

With just his first two films, Seagal had set the stage for his entire career. On the one hand, he seemed to enjoy making straightforward action films where his heroes were never in doubt or bettered. On the other hand, as evidenced by *The Making of Hard to Kill*, Seagal was continually frustrated by his studios' apparent lack of cooperation with the budding auteur's vision. It was not surprising, then, that he parted ways with Warner Brothers for his third movie, *Marked for Death* (1990), where he took on Jamaican voodoo drug runners with his kinetic aikido. Seagal returned to the screenwriter role for his next movie, which was originally titled *The Price of Our Blood*. The studio, however, didn't want to lose the catchy three-word titles of his filmography, so when the movie reached cinemas in 1991 it was titled *Out for Justice*.

This one stripped down Seagal's desires to their basics. Basically a very busy twenty-four hours in the life of a very violent Brooklyn cop, the film's plot was just a string on which to hang Seagal's multiple scenes of aikido ass-kicking, climaxed by an extended sequence in which Seagal corners the villain (William Forsythe) in a tenement kitchen, then methodically takes him apart in a series of master shots (camera angles that take in the entire room) so you can see Forsythe systematically beaten through the power of aikido — creating one of the most pounding, brutal, and memorable scenes in Seagal's career.

Seagal seemed content with that direct, suspenseless approach,

Kung FU.S.A.

but the studio wanted more. So did Andrew Davis. Following *Above the Law,* he had had another few frustrating years. He managed to get *The Package* (1989) made, but it was a forgettable suspense thriller starring Gene Hackman as a military man trying to prevent the assassination of Russia's president. After that, nothing. So, taking a script by J. F. Lawton, Davis hired Tommy Lee Jones and Gary Busey to play villains, got the use of the USS Alabama museum ship, and fashioned *Under Siege* (1992). It was *Die Hard* on a boat, but a really good *Die Hard* on a boat.

It became Seagal's most critically and financially successful film, but also one of his most telling, thanks to an infamous magazine article by the scripter, who revealed that it was Jones' idea to disguise himself as a rock singer, Busey's idea to kill the captain of the ship while dressed in drag, and that Seagal's major contribution was the demand that a bare-breasted *Playboy* bunny be brought onboard in a hollow cake (instead of sticking to Lawton's subplot concerning a female Coast Guard officer's heroics). There is less aikido than ever before, but the stars and director try to make up for it with big booms and many, many bullets.

Taking credit where credit was due, Seagal sought to control his movie destiny. His next film didn't appear until two years later, but it was produced, directed, and starring Steven Seagal. *On Deadly Ground* (1994) was promoted as a serious ecological statement — being the story of an oil rig specialist who tangles with an apparently insane corporate polluter. But from the moment Seagal appears onscreen, background characters literally can't stop talking about how great he is. What at first appears to be an odd directing and editing choice becomes an annoying distraction by the middle of the movie. Finally, when an evil mercenary team's leader interrupts the climax to deliver a monologue on how incredibly talented Seagal's character is, it becomes a laughable sign of insecurity.

Adding fuel to that theory is a perplexing dream sequence in which Seagal's character is "reborn" in a river of life wearing neck-to-ankle leather while naked "Native American" girls undulate around him. Seagal single-handedly destroys an entire oil foundry, kills all the corporate executives affiliated with it, and what happens? Is he arrested and jailed like some sort of latter-day Billy Jack? Oh, no; he is celebrated and caps the film with a speech about alternate energy sources. Suffice to say that the film did not reach the box-office heights of *Under Siege*. Therefore, a sequel of that hit was hastily called for.

Thankfully, Andrew Davis did not need to direct it. He had gone on to direct the wildly successful movie adaptation of the television show *The Fugitive* (1993), starring Harrison Ford and Tommy Lee Jones, so *Under Siege 2: Dark Territory* (1995) was directed by New Zealander Geoff Murphy as "*Die Hard* on a train." Although far better than *On Deadly Ground*, it was considered a disappointment. Rather than see that as a setback, Seagal took the initiative to take an effective guest-starring stint in the suspenseful *Executive Decision* (1996), starring Kurt Russell and directed by longtime editor Stuart Baird. Playing a self-sacrificing government commando, Seagal appeared in only about fifteen minutes of the thriller, but to great effect.

That successful gambit completed, the next step was supposed to be a comic "buddy cop" picture along the lines of *48 Hours* (1982), but when *The Glimmer Man* appeared in 1996, it was light on the comedy, very light on the "buddy," and extremely heavy on the kind of action which had become associated with Seagal in the films prior to *Under Siege*. There was only one major difference: rather than film Seagal's aikido in one long shot, each of his fights were now torn by dozens of fast editing cuts, so the beauty and smoothness of the moves were all but obscured. It was hard to tell what was actually happening anymore, and even harder to care.

The good vibes Seagal had engendered in *Executive Decision* were

Kung FU.S.A.

all but dashed by his 1997 effort, *Fire Down Below,* which was, for all intents and purposes, an even more ludicrous sequel to *On Deadly Ground.* Here Seagal was a full-fledged Environmental Protection Agency agent (seemingly with a license to kill) going up against another, even more psychotic, corporate polluter. Only this time, producer Seagal throws in as much country music as he does aikido, seemingly trying to create a latter-day B Western in the tradition of Roy Rogers pictures. He even dons a buckskin jacket, pulls out an ol' guitar, and sings a couple of tunes he penned himself.

The film's lack of success at the box office made an orphan of Seagal's next movie, *The Patriot* (1999), so it had its American premiere on the Home Box Office cable channel. There, fans could enjoy Seagal as one of the world's top immunologists (?!) who becomes a small-town doctor to get away from the machinations of big government disease-control types. But when a militant crackpot spreads a deadly disease, he needs all his killing and healing skills to save the day. As a major motion picture it was sadly lacking but developed a life, and income, of its own on home video.

Finally, Seagal saw a way to do the movies he wanted to do the way he wanted to do them. By this time, the middle-aged star was thickening, and his reliance on aikido was thinning. But that didn't matter to his many fans throughout the world. No matter how he looked or acted, his brand of relentless justice could still find favor in multiple countries. So, after a few more feeble stabs at big screen relevance (2001's *Exit Wounds* and 2002's *Half Past Dead*) Seagal became king of the "Direct to DVD" world — making more than twenty in less than a decade. 2003's *Belly of the Beast* is notable in that it included kung fu and was directed by the exceptional choreographer Tony Ching Siu-tung (who also directed 1982's *Duel to the Death,* 1987's *A Chinese Ghost Story,* and 2002's *Naked Weapon*), but the rest were of a type.

There's a great man (played by Seagal). Someone messes with

the great man by threatening him or his family in some way. The great man goes out and takes care of the problem. Period. The end. It's clearly McMoviemaking, but there's a reason the fast food variant has billions and billions sold. One look at any of his "D2DVD's" audio set-ups tells you all you need to know about why Seagal keeps grinding them out — his down and dirty, bare bones, revenge flicks come complete with at least five different language tracks and seven different subtitles, including Korean, Thai, Spanish, and even Portuguese.

So don't cry for Steven Seagal, America. He's doing exactly what he's always wanted to do, in the way he's always wanted to do it — and making a tidy profit each and every time. He may not care what the mass audience wants, but he knows what he wants, and he delivers. Take this telling (slightly paraphrased) dialog from *Urban Justice* (2007) as he's confronted by a beautiful, pacifist woman while preparing to wipe out the people who killed his son:

Woman: "This is just for revenge."
Seagal: "Damn straight."
Woman: "The cycle of violence will never end."
Seagal: "I don't care."
Woman: "You're as bad as they are."
Seagal: "No ... I'm a lot worse."

Well said, Steven, well said.

But back in 1990, when Chuck was in *Delta Force 2: The Columbian Connection*, Jean-Claude was growling "wrong bet," and Steven was *Marked for Death*, kung fu managed to make its way into American cinemas in disguise. It started in 1989, when Jackie Chan was rebuffed by U.S. theater owners. His producer was told that they would never show a film with an all-Asian cast. Golden Harvest Studios considered its options and decided, "Well, what if they don't know that the heroes are Asian? What if the fighters were ... turtles?"

Kevin Eastman and Peter Laird had originally created the *Teenage Mutant Ninja Turtles* as something of a joke, but they wrote and drew their independent comic book seriously as an homage celebrating their love of great martial arts movies. The public responded to these "heroes on a half shell," and especially to Eastman and Laird's honest conviction. Once a savvy marketing genius ran with the idea, these pizza-loving creatures (Donatello, Leonardo, Michelangelo, and Raphael, named for famous artists), were everywhere — which was where producer Kim Dawson and writer Bobby Herbeck found them.

Making a deal with all concerned, they signed director Steven Barron. Barron became famous with a series of innovative music videos, including Dire Straits' *Money for Nothing,* A-ha's *Take on Me,* and Michael Jackson's *Billie Jean.* His first movie, however, was a different story. *Electric Dreams* (1984) was hobbled by a silly script, but there was no question that it was the work of an original thinker. His thought for the Turtles was simple: the more outlandish the characters, the more realistic the atmosphere and photography had to be. It would be a concept that he had to continually fight for, but one that helped make the first *Teenage Mutant Ninja Turtles* (1990) film the only one worth watching.

The animatronic suits for the leading characters were made by Jim Henson's Creature Shop. But to fill those tiny suits required very small, very capable martial artists. They were three Asians and three Americans: Yuen Mo-chow, Choi Nam-ip, Chi Wai-chiang, Reggie Barnes, Ernie Reyes Jr., and Kenn Troum.

"You could hardly see in there, and you could hardly breathe," Troum told me. "And, oh yeah, you sweat buckets as well."

While Pat Johnson, veteran of the first four *Karate Kid* pictures (1984, 1986, 1989, and 1994) handled the stunts, the kung fu consultants were Chun Wai "Brandy" Yuen (who worked with Sammo Hung on *Dreadnaught* and *Pedicab Driver*, among others) and Tak Wai "Billy" Liu.

"They all conferred together," said Troum, "but it was usually Brandy and Billy who worked with us on the more intricate kicks and hits."

This combination of American and Hong Kong experience lent an authenticity that audiences around the world appreciated. It came together in an international hit, which the producers then squandered with inferior sequels that upped the level of absurdity while diminishing the realistic look of the original.

The Turtles' success in theaters, TV, and toy stores made networks and studios far more receptive to Asian concepts that they had rejected in previous years. For instance, Tokyo producers had been trying to convince American television stations that the many teams of costumed superheroes that were beloved in Japan would also be as big a hit in America. The biggest costumed superhero in Japan, in both size and success was *Ultraman*, but despite many attempts to Westernize him, his truncated, dubbed appearances on English-speaking television, and in American comic books, were mostly forgotten.

The problem seemed to be the pesky differences between Eastern and Western cultures.

To see one of these Japanese superhero shows was essentially to see them all. They all started with an interchangeable alien villain deciding to take over the earth. The only thing standing in their way is a group of supernaturally powered teenagers. So every week a new monster is dispatched to defeat the heroes and destroy the population. The first half of these efforts was all setup and the second half was all action. Mobs of biodegradable thugs are thrown against the heroes to soften them up, only to be defeated easily. The main monster would then appear and trash the town as well as the

Kung FU.S.A.

costumed teens, until the kids banded together into a gigantic robot. The monster would then grow magically to giant size and slug it out until the team blew him up. Then there would be just enough time for a joke or important life lesson.

Television executives took one look at these redundant, silly shows — albeit colorful and action-packed — before dismissing them without a rational thought. Looking for any way in, the Tokyo entrepreneurs even tried getting American producers to laugh with them rather than at them. In the wake of Woody Allen's *What's Up Tiger Lily* (1966), in which Allen redubbed a bad Japanese espionage movie, members of the SCTV comedy troupe did the same for thirteen half-hour episodes of a high-flying Japanese television series. The result, *Dynaman* (1988), was shown on the USA cable network's *Night Flight* anthology music and comedy series, before disappearing.

Finally, the Saban company convinced Fox television to air what they were calling *Mighty Morphin Power Rangers* (starting in 1993 and still on the air as of this writing), hodge-podged from various seasons of the *Super Sentai* series (which has been running continually since 1975). They kept the Japanese action sequences while refilming the non-costumed moments with an interracial, English-speaking cast. In fact, to make it even more attractive to its young audience, they made one of the boy heroes (the yellow ranger) into a girl. It didn't matter. As the long-suffering Japanese producers figured, the series was a big success in the States, spawning two movies as well as many different series.

By the time of the first American film version, *Mighty Morphin Power Rangers* (1995), California (and, eventually, New Zealand) filmmakers were producing most of the material — allowing an actual woman in the yellow ranger's suit and more kung fu to carry the day. But just like the Turtles before them, subsequent films and TV series were not as good as the first, but, again, just like the

Turtles before them, new incarnations continue to be created. As of this writing, brand new versions of both the Turtles and the Rangers are being readied for the Nickelodeon Network, to air alongside the *Kung Fu Panda* TV show.

The question is, will enough people care? A notable percentage of new audiences were turning to videogames for their prime entertainment. There, martial arts in general, and kung fu in particular, is a mainstay. Naturally movie studios tried to get in on the act, with mostly disastrous results. *Mortal Kombat* (1995), in fact, was the only halfway decent movie adaptation of a video game. It helped that the video game itself had more of a back-story than most, but it didn't help that the game featured more blood than a date with a starving vampire.

The filmmakers, led by director Paul Anderson, wanted to attract the under-seventeen crowd, so meaningless movement replaced the bone-snapping thrills of the game. Aiding greatly in the film's acceptance was the game's driving musical themes, not to mention co-star Robin Shou — the only one of the leads who actually knew any kung fu. Although Shou contributed some decent wushu to the special effect-laden mix, nothing made much sense in the finished film, and the seemingly slapped-together script constantly undercut whatever involvement the audience might feel. It was even worse in *Mortal Kombat: Annihilation* (1997), which not only made almost no sense, but wasn't even remotely exciting. By then the kung fu had been reduced to empty movement, with no intellectual or emotional reason for being.

But then *Rush Hour* premiered in movie theaters, one month after the success of the martial arts-vampire movie *Blade* (1998), while, a month after that, *Martial Law* premiered on CBS television. Meanwhile, the samurai-sword stylings of the long-running *Highlander* movie series (1986-2007) were still going strong, and, despite the tragic death of Brandon Lee, *The Crow* was given new life on

Kung FU.S.A.

television in 1998, with Mark Dacascos — a veteran of many kung fu exploitation films and future host of *Iron Chef America* — as the avenger from beyond the grave.

But this was all just prelude to a game-changing event in 1999. Sure, everyone knew that Jackie Chan and Jet Li could do kung-fu, but what about that mythical audience the studio executives always talked about? The ones who would "never" accept a Chinese star? Who would be their hero? Would you believe Keanu Reeves? Actually it was more Yuen Wo-ping, because he was the one who choreographed the martial art action in *The Matrix*, the pioneering, influential science fiction epic.

Despite its disappointing sequels, *The Matrix* cannot be underestimated in terms of American kung fu. This time it was American-born actors who were able to learn enough to be almost credible as kung fu fighters. Their stances may be a bit off-balance and their actions more ice than water, but they were credible enough to convince viewers (and, maybe more importantly, other movie stars) that they too could, as Keanu put it on screen, "know kung fu."

Although the *Matrix* trilogy quickly descended into substandard superhero and sci-fi, that one fight between Reeves and Laurence Fishburne — mislabeled on screen as "karate" in true standard-operating-racism ignorance — was enough to whet whole new audiences' appetites for kung fu ... appetites that *Crouching Tiger Hidden Dragon* quickly satisfied. Tragically, however, Hollywood raced forward to staunch the hunger as quickly and effectively as they could. The descent started, as many cinematic descents did, with *Star Wars I: The Phantom Menace* (2000).

The non-spaceship action in the original Star Wars trilogy — *Star Wars* (1977), *The Empire Strikes Back* (1980) and *Return of the Jedi* (1983) — was clearly based on samurai films. The action in the Star Wars prequel trilogy — *The Phantom Menace*, *Attack of the Clones* (2002) and *Revenge of the Sith* (2005) was clearly based on kung fu films — specifically *Moon Warriors*, the 1993 "*Crouching Tiger* meets *Free Willy*" film directed by Sammo Hung, which was screened at Lucasfilm prior to the prequels' production. That film's acrobatic action was solidly translated into light-saber terms, but the fight choreography, credited to stunt coordinator and sword master Nick Gillard, was the very model for the internally-closed, pod people version of "kungfoo" known in the trade as "empty movement."

This style of "empty movement" kungfoo fighting was not just embraced by Hollywood, but bear-hugged with ferocity. It eliminates substance, drama, variability, and inner energy (chi) from the battles, leaving only pretty, nonsensical, repetitive, monotonal, and ultimately, boring combat behind. *The Matrix* sequels quickly added insult to injury by having Wo-ping do soulless variations on Jackie Chan classics (like the *Project A* fight on the nightclub staircases). But tinseltown wasn't done with the Yuen family yet. Drew Barrymore's film version of the *Charlie's Angels* (2000) TV series brought in Yuen Cheung-yan to design, supervise, and train the actors for the film's lighter-than-air "wire-fu" fights.

Not surprisingly, American filmmakers are far more comfortable with this special effect-assisted fantasy superheroic type of flying, floating, and spinning than gravity-based, chi-powered kung fu. They also far prefer their heroes to be emotionless or angry rather than communicate the kind of serenity great kung fu requires. American movie producers seem intent on almost always showcasing the "biggest s.o.b. in the valley," leading to endless, increasingly implausible scenes of blank-faced sorts walking away from elaborate explosions without flinching, blinking, tensing, pausing, or reacting with any sort of logical realism. To U.S. producers, this denotes "cool" … rather than ridiculous, pitiful, stupidity.

At least Jason Statham earned his "cool." Although an Englishman toiling in Luc Besson's French-financed thrillers, his history of kickboxing, Olympic diving, and street wisdom gave his screen

Kung FU.S.A.

work credibility. Already appreciated for his performances in director Guy Ritchie's *Lock, Stock, and Two Smoking Barrels* (1998) and *Snatch* (2000), it was his going mano a mano against Jet Li in *The One* (2001) that led to his being cast as the title character in *The Transporter* (2002) — co-directed and choreographed by Corey Yuen Kwai. Its success led to several sequels, as well as a rematch with Jet in *War* (2007) and a memorable team-up with Jet in *The Expendables* (2010).

"I'm impressed with the likes of Jackie Chan, and Bruce Lee was a big hero of mine for many years," Staham said. "[But] martial arts isn't just about physicality. As Jet told me, it's the spirit and the mind that breeds an inner confidence and knowledge of life, people, and the world around you ... if you keep practicing this kind of thing all your life."

With Statham's words of wisdom fading away, American audiences were left with occasional sparks supplied by Jackie, Jet, Corey, Yuen, Zhang Yimou, and Stephen Chow (see next chapter), but mostly fizzles supplied by the same people, as well as many blissfully ignorant American screenwriters, producers, and directors. But the man who was ready, willing, and able to change it all was Quentin Tarantino. Having already wrestled film noir (1992's *Reservoir Dogs*, 1994's *Pulp Fiction*) and blaxploitation (1997's *Jackie Brown*) to the ground, he set his sights on kung fu with *Kill Bill Volume 1* (2003) and *Volume 2* (2004). U.S. kung fu film fans already had ample reason to be grateful to him. Without his support, it is possible that such classics as *Iron Monkey* (1993), *Shaolin Soccer* (2001), *Hero* (2002), and other kung fu greats in Miramax's DVD home video library would never have seen the light of American day.

As is his film-loving wont, he hired the best people: Yuen Wo-ping as choreographer, with David Carradine, Gordon Liu Chia-hui, Shinichi "Sonny" Chiba, and Michael Jai White as action actors. He also borrowed from the most memorable sources: the general plot from *Lady Snowblood* (a 1973 chanbara/samurai film), characters from *Kage No Gunden* (a Japanese ninja TV series), *They Call Her One Eye* (a 1973 Swedish exploitation thriller), and *Executioners from Shaolin*, costumes from *Game of Death*, and fight scenes from *Sex and Fury* (a 1973 Japanese erotic action film), the Japanese Baby Cart/ *Shogun Assassin* series, and many others.

Although starting with the Shaw Brothers Studio logo, the *Kill Bill* films are best remembered for their samurai sword fights, which is a slight shame, since they are actually Chinese sword fights using Japanese swords (akin to watching a team play football with a baseball, or baseball with a football). Although Tarantino had one of the film world's great samurai action choreographers on set (Chiba), it's possible that the globe-hopping production couldn't afford him and Wo-ping, so the latter did all the action. Therefore, even though samurai sword fighting is as intrinsically different from Chinese sword fighting as fencing is from broadsword battles, the *Kill Bill* characters always squander the single most important move in Japanese samurai sword fights — the draw.

Ironically, the far more violent Japanese version of *Volume 1* is better than the American edit, but both showcase the director's now established approach. He was no longer really interested in making believable "real world" movies. Now all his films existed in Tarantino-land, where the cinema references are rife, the environment is artificial, the plot is contrived, the heroine's bare feet are always nearby, and the dialogue is quippy, self-consciously mannered, and purposely-paced. Sadly, a kung fu fight scene between Carradine and Jai White never made it into the finished film (in fact, Jai White's entire character was left on the cutting room floor), but it didn't keep the *Kill Bill*s from being superficially entertaining throughout. Unfortunately, despite the presence of Wo-ping and the acknowledgements to Chang Cheh, Lo Lieh, and the Liu Chia family, Tarantino apparently didn't learn much about kung fu from them.

Kung FU.S.A.

Although the films did respectably at the box office, they didn't open a floodgate of kung fu fun, despite several studios buying, and shelving, as many Hong Kong action films as they could. Tarantino, like most of the L.A. action filmmakers, moved on to comic books (where, coincidentally, Western superheroes get their powers from without — the sun, radioactive spiders, etc. — while Eastern superheroes get their powers from within). The kung fu in Tim Burton's original *Batman* (1989) — attributed to stunt coordinator Eddie Stacey — is actually quite good. He only moves as much as he has to (which may be attributable to the stiff Batman costume that didn't allow him to even turn his head), and his basic, open-handed stance is right on. The fighting (credited to stunt coordinator Simon Crane) is also accurate and excellent in *GoldenEye* (1995) — Pierce Brosnan's first, and best, 007 film.

But, for the most part, action films were frozen in ice during the last decade of the 20th century and the first decade of the 21st century. Even subsequent Batman and James Bond films lost their kung fu, content to wallow in round house punches and flawed kicks. Clawing for their section of the spotlight was M.M.A., aka Mixed Martial Arts, exemplified by the UFC, aka the Ultimate Fighting Championship — a "biggest s.o.b. in the octagon" competition that mixes boxing with equal amounts of World Wrestling Entertainment-style promotion and barroom brawl ambiance. For audiences who loved anger and muscles, it was a godsend, and, in marketing parlance, "so popular with the kids" that it infected Jackie, Jet, and Wo-ping's *Forbidden Kingdom*.

Miraculously, however, another film was in production parallel to *Forbidden Kingdom* — one that critics, journalists, audiences, and even its own studio was seemingly overlooking and/or underestimating. It started almost a decade before with an idea from a studio executive, but his idea didn't start developing until the early 2000s. By then I had been doing my San Diego Comic Con Superhero

Kung Fu Extravaganza for nearly a decade. Apparently someone from the studio had seen one or more of these events, because, out of the blue, I was asked to visit the studio to give a private seminar on what kung fu was, and, perhaps more importantly, what kung fu wasn't.

That was my first experience with DreamWorks Animation's *Kung Fu Panda* (2008). Once there I asked the producer and crew if they had already done any research. They said, "Oh, sure, we watched *Seven Samurai*." My reply: "With all due respect, you're making a football film and you're watching baseball movies." What was scheduled to be a ninety-minute chat became a nearly four-hour seminar. I was pleased with the tutorial and impressed by the production drawings I saw, but the next time I got word of it, everything, except the concept, had changed. The people I had talked to (except a single important one) were no longer with the project.

But that's where the character designer, storyboard artist, head of story department, layout artist, layout supervisor, puppeteer, visual effects designer, sfx supervisor, art director, writer, producer, and director John Stevenson comes in. He had started his career on *The Muppet Show* (1976-1981), and considered Jim Henson his mentor and, in kung fu terms, his sifu. "It was early 2004 when I was asked to take a look," he told me. "I had been at DreamWorks for a while and had asked (boss) Jeffrey Katzenberg for my chance to direct a feature film. I had been aware of the project, as it had been in development at the studio for some time, but it had only been officially in pre-production for a few months. At that point, it was a very different movie. Po (the Panda) was actually the least interesting character in that version of the story, which was much more about the efforts of The Furious Five to create the illusion that he actually had martial arts skills."

But the Panda's karma was strong. Of all the hopeful directors in all the world, Katzenberg had somehow anointed a knowledge-

Kung FU.S.A.

able, insightful kung fu movie fan. A real kung fu movie fan. "I've loved kung fu movies since childhood," he explained. "Growing up in a little rural village in Sussex, England, nothing could have been more alien. I was attracted to the philosophy and spiritual side of the stories as much as the fighting. I remember Tsui Hark's *The Butterfly Murders* as being the martial arts film that blew my mind. I was utterly confused and completely captivated at the same time. I had to know more. The next wuxia film I saw was a life-changing experience. It was a revival of King Hu's 1971 masterpiece *A Touch of Zen* — still my very favorite kung fu movie ever. It convinced me even back then that kung fu films could be art."

But exactly how would this first-time movie director bring art to a lowly "chop-socky" film at a studio whose previous computer-animated features were seemingly designed only to satirize Disney? "I did not want to make a parody, but a real kung fu movie that was funny," Stevenson said. "I did not want any pop culture references or popular music cues to break the spell of that world. And no fart jokes! I wanted to try and make the most beautifully designed movie DreamWorks had ever made, and to honor the art and culture of China. And I wanted to have real kung fu sequences, as well thought out and executed as any live action movie."

A seemingly impossible task in an industry that appeared to be Bruce and MMA-obsessed, but Stevenson had three things going for him. First, Bill Damaschke, president of creative for DreamWorks Animation, supported his vision, then, second, and third, Mark Osborne and Melissa Cobb joined him as, respectively, co-director and producer. "Bill was a great friend and supporter of the film all the way through production," Stevenson said. "The burden of proof was on us early to prove that all the things we wanted to try that were a bit different from the (then-circa 2004) current crop of films in production were actually going to work. But once we had shown them enough material, they totally got what we were going for and helped us get there. Honestly, it was a very happy and supportive atmosphere all the way through production."

The Panda's karma continued to hold throughout the hundreds of crew members. "I picked a brilliant designer called Nicolas Marlett who had worked at DreamWorks for many years, but had never been given the chance to design a whole movie. I was also blessed in that I had a superb visual development team headed by production designer Raymond Zibach and art director Tang Kheng Heng. Once we had our cast of characters from Nico, Ramone and Tang designed a mythic Chinese world to compliment them. We were insistent that we were culturally specific; this is China (albeit a fanciful version of a China that never existed), not a generic 'Asia world' that would blend elements from Japan and Korea. Although the mythic world of *Kung Fu Panda* is set in no particular time, we went to great pains to make sure that all the details in terms of architecture, landscape, clothing, and artifacts are authentically Chinese, even if sometimes we blended elements from different dynasties together.

"We spent the first eighteen months concentrating on the story with Jen Yuh Nelson, our head of story, and our story team. Mark and I were in every meeting and made all the final decisions together about the creative direction of the movie while Melissa ran the production in a marvelously efficient way. Mark's background is in stop motion animation (he directed the wonderful Academy Award-nominated short film *More*), so it was natural for him to work closely with the animators. Since my background is art-based and I had guided the visual development of the film, I was in charge of ensuring that the world and visual style we had created in the art department was translated accurately to the screen."

That was all well and good, but there was still one big elephant in the room (along with all the bears, monkeys, tigers, snakes, and cranes) ... and it comprised two words out of their three-word film title. If there's one thing this chapter shows, it's that America, when

Kung FU.S.A.

left to its own devices, doesn't know its kung fu from its karate. "Our goal with our kung fu scenes was to create something that had not been seen before," Stevenson said, "legitimate martial arts action done in animation, covering the whole spectrum of styles from humorous to very dark — with every fight scene having its own distinct visual design and color theory.

"The key people responsible for designing our kung fu sequences were Jen Yuh Nelson, Simon Wells and Rodolphe Guenoden. Jen was our head of story, but also a brilliant storyboard artist in her own right with a particular flair for action sequences. Simon Wells is a gifted writer/director and a superb draughtsman. For years Simon and Jen, independently, were the 'go-to' people for action scenes (I think Simon has storyboarded and designed almost all the climactic scenes in every DreamWorks movie). We made them into a unit charged with the task of designing and storyboarding each of our main kung fu sequences.

"Rodolphe Guenoden is a master storyboard artist and animator who has also trained in martial arts for many years. Rodolphe was a key part of our story team and developed many of the ideas that found their way into our kung fu scenes. Rodolphe would take Jen and Simon's sequences, and design specific kung fu moves that adapted the real animal fighting style to the animal's anatomy. One of the conceits of the film was that our kung fu masters were the living embodiment of the many animal-inspired styles of fighting. But working out how a snake or mantis does kung fu in those styles was no easy thing. Because Rodolphe had an intimate first-hand knowledge of martial arts, and was a superb draughtsman, he was able to break down the complex actions into easy to understand drawings, which could be shared with our brilliant animation team led by master animator Dan Wagner."

Rodolphe was also the one remaining crew member who had attended my seminar years before. Thankfully for the film, I was preaching to the choir. But the rest also wanted to walk the walk. "We also had the whole crew (including Mark, Melissa and I) take an intensive (and painful) kung fu class with martial arts consultant Eric Chen, just so that all of us would experience first-hand some of what Po undergoes in the film," Stevenson clarified. "Most of us were horribly out of shape, but we told Eric not to take it easy on us — and he took our directive to heart. We were all black and blue for weeks. We also had regular lunchtime kung fu classes for the animators led by Rodolphe. We found that only by physically doing kung fu and understanding the stresses and strains first hand could our animators animate kung fu convincingly. They had to feel it in their bodies first before translating it in their imaginations. We had an amazing unit in Jen, Simon and Rudolphe, who collectively were our action director."

That took care of the external, martial applications of kung fu, but there was still the pesky question of the internal, healing reality of real kung fu. Any other American production would (and many did) ignore that, or make excuses for omitting it. This was, after all, a "kid's film." Even DreamWorks' own marketing department and the Mattel Toy Company, who produced the film's tie-in merchandise, seemed committed to that juvenile, unbalanced, approach. But not John, Mark, Melissa, and company.

"In Bruce Lee's *The Silent Flute* (aka *Circle Of Iron*), the main character goes on a quest for the Book Of Enlightenment, only to discover that the book is a mirror, showing that the secrets to self-knowledge are already within him," Stevenson remembered. "We experimented with variations on this idea. We had a box that bore the inscription 'True Power Lies Within' that proved to be empty; we had a gauntlet of trials that had the same inscription above the door where Po would fight his way through to a room with a mirror; we had a legend about the all-powerful Dragon Sword that made the bearer invincible hidden behind massive doors that bore the same inscription in a chamber below the Jade Palace that turned out not to exist, and many other experiments with the same basic concept. Eventually the Dragon Sword became The Dragon Scroll containing 'the secret to limitless power.'"

That power is your own chi energy, waiting for each individual to use it properly. "There is no magic, just you. In our minds, Po was the only one who could understand this message; it is clear that neither Shifu nor Tai Lung (or probably any other conventional warrior) can grasp the idea. Po is the only one who gets it, which is why he is The Dragon Warrior; something Oogway realized when Po crashed in front of him at the tournament 'by accident.'"

That only left the ultimate kung fu film conundrum: if kung fu is self-improvement where the highest form is not to fight, how do you create a kick-ass climax that satisfies both the blood-thirsty and the benevolent? For *Kung Fu Panda*, that came in one defining battle. "The origins of the showdown came from our experiments with how we could have Po legitimately defeat Tai Lung without turning him into Bruce Lee. Po had to beat Tai Lung by being the best version of himself. I had taken taichi and aikido in my youth, so was familiar with the ideas of 'hard' versus 'soft' forms of martial arts. Obviously Po had to epitomize 'soft' while Tai Lung would be the living embodiment of 'hard.' Soft style martial arts seek to redirect the force of an attacker back against them, and upset their balance. In aikido, there are no offensive moves, you cannot instigate an attack, only defend yourself from one.

"This seemed appropriate for Po ... and reminded me of another of my cartoon heroes: Bugs Bunny. In the Bugs films directed by Chuck Jones, he never provoked or started a conflict. But when trouble found him, watch out. Bugs would demolish the guy. We had also read the *Tao Te Ching* by Lao-tzu and had found in the seventy-sixth verse the stanza 'the hard and strong will fall, the soft and weak will overcome' — which gave us the philosophical underpinnings to go along with our martial arts approach."

Not only did they have their approach, but they also included foreshadowing to the monumental moment. "Rodolphe had drawn extensive boards of Po fighting the training dummy when he first meets The Furious Five. Originally this was a much more elaborate scene with Po launching repeated assaults on the dummy and getting bounced off. That scene eventually got boiled down to just one punch from Po in the final movie. Then we also used to have a protracted scene of Tai Lung attacking Po in front of his gang of wolf bandits (before we realized Tai Lung was so tough he didn't need a gang), and Po just kept on bouncing back like the dummy until Tai Lung was humiliated.

"As in the dummy training scene, this got refined down to one huge blow from Tai Lung (provoked by his anger at not understanding the secret of the Dragon Scroll), and Po acting like the training dummy — returning Tai Lung's force ten-fold. Simon Wells did the final boards for this scene. Po looks at his hands in wonder, because that is the moment when he finally believes without any doubt that he can do it. He accepts that he is the Dragon Warrior, a kung fu master and the only one able to stop Tai Lung. And that makes him happy."

It also made kung fu students, kung fu teachers, kung fu film fans, and moviegoers happy all over the world. Despite the fact that projections for its opening weekend topped out at about thirty million dollars, *Kung Fu Panda* made twice that in three days — making it DreamWorks Animation's biggest opening for a non-sequel film. It went on to become the highest grossing animated movie of the year (and the third-highest overall, animated or live action). But in terms of this book's subject, it also did something unprecedented: it was reported that the Chinese Government chided its own film industry for not doing something like it first. And, unlike *Forbidden Kingdom* or even *Crouching Tiger*, the film was also a big hit in China.

Kung FU.S.A.

It has now spawned a sequel, as well as a TV series on Nickelodeon (for which I was asked to do a second seminar – one of the unexpected rewards for which serves as my "about the author" picture on the back cover). "*Kung Fu Panda* was a huge labor of love for everyone who worked for more than four years to bring it to the screen," John Stevenson concluded. "It was always hard work, but it was work we loved. It will always be a happy memory for me. I hope King Hu and Jim Henson would have liked it."

CHAPTER TEN
KUNG FUTURE

Picture identifications (clockwise from upper left):
Sammo Hung vs. Donnie Yen in *Ip Man 2*; Wu Jing in *Master of Taichi*; Stephen Chow in *Kung Fu Hustle*; Michael Jai White in *Blood and Bone*; Tony Jaa in *Ong Bak 2*; Andy Lau and Nicholas Tse in *Shaolin*.

Kung Future

At the end of the first decade in the 21st century, kung fu films are back to where they started. Although an animated Panda has shown Westerners the way, for the most part, kung fu films have retreated from Hollywood — which has made it clear that they not only do not understand, but don't particularly appreciate the cinematic technique involved. One of the very few who does is Michael Jai White.

Born in Brooklyn, New York, then raised in Bridgeport, Connecticut, he started soaking in martial arts at the age of seven. "I was taken by it from the first moment I saw a kung fu movie," he told me. "It was *Five Fingers of Death,* and it scared the life out of me! I was too young to see a picture where they were tearing eyes out of people. After that there was a kung fu craze. I had a picture of Joe Louis on my wall, and I said when I grow up I want to look like that! I wanted to be powerful and have that prowess."

By the time he was fourteen, he had worked extensively with Eric Chen and his teacher Wu Bin, who was the coach of the prestigious Beijing wushu team — as well as sparred with Bill Wallace, among many other world champion boxers and kickboxers. Through all of them, he not only learned about the external martial aspect, but the internal, self-improvement aspect as well. "When I was a celebrated fighter, I was less of a martial artist. I didn't want to win as much as I wanted to learn something. I respect every opportunity to better myself. It's really about that."

All along, White was winning multiple contests, and teaching. His desire for learning developed as fast as his physique. "When I got a chance to start martial arts I trained incessantly. I didn't play basketball or baseball, I practiced martial arts. Meanwhile I would take acting and filmmaking classes for fun. Started going on auditions, and landed three things at the same time. At that point I figured I had better start paying attention to this."

Producers and directors had certainly already started paying attention to him. After extensive experience in New York plays, White followed his agent out to Hollywood where he found parts in cheap movies (1989's *The Toxic Avenger Parts II* and *III*, for example) and TV series before nailing the lead role of boxing champ Mike Tyson in the *Tyson* (1995) TV movie. That led to playing the title superhero in the live action movie version of the comic book *Spawn* (1997).

To his fans and peers, he was best known as an actor, but his friends knew his consummate kung fu skills. Throughout his career, White wanted to meld both, and it would look like he would be able to do just that when Quentin Tarantino came calling with a major supporting role in *Kill Bill*.

"At first I was supposed to do a much larger role in the movie," he revealed. "There was a whole casino sequence where Bill (David Carradine) was originally going to be introduced. I was the guy running the place, and Samuel L. Jackson was going to do a cameo as the piano player. I was going to be a tuxedo-and-Hanzo-sword-wearing boss who's partnered with the piano player's wife. But later on, Quentin changed it. I didn't take that personally, because we were friends before I went to work with him. Then, later, he called with the idea of a flashback to highlight David Carradine's skill because, one, he wanted a fight scene with me, and two, the audience had never seen David's prowess. Although it didn't really fit even then, I still got to go to Beijing, meet Gordon Liu, and had a great time. But I wasn't surprised when it didn't make the final cut."

Happily, the edited fight scene is available for viewing on the *Kill Bill Volume 2* DVD, and it inspired White to take an even greater role in shaping his own destiny. "I've always been a writer, so when I'm not satisfied with scripts I'm getting I write my own." *Blood and Bone* (2009) was a prime example, and White's first major showcase displaying both external brawn and internal skill. "It's not the muscle," he said, "it's the technique."

It was also a satisfying experience, and, even before he finished making the film, he already had his next film prepared. "I finished *Blood and Bone* and started *Black Dynamite* ten days later," he said. "I knew I had to take the reins on it because all too often people in power at the major studios can't admit when they don't know how to do something right. I knew how to do this movie, so I didn't want to go the studio route." *Black Dynamite* (2009), a delightful satire of the blaxploitation genre, became an international phenomenon — showing White the way to make a childhood dream come true.

"I want to continue this way, especially for kung fu films," he explained. "Usually the best martial artists are not self-promoters, so a lot of Hollywood martial art films are choreographed by people who really don't know a lot of, or a lot about, martial arts. I'd love to change that. In fact, I feel like I haven't even gotten in my stride yet. Martial arts is pervasive all over the world and is a great money maker. Great kung fu, and how it should be depicted, is not going to come from the studio system. I want to find good people, stick with them, and do great work."

As Michael Jai White uses his many talents to change the course of live action American kung fu films, John Woo slowly reclaimed his reputation by returning to China to make *Red Cliff Part One* (2008) and *Two* (2009). An epic examination of the battles that ended the Han Dynasty in 209 AD, it cost more than any Asian-financed film in history, and presented Woo with incredible obstacles and challenges — not the least of which was Chow Yun-fat exiting the lead role. He was replaced with Tony Leung (as he had been before during *Bullet in the Head*).

As exciting as the sweeping saga was — with Woo filling the screen with extraordinary beauty, and deftly resting the fate of a war on a change of wind and a cup of tea — the real treat for kung fu fans was the production's realization of several historical martial art icons. Generals Guan Yu and Zhang Fei will be familiar to anyone who's ever visited a Chinese souvenir shop ... although they might not recognize their names. Both men are the models for multiple sculptures in every medium.

But, as realized in *Red Cliff* by actors Ba Sen Zha-bu and Zhang Jin-sheng, respectively, then choreographed by Corey Yuen Kwai, these seemingly mythical characters are brought to life in several show-stopping "battlefield-fu" sequences — ala Orlando Bloom's Legolas in the *Lord of the Rings* movies (as you may recall, Legolas was really the only character given a virtuoso fighting scene in all three films). But, as previously stated, it was these terrific displays of kung fu prowess that were either eliminated or homogenized in the two-hour-thirty-minute U.S. version of the original three hundred and twenty-minute, two-part Chinese version. The reported reason for the editing was that these superlative kung fu displays were "unrealistic." So, again, "standard operating ignorance" takes its place alongside "standard operating racism."

In any case, both the Chinese and American versions of *Red Cliff* were worthwhile and successful — winning awards and setting new box office records in Asia. John Woo recovered from the arduous production by helping out with *Reign of Assassins* (2010), his first flat-out wuxia film, co-directed by Su Chiao-pin and starring Michelle Yeoh. Premiering at the Venice Film Festival, it took another great step in reinstating Woo's cinematic standing, garnering rave reviews for its action, humor, and filmmaking verve in every corner of the world.

But Woo, then sixty-four years old, is just one of the old guard still fighting his way into the new century. Zhang Yimou, having illuminated kung fu and wuxia films with the magnificent *Hero*, mysterious *House of Flying Daggers*, and maddening *Curse of the Golden Flower*, has moved on to other genres. Yuen Wo-ping, sixty-five years old in 2010, and Liu Chia-liang, seventy-four, started collecting lifetime achievement awards. Jackie Chan, fifty-seven, loves making movies, but keeps announcing his eventual exit from doing

Kung Future

elaborate on-screen kung fu. Same with Jet Li, forty-seven.

So what is a genre to do? Well, there's always China. Although the Peking Opera Schools are closed in Hong Kong, the China Sports Universities are still going strong. China's history is all about kung fu, and, although the government stresses the sports version, wushu, that's more than enough for filmmakers and action actors. It's also more than enough for the Asian movie industry, which finds kung fu films far easier to get approved by the ever-vigilant Chinese Communist Party than almost anything else. So, if any actor knows kung fu, they have a great shot at longevity. Just ask Sammo Hung, Yuen Baio, Chen Kuan-tai, Lo Mang, and Fung Hak-on — all old school stars who work as much as they want to.

But 21st century China is a double-edged sword for kung fu film hopefuls. While the old guard are back at work, the men who might have been Jackie or Jet are in a holding pattern. Clearly the biggest kung fu-star-waiting-to-happen is Jacky Wu Jing, aka Jason Wu. Another graduate of the Beijing Sport University, he was discovered by Yuen Wo-ping, who was looking for someone to help him better capture the power and beauty of taichi on screen. He looked no further than Wu Jing.

Born in 1974 into a royal Manchurian family, his father was an assistant coach of the Beijing Wushu Team who sent his son to start training at the age of six. That's where Wo-ping found him fifteen years later. Following *The Tai Chi Master* with Jet and Michelle Yeoh, Master Yuen wanted to try again with *Tai Chi II* (1996). It was within this film that Wu's character took on the first name Jacky, and it stuck. Although Wu's charm was obvious, and his kung fu technique phenomenal, the plot was even goosier than in the original.

Even so, Yuen Wo-ping signed Wu to a three-year contract, and kept them both busy with the landmark television series *New Shaolin Temple* (1998), *Swordsman of Flying Dagger* (1999), and, most notably,

Master of Taichi (1997) — which contains the finest taichi ever put on screen. Although available in a complete form on DVD, when Tai Seng Entertainment cut the series down into an American TV movie, they inexplicably changed the title to *The Tai Chi Master* ... creating endless confusion with the Jet Li version.

Under any name, it contains some of the finest fights in kung fu film history. Using much the same cast as *Tai Chi II*, there is authentic taichi throughout, as well as two taichi versus ba qua battles that remain the industry standard. The movie's central sequence puts Wu in a Bruce Lee situation: having to fight five true martial art masters, each on a different floor of a pagoda, but Yuen takes the *Game of Death* conceit and turns it into a magnificent kung fu lesson in both physical and mental martial arts.

Although the pagoda fights are the most memorable, the final fight is the most interesting and telling. Forced to face an obstinate, rage-full general (expertly played by Billy Chow), the entire confrontation is the finest "hard" versus "soft" kung fu fight ever conceived and executed — from the pre-battle stretching to the post-battle realization. All three TV series were hugely successful throughout Asia. At any other time in modern history, they would have heralded the discovery of a new kung fu star, but when Wu Jing left Yuen's wing, the Hong Kong film industry was in deep, post-1997 takeover, post-Japanese-economic-meltdown, post Triad-mobster-infiltration funk.

More than fifty percent of the industry was looking for work, and those working were in somewhat uninspired fare, to say the least. Wu appeared in Tsui Hark's technologically exceptional, emotionally vacant remake of *Zu Warriors*, *Legend of Zu* (2000), but his kung fu skills were not required. He was further anointed as a kung fu star by being personally chosen to co-star in Liu Chia-liang's farewell feature *Drunken Monkey* in 2002, but, although he got to strut Master Liang's stuff, the film was not the consummate classic everyone was hoping for. Wu had little choice but to return to TV and await further developments. He made good use of his time back on the small screen, however, developing his own skills as a choreographer.

Money began to flow again in 2004 when Wu was signed by a new talent agency. Seeing the genre turn toward more modern crime tales, Jacky was cast as an extremely dangerous villain, starting him on a string of minor thrillers — *Fatal Contact*, *Twins Mission*, *Invisible Target* (all 2006), and *Fatal Move* (2007) — all with exceptional kung fu. He even got to fight Jet Li on screen in *Mummy 3: Tomb of the Dragon Emperor* (2007). Finally, as of this writing, Jacky Wu is starring alongside Jackie Chan in *Shaolin* (2010), the official sequel to the 1981 *Shaolin Temple* film that started it all for Jet. Wu Jing is clearly the genre's new kung fu star ... now all he needs is a leading role worthy of him.

The new century is also a time when actors who were previously minor stars get to take their place as major stars. Just ask Vincent Zhao, aka Zhao Wen-zhou aka Chiu Man-cheuk, who had to carry the stigma of being the George Lazenby to Jet Li's Sean Connery for years before Chinese studios became beggars who couldn't be choosers. Another graduate of the prestigious Beijing Sport University, Zhao was discovered by Corey Yuen to be the villain in *Fong Sai Yuk*, then got saddled with the Wong Fei-hung yoke after Tsui Hark's declaration that Jet Li was nothing without him.

Retreating to television roles to lick the wounds inflicted by critics, Zhao was chosen by Yuen Wo-ping to star in *True Legend* (2010), a new take on the Beggar Su character immortalized by Yuen's father, Simon, in *Drunken Master*. Although unfocused, the disjointed tale of Su's rise, fall, and rise, filmed partially in 3D, was a monument to kung fu, featuring myriad fight and training sequences that only improve with repeated viewing. It also served as a showcase for MMA fighter Cung Le as a barbarian, Gordon Liu as a mad monk, Jay Chou as the "God of Wushu," and especially Andy On Chi-kit as a truly demented, truly dangerous villain.

Speaking of villains, there's Fan Siu-wong. Born in 1973 Hong Kong, he was the son of popular, famed supporting actor Fan Mei-sheng, who was the man they brought in to replace Simon Yuen when he passed away during the filming of *Magnificent Butcher*. Sent away at the age of fourteen because he was so scrawny, the younger Fan bulked up by studying martial arts, then followed in his father's footsteps.

Known for his round, dark eyes, he first came to major international fame at the age of eighteen as "Terry Fan" in *Story of Ricky* (1991) — the Chinese live action adaptation of an absurdly violent Japanese manga called *Riki-Oh*. With his father playing a demented, hook-handed assistant prison warden, the Chinese Ricky uses growing powers to take on stupendously sadistic guards (including a psycho-sexual whiptress played by Yukari Oshima) until the jail staff mutates into monsters, and Ricky punches them into chopped meat and jelly.

Terry continued working in the movie industry in such efforts as *Project S: Once a Cop*, but the quality of his roles lessened as the film industry struggled post-1997. Where once he did five movies a year, he was reduced to none in 1999. But all good things come to those who wait (and train), so when China started pouring money into the local film industry early in the 21st century, the actor, now known as "Louis Fan," returned with a vengeance. He made twenty movies in the first six years of the decade and became action choreographer for *Kung Fu Fighter* in 2007. With the semi-retirement of Jackie and Jet, Louis has become the go-to supporting "best friend" or "villain" actor for the Chinese kung fu film. He did eight films in 2010 — including *Kung Fu Chefs* with Sammo Hung and *Future X Cops* with Andy Lau — and made an excellent impression in every one.

Kung Future

All of these performers could be the new "king of kung fu," but none of them are. The one who is was born the same year as Jet Li, 1963. But Jet Li's mother was not one of the world's greatest taichi practitioners and teachers. That would be Bow Sim-mak, who moved with her newspaperman husband, Klyster Yen, to Massachusetts in 1975. While Bruce Lee started teaching gweilo outsiders kung fu on the west coast, Bow started teaching them on the east coast. She also started teaching her son, Donnie Yen.

"I started training with my mom when I was very little," he told me. "I learned some taichi, but mainly Northern Shaolin. But I've always been a rebel. When I was young, all sorts of students from different fields used to come in and kind of worship my mom, you know. And I would challenge that. I would run off to other people's martial arts schools to train in different styles. I had a lot of friends who studied karate and a mixture of kung fu stylings, so I was exploring that. A lot of kung fu masters in Chinatown used to say to me about how my mom was so famous and so good at what she does, so why would I train in other styles? But my mom was actually kind of open to what I was doing."

Like others, Donnie looked at the "soft" but powerful things his mom did, then looked at the "hard" things Bruce Lee did on screen, and made his decision. But that was the least of the fourteen year-old's problems. "I ran away from home because I was having trouble at school. At about the same time the Beijing Wushu Team came to the states and were visiting every martial arts school in Chinatown. When they visited our school, my mom asked me to perform for two of their head coaches. They were very impressed and told my mother if I was trained by them for a year or two I could be a champion in China. A few months later, my mom asked if I wanted to go to China. Well, I knew that if I stayed I'd just get into more trouble, so I agreed."

Only one problem: they didn't check with the head coaches.

"They were shocked," Donnie explained. "They hadn't expected me to actually arrive at their doorstep! Their training an American would get them into trouble. We went through all kinds of departments and making connections here and there. And they finally changed their policy! I was the first Asian not born in China to train with the wushu team."

Donnie trained for two years, then was ready for the next big change in his life. "I visited Yuen Wo-ping's sister, who used to study with my mom when she taught in Hong Kong. Her brother was making *Drunken Tai Chi* and was looking for a young unknown to cast in it. She told him about me, and he said, "Show me what you can do." The whole Yuen clan was there and they shot my performance on film. About a couple of weeks later, I got the part."

Drunken Tai Chi (1984) filmed in Taiwan for almost eight months, and reflected the crazy and corny approach Wo-ping was using at that time. "It was released head on with *Project A*," Donnie remembered. "It did okay, but not as good as they wanted to. It was the end of the old-fashioned kung fu movie, and, to make matters worse, Yuen Wo-ping would think nothing of taking two years to make a film. The competition was getting a lot harder, and the audience seemed more interested in the more modern type of action flick."

But instead of doing one of those, Donnie tried a change of pace. *Mismatched Couples* (1985) was a freaky and funky mid-80s romantic comedy romp that put the budding star in spandex and had him popping and locking. Little wonder that he returned to America to hide out for a year or two. "When I got back to Hong Kong, the whole dynasty of martial arts movies was divided and, clearly, Jackie Chan, Yuen Baio, and Sammo Hung were dominating the whole circle."

So Yuen Wo-ping decided to try one of the more modern types of action flicks, helming what turned out to be one of the great "new wave" crime and corruption thrillers of the era, *Tiger Cage*

Kung Future

(1988). Although the 1997 Chinese takeover of Hong Kong was still almost a decade away, the fear of what might happen was growing, and *Tiger Cage* tapped into that fear. It also presented a new way to picture kung fu fights.

"Yuen Wo-ping filmed Donnie's climatic fight as if it were almost one of those fighting videogames," recalled Vincent Lyn, who played the half-breed gweilo villain in the film. "He and his adversary were on a quay by the beach and went at each other using classic kung fu techniques while the camera tracked alongside in full body shots. I don't know if the audience picked up on it, but they really responded, and it was perfect." It was Donnie's most powerful part yet, and he wanted to take full advantage of it.

"After a couple of years away, I wanted to start again as a bit more mature personality," Donnie said. "I studied all of Jackie and Sammo's films, looking for a way to make my own name. We had very limited budgets, so I was training very hard to bring the real flavor of martial arts into the films. When you study the Sammo Hung style of filming — which includes Jackie Chan and Yuen Kwai — you might notice a kind of concentration on the stuntman ... on the reaction rather than on the person actually throwing the kick. So I decided to have a very strong personal flavor. I'm going to try to break the rhythm of the choreography and have a lot of pre-movement before the actual kick."

The problem there was that only Jackie and Sammo were getting the kind of filmmaking freedom Donnie, as a newcomer, was deprived of. 1989's *In the Line of Duty IV* and 1990's *Tiger Cage 2*, although each featuring exceptional kung fu, were uninspired otherwise. Then, because he wanted more freedom, Donnie parted company with Yuen Wo-ping, eliciting some bad feelings. Whatever the cause, he was relegated to the likes of the ludicrous *Holy Virgin vs. the Evil Dead* (1991) the middling *Crystal Hunt* (1991), and the rough *Cheetah on Fire* (1992).

"But then Yuen Wo-ping came back and asked me to help him out on *Once Upon a Time in China II*," Donnie reported. "So I met with Tsui Hark and said okay. I also helped them choreograph the fight scenes." It resulted in (arguably) the best of the series. "It only took us three days to finish the fight scenes, even with all the waiting for the fans and lighting and all the effects," Donnie revealed. "It was actually kind of easy. Fighting in *Drunken Tai Chi*, with thirty-five to forty movements in one shot ... now, that was tough! I think fighting with Jet was much easier. In fact, some of it wasn't even choreographed. We just went at it!"

Knowing a good thing when he fought it, Donnie was content to jump back and forth between Tsui Hark and Yuen Wo-ping projects for the next few years. He played another memorable villain in *Dragon Gate Inn* (1992), and a supreme hero in the exceptional "Young Wong Fei-hung" film, *Iron Monkey* (1993). "I liked doing that because it was a challenge for me to play a heroic role in the vein of Jet Li. He had already made Wong Fei-hung famous again, and although I was playing his father, I was basically playing another Wong Fei-hung. So the challenge was; how would I fight differently and still be just as impressive as Jet? So I told Yuen 'let's not do the no-shadow-kick technique with a lot of editing, let's speed up the frame.'"

Donnie continued to work with Yuen in *Hero Among Heroes* (1993) and *Wing Chun* (1994), but he also continued studying film, and looking for opportunities to produce and direct his own projects. That desire led to some critical drubbings. "*Iron Monkey II* was a big mistake," he admitted, "but I needed the money. Unfortunately I did a number of pictures I'm not proud of simply because I needed the paycheck. In Hong Kong, I had a reputation for turning down films, but when I needed the paycheck, I had to sell my soul. But I still think that I have done less poor films than many others, so that makes me feel a little better."

Kung Future

His fans also felt much better when he turned to good television rather than bad films like *Circus Kids* (1994), *Satan Returns* (1996), *High Voltage* (1997), and *Black Rose 2* (1997). "I didn't want to do TV because I didn't expect to have the kind of freedom in terms of choreography and production support that I had in films. But when they told me I would be working with my good friend Benny Chan, the director of *The Big Bullet*, I agreed to talk about it. So I did *The Kungfu Master* and the ratings went straight up. So they asked me to do another series. And I said, if I'm going to do another one I'm going to have more control. Let's do a Bruce Lee series, because he's my idol.

"Everybody was affected by Bruce Lee. At first I just watched his films, but stayed away from his style in real life. Then, as my martial art skill matured, I came back to his philosophy. So I worked on the *Fist of Fury* TV series for seven months, even though I was only being paid for three months' work. I wanted to revolutionize TV action fighting editing. I had total control on the action editing, and was very proud of it, because the *Fist of Fury* series had the highest rating ever, and made the most money of any series ever telecast on the ATV channel."

Donnie wanted to keep that feeling of freedom going, so he directed and choreographed his next three personal projects: *Legend of the Wolf* (1997), *Ballistic Kiss* (1998) and *Shanghai Affairs* (1998). "I'm very proud of *Legend of the Wolf* and *Ballistic Kiss*, because both were made for less than $HK4,000,000, and, pound for pound, they look far more expensive in terms of production value. *Once Upon a Time in China II* cost $40,000,000! There were a lot of problems getting them made and distributed, so I was quite proud to get them out. I only made *Shanghai Affairs* because I needed the money for *Ballistic Kiss*!"

By then it seemed that Donnie had done everything he wanted in Hong Kong, so he broadened his horizons ... with a little help from his friends. "Michelle Yeoh is a great friend and, indeed, the best female martial artist actress in the world. She's a workaholic — very tough and daring. A complete woman — sincere and down to earth. She told everybody in Hollywood about me." And they responded by giving Donnie parts in *Highlander: Endgame* (2000), *Blade II* (2002), and *Shanghai Knights* (2003) with Jackie Chan. But Yen quickly discovered that if working in Hong Kong was a rocky field, working in Hollywood was a fur-lined prison. The freedom to experiment and create was just not tinseltown's way.

Thankfully by then, Zhang Yimou had come calling, and Donnie was to add his small, but integral piece to *Hero*. "Obviously it was pretty clear that they wanted the most anticipated action scene between Jet and I since *Once Upon a Time in China II*," he told me. "So we had a lot of discussion on how best to do that scene. We actually spent twenty-two days shooting that. Normally, especially in Asian films, the time and budget is always constrained. But when we were there, the producer would come in and say 'Take your time. We don't want the best scene … we want the best of the best scene!'

"So, with every shot, both Jet and myself would really work at doing the absolute best possible and decide the right way to do it. Because we knew we not only have to top ourselves in *Once Upon a Time in China II*, but we also, half-jokingly, half-seriously, wanted to top the Michelle Yeoh/Zhang Ziyi fight scene in *Crouching Tiger Hidden Dragon*. So a lot of times Jet and I would joke around, saying, hey, no offense to the women, but we can't lose it to Michelle and Zhang! So we really took our time to really nail every shot."

It paid off, but, ironically, it required the filmmakers to lessen Donnie's contribution to a previous scene, so as not to lessen the power of his sequence with Jet. "They cut down the sequence between me and the seven Qin warriors," Donnie recalled. "At first, after I defeated all of them, I went to the blind musician, gave him some money and asked him to play another song. Only after that did I start to walk out, and then stop when I hear Jet calling me. But when I saw the film, I knew something was missing."

Hero's international success gave Donnie's career even more credibility, which he had already taken advantage of by choreographing both a Japanese film (2001's *The Princess Blade*) and a German TV show (2000's *Code Name: The Puma*). As much as he enjoyed the experiences in Europe and America, there was no place like home, so Donnie returned to South China with renewed vigor and intent. His work began to pay off with *The Twins Effect* (2003) — a film originally designed just to exploit the fame of a popular singing duo (Charlene Choi and Gillian Chung).

"I really put in a lot of effort to train and mold the girls there — trying to really bring up the level of Hong Kong-style action films. Now, I've shot a lot of action involving women before, but *Twins Effect* was something else. They'd never shot any action films before, not to mention they're very new at this. It was a big challenge, because I really wanted them to look convincing. You know, a lot of Hong Kong films are known to be able to shoot anybody doing a kung fu scene and make them look half-decent, but I didn't want to do that. I really wanted them to shine and make them unique. I really wanted to bring out the best in them and challenge myself."

The same was true with co-star Ekin Cheng. "He's done a lot of action movies, but I didn't want him to look like he was just doing another one, I wanted him to look new and refreshed and different. Then, there was the pressure of action-directing Jackie Chan's cameo sequence. You know, either he's choreographed himself or by Sammo Hung, so there's a certain expectation and standard there. So I wanted to shoot Jackie so I could retain his style while blending it into my own vision. Well, shooting Jackie and Ekin and the Twins was a great challenge, which I'm very pleased with. The Twins are known as little, petite, fragile girls. But they really kick butt."

The newly anointed action stars took Donnie's lessons to heart in their subsequent film, *House of Fury* (2005), co-starring and directed by Jackie Chan protégé Stephen Fung, and choreographed by Yuen Wo-ping. Donnie, meanwhile, made a career-defining alliance with director Wilson Yip Wai-shun. Yip, who had been known for his eclectic career of horror, erotic, and comedy, collaborated with Donnie on a crime thriller that bore an odd and awkward name: *Sha Po Lang* (aka *Kill Zone*, 2005) — words that represent three stars in Chinese astrology: the "Seven Killings" power star, the "Army Breaker" ruinous star, and the "Greedy Wolf" flirting star.

Originally the film, aka *SPL*, was going to be a straight thriller, but once Sammo Hung was cast as a family-loving mob boss, Wu Jing as a mainland Chinese hitman, and Donnie was also on board as choreographer, superlative kung fu was added in the form of three remarkable fight scenes. The first occurs a full half-hour into the film and seems to spark off like a small physical explosion when Sammo and Donnie suddenly go at it. Having been intrigued by the possibilities of mixed martial arts being integrated into modern movies, Donnie took the opportunity to incorporate superlative ground fighting into his arsenal.

Great ground fighting returned in the climatic rematch between Donnie and Sammo, but possibly the film's best fight occurs just prior to that, as Donnie takes on the knife-wielding hitman with only a short police baton (but, tellingly, a short baton that was still longer than a knife — in most evenly matched kung fu fights, the longer weapon wins). Donnie and Wu Jing, having both been classically trained, were beautifully matched, and meticulously slaved to create the best fight of its kind. In a season of tepid, unimaginative films, *SPL* stood out like the flash on a blade. Although Donnie took some time to co-star in Tsui Hark's disappointing *Seven Swords* (2005), he quickly reunited with Wilson Yip for a string of increasingly successful efforts.

First out of the gate was, fittingly, *Dragon Tiger Gate* (2006), an attempt to have Chinese manhua (comic books) take their place alongside the likes of *Batman Begins* (2005) and *Spider-Man* (2002). The *Dragon Tiger Gate* comic is as successful in China as *Superman* was in the U.S., and Donnie did a great job training Nicholas Tse as Tiger Wong — ostensibly the star of the story — but Yen's powerful presence shifted the film's focus onto his character, Dragon Wong, which threw off the story's balance. And, despite some exceptional on-screen action, Dragon's unparalleled kung fu superiority over everything and everyone on screen also served to diminish the effectiveness of the villain.

No matter. Wilson and Donnie next tackled *Flash Point* (2007), which looked and played like a prequel to *Sha Po Lang*, although the filmmakers deny any connection. Even so, it once again featured Donnie as a superlative kung fu cop, this time taking on three vicious criminals led by Collin Chou. Chou, a Taiwan-born actor, made a sizeable impression as the villain in Jet Li's *Bodyguard from Beijing* (aka *The Defender*) under the name Ngai Sing, then wound up playing the part offered to Jet in *The Matrix* sequels, as well as portraying Jet's father in *Fearless*. As such, he was well-matched with Donnie, and their face-off in the film's final third is worth the price of admission to the otherwise familiar thriller. Taking the opportunity to further explore ground fighting's place in kung fu action, Donnie designed a literally knock-down, drag-out, Hong Kong Film Award-winning fight that left audiences exhausted and exhilarated.

But the best was still to come. Gratified by the hard-won respect the burgeoning Chinese film industry was showing him, Donnie took some time to co-star in Ching Siu-tung's familiar war epic *An Empress and the Warriors* (2008) and Gordon Chan's uninspired historical horror fantasy *Painted Skin* (2008) before returning to the Wilson Yip fold for, quite possibly, the most important film of his transformed career.

Many of the people who Bruce Lee most influenced and inspired were saddened that the icon never got the opportunity to fully mature. Many true kung fu sifus recognize the classic pattern: youthful aggression (wanting to win everything), adult denial (straining your body in an attempt to ignore age), middle-aged acceptance (inward exploration to fully develop your chi), and mature wisdom (using your ever-developing balance to attain ultimate ability). Given that Bruce died at the height of his aggression, his followers continue to pay homage to that version of him ... including Donnie. But then art-filmmaker extraordinaire Wong Kar-wei announced that he intended to make a movie about Bruce Lee's wing chun teacher, Yip Man.

The industry was galvanized by this news. Although the idea of a bio-pic about this venerable sifu had long been considered, it took a director of Wong's stature to kick-start several competing productions. The one with the most momentum was to be directed by Wilson Yip and star Donnie Yen. It was the culmination of their collaboration. Edmond Wong, who scripted *Dragon Tiger Gate*, wrote the screenplay (borrowing many tones and shadings of several Jet Li films like *Fearless* and *Once Upon a Time in China*). Sammo Hung, who played the villain in *SPL*, was chosen as choreographer because he had made the greatest wing chun film up until that time, *The Prodigal Son*. But to avoid conflict with Wong Kar-wei's vision, the assembled producers changed their film's name to *Ip Man* (2008).

By playing the revered sifu, Donnie was able to act from a place of serenity and center he hadn't previously hinted at. Always the soul of aggression, he was now performing the soul of discretion, and he wore it extremely well. In fact, the first hour of *Ip Man*, before it descends into yet another insidious Japanese versus intrepid Chinese World War II saga, ranks among the absolute best — especially an extended confrontation between a raging Northern martial artist (Louis Fan) and the balanced Ip, who brilliantly teaches him that

Kung Future

it's not about the sword ... it's about the sword-holder. This scene displays all concerned — the director, writer, choreographer, and actors — at their absolute finest.

It also firmly established Donnie Yen as the new king of kung fu films. For the first time he was nominated for "Best Actor" awards, and he was now number one on every action film producer's list. *Ip Man* won most major Asian film awards. *Bodyguards and Assassins* (2009), the powerful drama Donnie co-starred in, won the major film awards the following year. Boasting an almost unbelievably difficult production history (which spawned an impressive documentary of its own called *Development Hell*), this tale of ordinary people sacrificing themselves to protect freedom fighter Sun Yat-sen from government killers was a brutally beautiful film — highlighted by Donnie's on-screen match with famed mixed martial arts fighter Cung Le (not to mention Donnie's unforgettable final moment running face first into a galloping horse).

After all his years finding his place in the film world, Donnie seems to be reveling in his freedom to choose any project he cares to. In 2010 he starred in *Ip Man 2, 14 Blades* (a remake of Lu Chin-ku's Shaw Brother Studio production of *Secret Service of the Imperial Court*), and the frenetic, nearly farcical *Legend of the Fist: The Return of Chen Zhen* — a seeming sequel to Jet Li's *Fist of Legend* in which Donnie gets to redo *Fist of Fury* once again while also dressing up like Kato.

At the time of this writing, he is also playing The Monkey King in a film of the same name, General Guan Yu in *The Lost Bladesman* (2011) and a film that spans the history of kung fu entertainment, *Wu Xia* (2011). At one time he even spoke of teaming up with Tony Jaa (aka Panom Yeerum) before the Jackie Chan-inspired, Bruce Lee-worshipping, inordinately promising muy thai artist and filmmaker threatened retirement after starring in the *Ong Bak* series (2003-2010) and *Tom Yum Goong* (aka *The Protector*, 2005).

But whatever he does, it's safe to say that he will be giving it his all. "Martial art is a form of expression, an expression from your inner self to your hands and legs," Donnie has said. "When you watch my films, you're feeling my heart."

So what will the future of kung fu films look like? You've probably already seen it. It was in the book-ending sequences that began and ended *Shaolin Soccer* (2001) — a classic kung fu comedy directed, written, and starring another Bruce Lee idolizer, but one where, when you watch his films, you are feeling his funny bone as well as his heart.

Stephen Chow Sing-chi loves kung fu. More specifically, Stephen Chow loves kung fu movies. More generally, Stephen Chow loves Bruce Lee. "Bruce Lee's wushu theories heated up my heart like a fireball," he said, "helping me through many difficult times."

And the now internationally famous filmmaker had many difficult times to get through. Raised in poverty, Chow's one glimmer of hope came from inside a movie theater where Bruce Lee broke a "No Dogs or Chinese" sign outside a park, and made clear to all comers that the Chinese were not the "weaklings of Asia."

"I remember it like it was yesterday," he told me. "Behind wushu is the spirit of always heading forth and never giving up. This spirit, the fighting will, is what I learned from Bruce Lee films."

And he used it well. At first he dreamed of being a great martial artist, but he soon realized that the Bruce he loved was also a great actor (and, of course, intrinsically knew that the road to financial reward was littered with film stars, not kung fu masters). Getting by with a little help from his friends, he managed to get into the local television training school, and wound up the host of a children's program called *430 Space Shuttle*.

"He was known as being a little tough on the kids," recalls Frank Djeng, who was the "master of remaster" at Tai Seng Entertainment when they distributed several of Chow's comedies on DVD.

Kung Future

"Really, almost rude, but it was the same kind of dry comedy he's famous for now."

Ironically, when Chow got his big break into films, it was about as far away from comedy as he could get. He fought alongside such stars as Danny Lee in *Final Judgment* (1988), David Chiang in *Just Heroes* (1989), and even Jet Li in *Dragon Fight* (1989), but displayed far more acting chops than comedy or kung fu chops. In fact, he won a supporting actor award for the first film.

That, happily, led to roles in eight more films in 1990 alone, before visionary producer Ng See-yuen tapped Chow to star in his satire of Chow Yun-fat's *God of Gamblers*. *All for the Winner* (1990) was that rarest of creatures: a lampoon that made more money than the film it was making fun of. Much of its success undoubtedly came from the writing and directing skills of Jeffrey Lau and kung-fu choreographer Corey Yuen Kwai, but there was no denying the invaluable contribution of Chow, whose charm, wit, and obvious pleasure was infectious.

His joy at "making it" was also obvious, especially since he appeared in nearly a dozen movies the next year alone, including two *God of Gamblers* sequels. More importantly, he starred in the hitherto fore unthinkable homage to his childhood idol Bruce Lee, *Fist of Fury 1991*. *Fist of Fury*, of course, was the original title of the film Americans have come to know as *The Chinese Connection*, and was considered sacrosanct to Hong Kong moviegoers. So it's a clear measure of how loved Chow had become that the audience flocked to, rather than ran from, the undeniably hilarious film.

It was in this film that all the ingredients of Chow's burgeoning genius were on display: his manic-depressive/passive-aggressive screen persona and uncategorizeable charisma as well as the balance of sympathy and pathos within ingenious plotting. In this case Chow played a man with the most powerful right arm in all of China ... as well as the weakest left one. By the time he instituted another popular film series with *Fight Back to School* (1991) — nominally a comedic combination of *Fast Times at Ridgemont High* with *Kindergarten Cop* — his new brand of screen comedy, known as "Mo Lei Tau," was in place.

It meant that anything could, and often did, happen, from unexpected musical numbers to sudden satires of any commercial, music video, TV show, or other movie that came to mind. That much was obvious. What wasn't, to Western ears, was how much humor came from what Chow said and how he said it. Literally lost in translation were his brilliant wordplay, puns, insults, local slang and risqué jokes.

It didn't seem to make much difference. As Chow targeted the legal system (*Justice My Foot*, 1992), Chinese history (*Royal Tramp*, 1992, *King of Beggars*, 1992), James Bond (*From Beijing with Love*, 1994), television (*Sixty Million Dollar Man*, 1995), the gods (*Mad Monk*, 1993, *A Chinese Odyssey*, 1994), and many other things, he did it with revelatory invention and unrestricted imagination, often creating satires within satires that were understood wherever they were shown. He also took every opportunity to both spotlight and satirize martial arts, whether it was suddenly fighting like Bruce in *Out of the Dark* (1995) — his spoof of both *Ghostbusters* and *Leon: The Professional* — or turning a karate confrontation into a cha-cha during several films.

He had been involved in the creation of all his films, whether through ad-libs or dallying with co-writing and co-directing credits, but 1996's *God of Cookery* (seemingly a parody of Tsui Hark's 1995 culinary comedy *The Chinese Feast*) could truly be called a "Stephen Chow Film." It was so popular that Jim Carrey was set to star in an American remake with Chow directing. But that was not to be. Instead, Chow appeared in five more Asian films (even fighting Jackie Chan's bodyguard Ken Lo in *Tricky Master 2000*) before launching his next full-fledged personal production: an homage to the then-

Kung Future

dying Hong Kong film industry called *The King of Comedy* (1999).

It was that film that cemented Chow's intention to get off the cinematic treadmill. Finally, after starring in more than thirty movies in a dozen years, he decided to take the next step. It was time for Chow to utterly control his destiny and take over the world through the power of cinema. Rather than make one movie a month, he labored on his next for two years. But it was worth it. *Shaolin Soccer*, his love letter to kung fu (that started by showing everyday problems and ended with kung fu solving all the problems) won every Asian film award that wasn't nailed down and broke every box office record … until it hit an American wall.

Despite soccer's World Cup being played out on the world stage, for reasons still unexplained, the studio which owned the American distribution rights shelved Chow's delightful movie for years, then gave it only a nominal release with little promotion. It was a distribution mistake Chow had no intention of making again, no matter how much was offered. Three years later, partnered with Sony Pictures Classics, he proved it with *Kung Fu Hustle*, his flat-out valentine to kung fu cinema.

In order to include every kind of screen wushu, Chow initially hired Sammo Hung to be its action choreographer. "He did the first fight between the Axe Gang and the people of Pig Sty Alley," Chow told me. The one where the baker, tailor, and coolie reveal their skills. "I think he did a great job."

But after that, it is rumored that Sammo wasn't as interested in being involved in the heavily wired and digitalized subsequent sequences. These were not such a problem for the internationally renowned Yuen Wo-ping. And, even if they were a problem, Master Yuen didn't let it stop him. "He was always open to new ideas and suggestions," Chow reported, "no matter how outrageous." And they did get outrageous, from satirizing *The Matrix*'s mass slaughter of men in black suits, to making a Wile E. Coyote/Road Runner chase sequence come to live-action life.

"Oh yes," Chow admitted. "I saw Warner Brothers cartoons as a kid, and this sequence was inspired by it. It was originally a little longer — showing me jumping on a motorcycle and then crashing it — but I don't think that part worked, so I took it out. I am actually very happy I did."

He was also very happy to cast some of his childhood idols in supporting roles. He had always admired Bruce Leung Siu-lung's vertical kick — the one he used to great effect in *Kung Fu Hustle*'s casino battle — and was overjoyed to discover that the popular star of *My Kung Fu 12 Kicks* (1979) and *The Fists The Kicks and The Evils* (1979) was not only still in good shape, but also bald.

"At first I thought he had better hair than I do," he joked. "But then I found out he was wearing a wig. I was very relieved. I thought we'd have to cut his hair to make sure he didn't look better than me."

Chow completed his cast with his usual mix of striking faces (Bruce Lee look-alike Danny Chan), amusing attitudes (rotund sidekick Lam Chi-chung), innocent female beauty (Eva Huang) and great kung fu stylists (Yuen Wah, Chiu Chi-ling, Dong Zhihua, Xing Yu, and Fung Hak-on). Initially, it was reported that Chow also sought out retired film star Yuen Qiu, who appears as the landlady with the all-powerful "Lion's Roar," but in truth, the girl who saved James Bond's butt in *The Man with the Golden Gun* (1974) came to him entirely by accident.

"She had come with a friend who wanted to audition," he recalled, "but when I saw her across the room with a cigarette dangling from her lips, she looked exactly like the character I had created in my mind. I was very happy she turned out to be who she was."

He was also extremely happy to incorporate many different aspects of kung fu as well as a definitive Bruce Lee homage. In addition to spotlighting Shaolin, iron arm, staff fighting, *Deadful Melo-*

Kung Future

dy-style lyre killing, toad style, and taichi, he had the landlady make the exact same hand motions to the Axe Gang leader as Bruce made to the Italian mafia don in *Way of the Dragon*.

The final joke was on us. *Kung Fu Hustle* went on to become the most successful film in Hong Kong film history because nearly every scene either was, or contained, a satire of a specific Chinese action film ... that virtually no Westerner living outside of Hong Kong had ever seen. That much was obvious to me when I was asked to interview Chow for the *Kung Fu Hustle* DVD, but by then I already knew that there were two Stephen Chows. There was the private Stephen, who I already had several great talks with, and the public Stephen, who, as soon as the camera light went on, wickedly grinned and clammed up.

Take a look at the DVD interview and guess which Stephen showed up (and watch for the moment late in the talk when he suddenly looks to the left and smiles while still talking ... that's because when, again, he knows the answer to my increasingly desperate, elaborate question, but refuses to elucidate, I silently mouthed "I hate you" at him). Even though we were under strict time constraints, it's always great to talk to this remarkable filmmaker, even if, like most of his peers, he occasionally enjoys watching gweilo twist in the wind (all had learned that, while Asian fans usually say "what can I do for you," American fans usually say "what can you do for me?").

Actually, just about the only thing that makes Stephen Chow unhappy these days is that he has too much time for hustle, but not enough for kung fu. "I don't have as much time as I would like to practice," he lamented. "But I love kung fu. [Famed, pioneering taichi sifu] William C.C. Chen [www.williamccchen.com] is my ultimate master, and I respect him more than I can say. And now it's time to start thinking out films about *Journey to the West*, *Taichi*, and *Kung Fu Hustle 2*. Got any ideas?"

Look who's asking. Because "kung fu" actually means "hard work" or "concerted effort toward a specific goal," good ideas will keep coming from the people who balance eternal, external, martial applications with interminable, internal, personal power. It's just the nature of human physiology and psychology. Kung fu is harder, more exacting, and takes longer to master than other martial arts, but the life-long rewards are worth it.

So are the films. Again, it's like comparing all other dance movies to the films of Fred Astaire and Gene Kelly. No one can really recreate what those two dance giants did, but it is them who, and their films which, have stood the test of time. The same will be true for Bruce, Liang, Jackie, Jet, Donnie, Stephen, and all the others who take the time to do it right.

Why the kung fu film? Because it can excite, engage, inspire, and free an audience like no other genre. Because kung fu is, quite simply, the optimum in human development. There is no better, or more effective, way for a person to use their body and mind to set things right. Besides, when done correctly, it's glorious to watch. Why? Because, whether you know it or not, the power in kung fu films is also in each and every member of the audience. Now that's exciting to contemplate. And, as always and ever, watching films of fury is all about exhilaration.

THE TOP 100 KUNG FU MOVIES 1966 - 2010

COME DRINK WITH ME (1966)
Directed by King Hu
Choreographed by Han Ying-chieh
Starring Cheng Pei-pei
King Hu alerts the world that there's more to kung fu films than meet the eye.

THE ONE-ARMED SWORDSMAN (1967)
Directed by Chang Cheh
Choreographed by Liu Chia-liang, Tang Chia
Starring Jimmy Wang Yu
Chang Cheh changes the way kung fu movies are made and watched.

RETURN OF THE ONE-ARMED SWORDSMAN (1969)
Directed by Chang Cheh
Choreographed by Liu Chia-liang, Tang Chia
Starring Jimmy Wang Yu
Chang Cheh reveals his desire to make snappy populist cliffhangers.

A TOUCH OF ZEN (1969)
Directed by King Hu
Choreographed by Han Ying-chieh
Starring Ying Bai
King Hu makes the first kung fu art film with symbolism to spare.

THE CHINESE BOXER (1970)
Directed by Jimmy Wang Yu
Choreographed by Tang Chia
Starring Jimmy Wang Yu
Wang Yu sets the stage for Bruce Lee's patriotism.

Vengeance (1970)
Directed by Chang Cheh
Choreographed by Tang Chia
Starring David Chiang, Ti Lung
Chang Cheh bridges Peking Opera drama with his yang gang bloodshed.

New One-Armed Swordsman (1971)
Directed by Chang Cheh
Choreographed by Liu Chia-liang, Tang Chia
Starring David Chiang
Wang Yu out, David Chiang, Ti Lung, and Liu Chia-liang in.

The Water Margin (1972)
Directed by Chang Cheh
Choreographed by Liu Chia-liang, Tang Chia
Starring David Chiang, Ti Lung
Chang Cheh does for wuxia epics what he did for yang gang kung fu.

Fist of Fury (1972)
Directed by Lo Wei
Choreographed by Han Ying-chieh
Starring Bruce Lee
No Dogs or Chinese? Not anymore.

Way of the Dragon (1972)
Directed by Bruce Lee
Choreographed by Bruce Lee
Starring Bruce Lee
The purest Bruce ever.

THE TOP 100 KUNG FU MOVIES 1966 - 2010

INTIMATE CONFESSIONS OF A CHINESE COURTESAN (1972)
Directed by Chu Yuan
Choreographed by Simon Chui Yee-ang
Starring Lily Ho Li-li
Softcore erotica plus cool kung fu equals a unique classic.

ENTER THE DRAGON (1973)
Directed by Robert Clouse
Choreographed by Bruce Lee
Starring Bruce Lee
Real kung fu, meet the world. World, meet real kung fu.

BLOOD BROTHERS (1973)
Directed by Chang Cheh
Choreographed by Liu Chia-liang, Tang Chia
Starring David Chiang, Ti Lung, Chen Kuan-tai
Finally, emotional drama matched up with great screen kung fu.

FIVE SHAOLIN MASTERS (1974)
Directed by Chang Cheh
Choreographed by Liu Chia-liang
Starring David Chiang, Ti Lung, Alexander Fu Sheng
Five times the star power, five times the kung fu goodness.

ALL MEN ARE BROTHERS (1975)
Directed by Chang Cheh
Choreographed by Liu Chia-liang, Tang Chia
Starring David Chiang, Ti Lung
The sequel to The Water Margin completes the sweeping wuxia story.

MASTER OF THE FLYING GUILLOTINE (1976)
Directed by Jimmy Wang Yu

Choreographed by Liu Chia-wing
Starring Jimmy Wang Yu
Tacky, silly, crazy? Yes. Influential and entertaining? Also yes.

THE MAGIC BLADE (1976)
Directed by Chu Yuan
Choreographed by Tang Chia
Starring Ti Lung
The best of Chu Yuan's eastern sword-slinger cliffhangers.

KILLER CLANS (1976)
Directed by Chu Yuan
Choreographed by Tang Chia
Starring Chung Wa
The best of Chu Yuan's convoluted "no-trapdoor-remains-unsprung" thrillers.

EXECUTIONERS FROM SHAOLIN (1977)
Directed by Liu Chia-liang
Choreographed by Liu Chia-liang
Starring Chen Kuan-tai, Lo Lieh
Master Liang's epic story of hung gar's birth (and introduction of the evil Pei Mei).

JUDGMENT OF AN ASSASSIN (1977)
Directed by Sun Chung
Choreographed by Tang Chia
Starring David Chiang
Crackerjack adventure with the best kung fu (but worst wig) David Chiang has ever done (worn).

THE TOP 100 KUNG FU MOVIES 1966 - 2010

36ᵀᴴ CHAMBER OF SHAOLIN (1978)
Directed by Liu Chia-liang
Choreographed by Liu Chia-liang
Starring Gordon Liu Chia-hui
Master Liang's masterful "love story with kung fu."

SHAOLIN MANTIS (1978)
Directed by Liu Chia-liang
Choreographed by Liu Chia-liang
Starring David Chiang
Master Liang's story of mantis style's birth, with nearly the best David Chiang kung fu.

HEROES OF THE EAST (1978)
Directed by Liu Chia-liang
Choreographed by Liu Chia-liang
Starring Gordon Liu Chia-hui
Master Liang's groundbreaking kung fu Kramer vs. Kramer.

FIVE VENOMS (1978)
Directed by Chang Cheh
Choreographed by Lu Feng
Starring Kuo Chui, Chiang Sheng, Lo Mang, Lu Feng, Sun Chien
The first, and many say best, of what were to become known as the Venoms movies.

CRIPPLED AVENGERS (1978)
Directed by Chang Cheh
Choreographed by Lu Feng, Chiang Sheng
Starring Kuo Chui, Chiang Sheng, Lo Mang, Lu Feng, Sun Chien, Chen Kuan-tai
Lively, clever, Venoms follow-up, with arguably their best kung fu.

THE AVENGING EAGLE (1978)
Directed by Sun Chung
Choreographed by Tang Chia
Starring Ti Lung, Alexander Fu Sheng
Sun Chung brings grandeur and superior cinematic mise en scene to his best loved kung fu film.

SNAKE IN THE EAGLE'S SHADOW (1978)
Directed by Yuen Wo-ping
Choreographed by Yuen Wo-ping, Hsu Hsia
Starring Jackie Chan, Simon Yuen
Jackie Chan alerts the film world to his ascension.

DRUNKEN MASTER (1978)
Directed by Yuen Wo-ping
Choreographed by Yuen Wo-ping, Hsu Hsia
Starring Jackie Chan, Simon Yuen
Jackie Chan becomes a superstar with this milestone kung fu comedy.

DIRTY HO (1979)
Directed by Liu Chia-liang
Choreographed by Liu Chia-liang
Starring Gordon Liu Chia-hui, Yung Wang-yu
Unfortunate, misleading title, but superlative kung fu in this class warfare landmark.

MAD MONKEY KUNG FU (1979)
Directed by Liu Chia-liang
Choreographed by Liu Chia-liang
Starring Liu Chia-liang, Hsaio Ho
Master Liang takes center stage in this monkey style showcase.

THE TOP 100 KUNG FU MOVIES 1966 - 2010

KID WITH THE GOLDEN ARM (1979)
Directed by Chang Cheh
Choreographed by Lu Feng,
Starring Kuo Chui, Chiang Sheng, Lo Mang, Lu Feng, Sun Chien
The Venoms make a fun "comic book style" Jiang Hu adventure.

THE MAGNIFICENT BUTCHER (1979)
Directed by Yuen Wo-ping
Choreographed by Yuen Wo-ping, Sammo Hung
Starring Sammo Hung, Kwan Tak-hing
Great Sammo Hung showcase, but it's Master Yuen's Huang Fei-hong scene that makes this eternal.

Knockabout (1979)
Directed by Sammo Hung
Choreographed by Sammo Hung
Starring Yuen Baio, Sammo Hung
The height of Jackie's Peking Opera schoolmates' kung fu comedy film work.

RETURN TO THE 36TH CHAMBER (1980)
Directed by Liu Chia-liang
Choreographed by Liu Chia-liang
Starring Gordon Liu Chia-hui
The love affair with kung fu continues.

CLAN OF THE WHITE LOTUS (1980)
Directed by Lo Lieh
Choreographed by the Liu Chia family
Starring Gordon Liu Chia-hui, Lo Lieh
Influential villain icon Pei Mei returns, along with a wickedly fun "acupuncture-kung-fu" style.

THE MASTER (1980)
Directed by Lu Chin-ku
Choreographed by Hsu Hsia
Starring Chen Kuan-tai, Yuen Tak
Shaw Brothers try their hand at Jackie-style kung fu comedy, with entertaining results.

THE YOUNG MASTER (1980)
Directed by Jackie Chan
Choreographed by Jackie Chan, Fung Hak-on
Starring Jackie Chan
Jackie's ultimate statement in his initial style of kung fu comedy.

ENCOUNTER OF THE SPOOKY KIND (1980)
Directed by Sammo Hung
Choreographed by Sammo Hung, Lam Ching-ying, Yuen Baio
Starring Sammo Hung
Sammo thrillingly combines his best kung fu with China's ornate supernatural mythology.

MY YOUNG AUNTIE (1981)
Directed by Liu Chia-liang
Choreographed by Liu Chia-liang
Starring Kara Hui Ying-hung
Master Liang's kung fu My Fair Lady.

MARTIAL CLUB (1981)
Directed by Liu Chia-liang
Choreographed by Liu Chia-liang
Starring Gordon Liu Chia-hui
Master Liang's crowning Huang Fei-hong achievement.

THE TOP 100 KUNG FU MOVIES 1966 - 2010

MASKED AVENGERS (1981)
Directed by Chang Cheh
Choreographed by Kuo Chui, Lu Feng, Chiang Sheng
Starring Kuo Chui, Chiang Sheng, Lo Mang, Lu Feng, Sun Chien
The Venoms have wicked, bloody good fun with nasty three-bladed tridents.

THE PRODIGAL SON (1981)
Directed by Sammo Hung
Choreographed by Sammo Hung, Yuen Baio, Lam Ching-ying
Starring Yuen Baio, Lam Ching-ying, Frankie Chan
Arguably Sammo Hung's masterpiece, showcasing superlative wing chun.

LEGENDARY WEAPONS OF CHINA (1982)
Directed by Liu Chia-liang
Choreographed by Liu Chia-liang
Starring Liu Chia-liang
Master Liang's quintessential kung fu film, capturing his kung fu at the height of his powers.

FIVE ELEMENT NINJA (1982)
Directed by Chang Cheh
Choreographed by Cheng Tien-chi
Starring Cheng Tien-chi
Chang Cheh's last great, sharply structured, kung fu thriller.

HUMAN LANTERNS (1982)
Directed by Sun Chung
Choreographed by Tang Chia
Starring Chen Kuan-tai, Lo Lieh
Slasher killers plus great kung fu equals the best (and maybe only) of

its kind.

THE SHAOLIN TEMPLE (1982)
Directed by Cheung Yam-yim
Choreographed by Yue Hoi, Ma Yin-tat
Starring Jet Li
Mainland China unbuckles its propaganda straitjacket for their first mainstream kung fu production.

A FISTFUL OF TALONS (1983)
Directed by Sun Chung
Choreographed by Tony Ching Siu-tung
Starring Billy Chong Chuen-lei
Sun Chung's swan song is a suitably imaginative, fast-moving kung fu adventure.

DUEL TO THE DEATH (1983)
Directed by Tony Ching Siu-tung
Choreographed by Tony Ching Siu-tung
Starring Norman Chu, Damian Lau
This tale of Chinese kung fu vs. Japanese cheaters is loads of fast-moving, brain-stretching fun.

PROJECT A (1983)
Directed by Jackie Chan
Choreographed by Jackie Chan, Sammo Hung
Starring Jackie Chan
Jackie drags the period kung fu film, kicking and screaming, into the 20th century.

DISCIPLES OF THE 36TH CHAMBER (1984)
Directed by Liu Chia-liang

THE TOP 100 KUNG FU MOVIES 1966 - 2010

Choreographed by Liu Chia-liang
Starring Hsaio Ho, Gordon Liu Chia-hui
Master Liang's energetic take on the story of Fong Sai-yuk.

EIGHT DIAGRAM POLE FIGHTER (1984)
Directed by Liu Chia-liang
Choreographed by Liu Chia-liang
Starring Gordon Liu Chia-hui
The only Liang film chosen as one of China's Top 100 Films of all time.

OPIUM AND THE KUNG FU MASTER (1984)
Directed by Tang Chia
Choreographed by Tang Chia, Yuen Wah, Yuen Bun, Li Hai-sheng
Starring Ti Lung
Tang Chia's last, and best, film, turns the Cantonese kung fu comedy inside out.

WHEELS ON MEALS (1984)
Directed by Sammo Hung
Choreographed by Chin Kar-lok, Mars
Starring Jackie Chan, Sammo Hung, Yuen Baio
Fun, modern day adventure, highlighted by a classic realistic fight 'tween Jackie and Benny the Jet Urquidez.

SHAOLIN TEMPLE II: KIDS FROM SHAOLIN (1984)
Directed by Cheung Yam-yim
Choreographed by Yue Hoi, Ma Yin-tat
Starring Jet Li
Exceptional kung fu makes up for some creaky silliness.

POLICE STORY (1985)
Directed by Jackie Chan

Choreographed by Jackie Chan Stuntmen Association
Starring Jackie Chan
Jackie drags the modern kung fu film, kicking and screeching, into the 20th century.

YES MADAM (1985)
Directed by Corey Yuen Kwai
Choreographed by Corey Yuen Kwai, Mang Hoi
Starring Michelle Yeoh, Cynthia Rothrock
The creation of the woman wushu warrior with automatic weapons genre.

RIGHTING WRONGS (1986)
Directed by Corey Yuen Kwai
Choreographed by Corey Yuen Kwai, Yuen Baio, Hsu Hsia, Mang Hoi
Starring Yuen Baio, Cynthia Rothrock
Yuen Baio adds his own effort to the list of Hong Kong's finest kung fu thrillers.

MARTIAL ARTS OF SHAOLIN (1986)
Directed by Liu Chia-liang
Choreographed by Liu Chia-liang
Starring Jet Li
Master Liang meets Jet Li in this kung fu lover's magnum opus.

PEKING OPERA BLUES (1986)
Directed by Tsui Hark
Choreographed by Tony Ching Siu-tung
Starring Brigitte Lin, Sally Yeh, Cherie Chung
Tradition-tweaking Tsui delights with this fun feminist adventure.

THE TOP 100 KUNG FU MOVIES 1966 - 2010

A Better Tomorrow (1986)
Directed by John Woo
Choreographed by Stephen Tung Wai
Starring Ti Lung, Chow Yun-fat, Leslie Cheung
Woo explodes the genre with his first great "gun fu" thriller.

A Better Tomorrow II (1987)
Directed by John Woo
Choreographed by Tony Ching Siu-tung
Starring Ti Lung, Chow Yun-fat
Woo discovers that the audience's appetite for extreme gun fu is insatiable.

Project A II (1987)
Directed by Jackie Chan
Choreographed by Jackie Chan Stuntmen Association
Starring Jackie Chan
What many consider Jackie's apex as a director of kung fu adventures.

Eastern Condors (1987)
Directed by Sammo Hung
Choreographed by Sammo Hung, Yuen Baio, Yuen Wah, Corey Yuen Kwai, Hsaio Ho
Starring Sammo Hung, Yuen Baio
Sammo shoots the works in this jumble of almost every modern day war classic.

Police Story 2 (1988)
Directed by Jackie Chan
Choreographed by Jackie Chan Stuntmen Association
Starring Jackie Chan
It's really two movies in one, but both features almost unbelievably fast,

intricate kung fu.

DRAGONS FOREVER (1988)
Directed by Sammo Hung
Choreographed by Sammo Hung Stuntmen Association, Jackie Chan Stuntmen Association
Starring Jackie Chan, Sammo Hung, Yuen Baio
The last of the "Three Brothers" films, with nearly every kung fu actor they could fit.

TIGER ON BEAT (1988)
Directed by Liu Chia-liang
Choreographed by the Liu Chia Family
Starring Conan Lee, Chow Yun-fat
Master Liang tries his hand at "gun fu," with some of his superlative kung fu thrown in.

PEDICAB DRIVER (1989)
Directed by Sammo Hung
Choreographed by Sammo Hung Stuntmen Association
Starring Sammo Hung
The best of Sammo's "dark period" kung fu thrillers.

THE KILLER (1989)
Directed by John Woo
Choreographed by Tony Ching Siu-tung
Starring Chow Yun-fat, Danny Lee, Sally Yeh
Woo raises the cinematic standard of gun fu with this smart, visually thrilling masterpiece.

GOD OF GAMBLERS (1989)
Directed by Wong Jing

THE TOP 100 KUNG FU MOVIES 1966 - 2010

Choreographed by Paul Wong Kwan
Starring Chow Yun-fat, Andy Lau, Joey Wong
Schlockmeister Wong Jing finally gets one right, thanks to Chow's superlative performance.

BULLET IN THE HEAD (1990)
Directed by John Woo
Choreographed by Lau Chi-ho
Starring Tony Leung, Jacky Cheung, Waise Lee
Woo's gun fu Apocalypse Now meets Deer Hunter ... which is as intense as it sounds.

ONCE UPON A TIME IN CHINA (1991)
Directed by Tsui Hark
Choreographed by the Yuen Family
Starring Jet Li
Wong Fei-hung, and Jet Li's career, is revived in this excellent effort.

POLICE STORY 3: SUPERCOP (1992)
Directed by Stanley Tong
Choreographed by Mak Wai-cheung, Stanley Tong
Starring Jackie Chan, Michelle Yeoh
Jackie finally lets a woman make equal time.

ONCE UPON A TIME IN CHINA II (1992)
Directed by Tsui Hark
Choreographed by Yuen Wo-ping
Starring Jet Li, Donnie Yen
Tsui gets the balance of action, comedy, romance, and politics exactly right.

Full Contact (1992)
Directed by Ringo Lam
Choreographed by Liu Chia-wing
Starring Chow Yun-fat, Simon Yam
Lam's best gun fu effort, with exceptional performances by Chow, Yam, and Anthony Wong.

Hard Boiled (1992)
Directed by John Woo
Choreographed by Kuo Chui
Starring Chow Yun-fat, Tony Leung
Woo says so long to Hong Kong (for now) with this satisfying gun fu extravaganza.

The Heroic Trio (1993)
Directed by Johnnie To, Tony Ching Siu-tung
Choreographed by Tony Ching Siu-tung
Starring Anita Mui, Maggie Cheung, Michelle Yeoh
The best woman wushu warrior comic book adventure Marvel Comics never made.

The Bride with White Hair (1993)
Directed by Ronny Yu
Choreographed by Kuo Chui
Starring Brigitte Lin, Leslie Cheung
Swooningly romantic, emotionally thrilling wuxia.

Iron Monkey (1993)
Directed by Yuen Wo-ping
Choreographed by Yuen Wo-ping
Starring Donnie Yen
Master Yuen makes the best "wire-work" kung fu film (so far).

THE TOP 100 KUNG FU MOVIES 1966 - 2010

FIST OF LEGEND (1994)
Directed by Gordon Chan
Choreographed by Yuen Wo-ping
Starring Jet Li, Billy Chow
Jet Li cinematically captures his kung fu at its height.

DRUNKEN MASTER II (1994)
Directed by Liu Chia-liang, Jackie Chan
Choreographed by Liu Chia-liang, Jackie Chan Stuntmen Association
Starring Jackie Chan
Jackie's kung fu masterpiece (so far).

ASHES OF TIME (1994)
Directed by Wong Kar-wai
Choreographed by Sammo Hung
Starring Leslie Cheung, Tony Leung, Brigitte Lin, Jacky Cheung
Kung fu returns to the art film realm.

THE BLADE (1995)
Directed by Tsui Hark
Choreographed by Stephen Tung Wai, Mang Hoi, Yuen Bun
Starring Vincent Zhao
Tsui's masterful remake of The One-Armed Swordsman.

THE TAICHI MASTER AKA MASTER OF TAICHI (1997)
Directed by Yuen Wo-ping, Cheung Sing-yim
Choreographed by Yuen Wo-ping, Yuen Cheung-yan
Starring Jacky Wu Jing, Billy Chow
TV movie, yes. Best taichi and baqua ever filmed (so far)? Yes.

THE MATRIX (1999)
Directed by the Wachowskis

Choreographed by Yuen Wo-ping
Starring Keanu Reaves, Laurence Fishburne
White men can't jump, or really do balanced kung fu ... or can they?

CROUCHING TIGER HIDDEN DRAGON (2000)
Directed by Ang Lee
Choreographed by Yuen Wo-ping
Starring Chow Yun-fat, Michelle Yeoh, Zhang Ziyi
Ang caps wuxia films with a simple, now obvious, conceit: his characters' bodies are doing what their hearts cannot.

SHAOLIN SOCCER (2001)
Directed by Stephen Chow
Choreographed by Tony Ching Siu-tung
Starring Stephen Chow, Vicky Zhao Wei
A riotous comedy, and a charming showcase of kung fu's possible contribution to the world.

HERO (2002)
Directed by Zhang Yimou
Choreographed by Tony Ching Siu-tung
Starring Jet Li, Tony Leung, Maggie Cheung, Zhang Ziyi, Chen Dao-ming
A cinematic masterwork of color and meaning that accurately compares kung fu to music, calligraphy, art, writing, creativity, and nature.

KUNG FU HUSTLE (2004)
Directed by Stephen Chow
Choreographed by Yuen Wo-ping, Sammo Hung
Starring Stephen Chow
Chow's love letter to kung fu, and kung fu movies (that most westerners haven't seen).

THE TOP 100 KUNG FU MOVIES 1966 - 2010

SHA PO LANG (2005)
Directed by Wilson Yip
Choreographed by Donnie Yen
Starring Donnie Yen, Sammo Hung, Wu Jing
Donnie adds ground fighting to kung fu's cinematic arsenal.

FEARLESS (2006)
Directed by Ronny Yu
Choreographed by Yuen Wo-ping
Starring Jet Li
Jet's version of Clint Eastwood's Unforgiven: putting his previous vengeance-fueled films in context.

KUNG FU PANDA (2008)
Directed by John Stevenson, Mark Osborne
Choreographed by Jen Yuh Nelson, Simon Wells, Rodolphe Guenoden
Starring Jack Black, Dustin Hoffman
Quite simply, the best American kung fu film of all time (so far). Everything, especially the kung fu, is on the money.

IP MAN (2008)
Directed by Wilson Yip
Choreographed by Sammo Hung
Starring Donnie Yen, Louis Fan
Donnie finds his serene center by playing one of history's best wing chun teachers.

RED CLIFF (2008-2009)
Directed by John Woo
Choreographed by Corey Yuen Kwai
Starring Tony Leung, Kaneshiro Takeshi

Woo can go home again with this epic, kung fu-filled, visualization of one of China's greatest battles.

BODYGUARDS AND ASSASSINS (2009)
Directed by Teddy Chen
Choreographed by Stephen Tung Wai, Lee Tat-chiu
Starring Donnie Yen, Leon Lai
Brutal, tragic, powerful tale of sacrifice and patriotism.

TRUE LEGEND (2010)
Directed by Yuen Wo-ping,
Choreographed by Yuen Wo-ping
Starring Vincent Zhao
Fragmented, sure, but brimming with Master Yuen's kung fu brilliance.

REIGN OF ASSASSINS (2010)
Directed by Su Chao-pin, John Woo
Choreographed by Stephen Tung Wai
Starring Michelle Yeoh
Woo cements his, and Yeoh's, comeback with this delightful, period, kung fu Mr. & Mrs. Smith.

SHAOLIN (2010)
Directed by Benny Chan
Choreographed by Corey Yuen Kwai, Yuen Tak
Starring Andy Lau, Nicholas Tse, Jacky Wu Jing, Jackie Chan
The actual Shaolin Temple gave its blessing, and contributed its expertise, to this tale of might vs. right.

Selected Index

Symbols

3 Ninjas 247
14 Blades 110, 307
36 Deadly Styles, The 157
36th Chamber of Shaolin 95, 96, 121, 244
48 Hours 266
430 Space Shuttle 308
1941 28, 104, 109

A

Abdul Jabbar, Kareem 57
Above the Law 179, 262, 263, 265
Accidental Spy, The 149
Aces Go Places 164
Adventures of Fong Sai-yuk, The 30
aikido 92, 241, 262, 263, 264, 265, 266, 267, 283
Airport 252
All About Ah-long 237
All About Women 261
Allen, Woody 144, 271
All for the Winner 309
Allin, Michael 52
All Men Are Brothers 80, 156, 317
Amos and Andy 164
Anderson, Paul 272
Angel 182, 183, 184, 185
Angel 3 183
Angel Force 183
Angels 2 183
Angel Terminators 2 183
Angry River, The 173

Animal House 107
Anonymous Heroes, The 79
Apocalypse Now 140, 329
Armour of God 134, 135, 136, 138, 140, 181
Armstrong, Vic 191
Around the World in 80 Days 150
Ashes of Time 166, 176, 331
Ashley, Ted 52, 55
Assassination of General Ma, The 80
Assassin, The 77
Astaire, Fred 34, 50, 63, 314
A Touch of Zen 34, 35, 160, 279, 315
Attack of the Clones 273
Attack of the Joyful Goddess 88
Avenging Eagle, The 109, 112, 320
Avildsen, John 253

B

Bad Boys II 132
Baird, Stuart 266
Baker, Joe Don 244
Ballistic Kiss 301
Balsam, Martin 252
baqua 89, 331
Bare-Footed Kid, The 237
Barnes, Reggie 269
Barr, James 66
Barron, Steven 269
Barry, John 134
Barrymore, Drew 274
Ba Sen Zha-bu 292
Basic Instinct 263
Bastard Swordsman 110, 111, 188, 254

Batman 23, 43, 44, 147, 277, 305
Bay, Michael 132
Beach of the War Gods 77
Beauty Investigator 182
Belly of the Beast 267
Berkeley, Busby 203
Berkley, Busby 110
Berry, Halle 191
Besson, Luc 217, 274
Better Tomorrow, A 205, 230, 231, 232, 233, 234, 235, 236, 237, 327
Big and Little Wong Tin Bar 117
Big Boss, The 46, 47, 48, 58, 158, 161
Big Brawl, The 126, 128, 131, 245
Big Bullet, The 301
Big Heat, The 237
Billy Jack 240, 243, 266
Birth of a Man 40
Bishop, Joey 252
Black Belt Jones 244
Black Belt Theater 74
Black Cat 184, 185
Black Dynamite 291
Black Eagle 256
Blackman, Honor 190
Black Mask 214, 215, 261
Black Rose 2 301
Blade 272, 302, 303, 331
Blazing Saddles 241
Blazing Temple, The 157
Blonde Fury 183
Blood and Bone 288, 290, 291
Blood Brothers 222, 227, 229
Blood Brothers, The 80, 317
Blood on the Sun 243
Bloodsport 256, 257, 260, 262

Bloody Fights 30
Bloody Fists, The 80
Bloom, Orlando 292
Boat People 189
Bodyguard 211, 305
Bodyguard From Beijing, The 211
Bodyguards and Assassins 307
Bond, James 52, 58, 134, 136, 174, 190, 216, 243, 277, 310, 312
Bong Soo Han 243, 245
Bonnie and Clyde 75, 231
Borgnine, Ernest 66
Born Losers, The 243
Born to Defense 202, 203, 204, 212
Bourbon Street Beat 44
Bow Sim-mak 297
Boxer from Shantung, The 80
Boyle, Danny 195
Brave Archer 82, 83
Brave Archer and his Mate, The 83
Breaker Breaker 248
Breakout from Oppression 104
Bride of Chucky 176
Bride With White Hair 170, 176, 221
Broken Arrow 259
Brosnan, Pierce 190, 191, 277
Brown, David 246
Brynner, Yul 244
Buddhism 22
Buddhist Fist, The 155
Burning of the Red Lotus Temple, The 29
Burton, Tim 277
Bury Me High 183
Busey, Gary 265
Butterfly Murders, The 205, 279
Butterfly Sword 187

Selected Index

C

Cagney, Jimmy 81, 243
Call of the Nightbirds, The 78
Cameron, James 213
Cannonball Run, The 126, 129, 130
Carpenter, John 254
Carradine, David 55, 240, 251, 275, 290
Carrey, Jim 310
Cat vs. Rat 104, 105, 135
Challenge of the Masters 93, 100, 119, 175, 244
Challenger, The 134
Challenge, The 93, 97, 100, 119, 175, 244, 262
Chambers, Terry 248
Champions, The 182
Chan, Benny 301
Chan, Danny 312
Chan, David 140
Chan, Frankie 181, 323
Chang Chan-peng 104, 105
Chang Cheh 73, 75, 76, 77, 78, 79, 80, 82, 83, 84, 86, 87, 88, 89, 90, 91, 98, 107, 112, 113, 119, 121, 131, 172, 173, 175, 221, 222, 227, 229, 231, 233, 235, 244, 276, 315, 316, 317, 319, 321, 323
Chang Ho-cheng 73, 76
Chang Hsin-yen 200
Chan, Gordon 212, 305, 331
Chang, Terence 189
Chang Yi 158
Chan, Jackie 49, 55, 64, 71, 73, 74, 109, 110, 116, 117, 123, 133, 140, 144, 146, 148, 149, 150, 151, 152, 154, 155, 159, 160, 161, 162, 166, 175, 178, 181, 182, 186, 187, 190, 191, 192, 199, 204, 214, 215, 216, 234, 243, 245, 249, 268, 273, 274, 275, 292, 295, 298, 299, 302, 303, 304, 307, 310, 320, 322, 324, 325, 326, 327, 328, 329, 331
Chan, Peter 227
Chan Po-chu, Connie 171
Chan Wai-lau 124
Chan, Willie 118, 123, 214
Chan Wui-ngai 160
Charlieís Angels 182, 274
Charlie's Angels 191
Cheetah on Fire 299
Chen Chi-hwa 119
Chen, Eric 282, 289
Cheng, Ekin 303
Cheng Pei-pei 172, 194, 315
Cheng Shao-chiu, Adam 104
Cheng Tien-chi 88, 227, 323
Chen Kuan-tai 79, 85, 92, 93, 94, 113, 158, 175, 293, 317, 318, 319, 322, 323
Chen, William C.C. 313
Chen Zhen 48, 49, 212, 220, 307
Cheung, Adam 205, 208
Cheung, Jackie 214
Cheung, Jacky 226, 234, 329, 331
Cheung, John 64
Cheung, Leslie 230, 235, 327, 330, 331
Cheung, Maggie 133, 138, 142, 170, 187, 218, 330
Chiang Chuan 112
Chiang, David 70, 73, 78, 81, 82, 84, 88, 96, 97, 112, 134, 175, 206, 233, 309, 316, 317, 318, 319

Chiang Kai-shek 29
Chiang Sheng 84, 88, 319, 321, 323
Chiang Wing-fat 124
Chiba, Shinichi 275
Chieh Yuan 61
Chien Tien-chi 87
Chi Hon Joi 57
Chi Kuan-chun 70, 81, 82, 88
Chinatown Kid, The 82, 131
Chinese Boxer, The 70, 77, 120, 315
Chinese Connection 2 158
Chinese Feast, The 310
Chinese Ghost Story, A 205, 267
Chinese Gung-Fu\
The Philosophical Art of Self-Defense 43
Chinese Odyssey, A 310
Chinese Zodiac 152
Ching Chia 101
Chingmy Yau 185
Ching Siu-tung 110, 186, 188, 205, 207, 215, 219, 267, 305, 324, 326, 327, 328, 330
Chin Kar-lok 138, 139, 165, 325
Chin Tsi-ang 171
Chiu Chi-ling 312
Chi Wai-chiang 269
Choi, Charlene 303
Choi Nam-ip 269
Cho, Margaret 55
Chong, Billy 109, 324
Chou, Collin 305
Chou, Jay 296
Chow, Billy 138, 184, 198, 213, 294, 331
Chow, Raymond 46, 47, 53, 58, 60, 61, 73, 173

Chow, Stephen 204, 233, 275, 288, 308, 310, 313, 332
Chow Yun-fat 178, 193, 226, 227, 230, 231, 232, 234, 235, 236, 291, 309, 327, 328, 329, 330, 332
choy li fut 89
Chung Chor-hung, Cherie 175
Chung, David 177
Chung, Gillian 303
Chungking Express 176
Chu, Norman 134, 188, 324
Chu, Paul 78
Chu Yen-ping, Kevin 175
Chu Yuan 104, 107, 109, 132, 137, 194, 254, 317, 318
Cinema City 230
Circus Kids 301
City Hunter 143, 245
City on Fire 236
Clan of the White Lotus 101, 321
Clouse, Robert 52, 61, 126, 244, 317
Cobb, Melissa 279
Cobo de Garcia, Eva 141
Code of Silence 251, 252, 263
Cohen, Rob 62
Come Drink with Me 172, 315
Concord Productions 50, 52
Confucianism 22
Confucius 22, 23
Connery, Sean 136, 216, 243, 295
Contract, The 229
Convoy 248
Cool Breeze 263
Cool Hand Luke 142
Coppola, Francis Ford 139, 215, 233
Corsican Brothers, The 143

Selected Index

Costner, Kevin 149, 211
Cradle 2 the Grave 217
Crane, Simon 277
Crime Story 143, 144
Crippled Avengers 85, 319
Crosby, Bing 104
Crow, The 38, 64, 66, 67
Crystal, Billy 165
Crystal Fist 110
Crystal Hunt 299
Cung Le 295, 307
Curse of the Golden Flower 219, 227, 292
Cuse, Carleton 166
Cyborg 256

D

Dacascos, Mark 273
Damaschke, Bill 279
Dance of the Drunken Mantis 155
Dancing Warrior 88
Danger Girl 191
Dangerous Encounters of the First Kind 205
Daredevils, The 85
Darker Than Amber 52, 53, 55
Davis, Andrew 262, 265, 266
Davis, Andy 251, 252
Dawson, Kim 269
Dead and the Deadly, The 154, 162
Dead End 79
Deadful Melody 176, 313
Deadly Breaking Sword, The 109
Deadly Mantis. *See* Shaolin Mantis
Dean, James 81
Death Warrant 257

Death Wish 179
Deer Hunter, The 163, 329
Delon, Alain 231
Delta Force, The 252, 253, 255, 268
Departed, The 237
Destroyer, The 249, 250
Detective Dee and the Mystery of the Phantom Flame 261
Development Hell 307
Diamonds Are Forever 216
Die Another Day 191
Die Hard 214, 231, 256, 260, 265, 266
Die Hard II 231
Ding Lan 200
Dirty Dozen, The 142, 163, 252
Dirty Harry 68, 235, 250
Dirty Ho 70, 99, 100, 120, 320
Dirty Kung Fu 159
Dirty Tiger, Crazy Frog 165
DiSalle, Mark 256
Disciples of Shaolin 91
Disciples of the 36th Chamber 107, 324
Djeng, Frank 308
Do Do Cheng 141
Dong Zhihua 312
Donner, Richard 216
Don't Give a Damn 164, 166
Double Impact 257, 258, 261
Double Team 261
Dozier, William 43
Dragon 38, 40, 55, 59, 63, 65, 73, 82, 90, 119, 120, 127, 128, 130, 133, 160, 162, 165, 171, 176, 177, 192, 204, 217, 218, 222, 241, 254, 273, 282, 283, 284, 295, 300, 302, 304, 306, 309,

Dragons Forever 138, 139, 164, 165, 212, 213, 245, 328
Dragon Tiger Gate 305
Dreadnaught 18, 156, 270
Drunken Fist Boxing 174
Drunken Monkey 116, 121, 145, 294
Drunken Monkey in a Tiger's Eye 116, 121
Drunken Tai Chi 157, 298, 300
Dr. Wai in the Scripture With No Words 215
Duel, The 79
Duel to the Death 267, 324
Dumbo 249
Dynaman 271

E

Eagle's Claw 158
Eastern Condors 163, 213, 327
Eastman, Kevin 269
Eastwood, Clint 108, 131, 140, 248, 255
Eat Drink Man Woman 192
Ebert, Roger 67, 194
Eight Diagram Pole Fighter 105, 325
Eighteen Darts, The 117
Eight Taels of Gold 165
Election 237
Election 2 237
Electric Dreams 269
El Mechri, Mabrouk 261
Emery, Linda 43
Empire Strikes Back, The 273
Empress and the Warriors, An 305
Encounters of the Spooky Kind 162, 165

Endoso, Kenny 254
Enforcer, The 250
Enter the Dragon 20, 33, 52, 55, 56, 57, 58, 61, 118, 161, 174, 242, 244, 245, 247, 256, 317
Executioners 94, 95, 101, 175, 187, 276, 318
Executioners from Shaolin 94–95, 101, 175, 276, 318
Executioners of Death 94
Executive Decision 266
Exiled 237
Exit the Dragon 59, 158
Exit the Dragon, Enter the Tiger 59
Exit Wounds 267
Expendables, The 222, 275
Eye for an Eye, An 250

F

Face/Off 259
Fan Mei-sheng 156, 296
Fan Siu-Wong 296
Fantasy Mission Force 130, 175
Farley, Chris 247
Fast Sword, The 160
Fast Times at Ridgemont High 310
Fatal Chase 182
Fatal Contact 295
Fatal Move 295
Fatal Needles vs. Fatal Fists 158
Fatal Termination 183
Fate of Lee Khan, The 160, 174
Fearless 123, 130, 220, 222, 305, 306
Fearless Hyena 123, 130
Few Dollars More, A 250
Fight Back to School 310

Selected Index

Fighting Fool 110
Final Destination 217
Final Judgment 309
Fire Down Below 267
Firewalker 252
First Strike 148
Fishburne, Laurence 273, 332
Fistful of Dollars, A 108, 250
Fistful of Talons, A 109, 324
Fist of Fury 48, 50, 55, 58, 77, 118, 119, 211, 212, 231, 301, 307, 309, 316
Fist of Legend 198, 212, 213, 227, 307, 331
Fists and Guts 159
Fists The Kicks and The Evils, The 312
Five Element Ninja 87, 227, 323
Five Fingers of Death 73, 289
Five Masters of Death 81, 83
Five Shaolin Masters 81
Five Super Fighters 110
Five Venoms, The. *See* Five Deadly Venoms
Flash Legs 91
Flash Point 305
Flying Guillotine, The 76
Fong, Mona 91, 113
Fong Sai-yuk 30, 32, 34, 107, 198, 295, 325
Fong Sai Yuk 208
Forbidden Kingdom 20, 150, 222, 277, 284
Force Five 245
Force of One, A 249
Ford, Clarence 185
Ford, Harrison 266
Forest Warrior 253

Forster, Robert 252
Forsythe, William 264
Founding of a Republic, The 151
Frand, Harvey 55
Freddy vs. Jason 176
Free Willy 274
Friedlander, Howard 54
From Beijing with Love 310
From Riches to Rags 230
From Russia with Love 243
Fugitive, The 266
Full Contact 226, 236, 330
Fu Manchu 52, 254
Fung Hak-on 132, 154, 181, 293, 312, 322
Fung Hark-on 138
Fung, Stephen 304
Fun the Luck and the Tycoon, The 237
Fu Sheng, Alexander 70, 81, 82, 83, 84, 86, 103, 104, 105, 106, 109, 119, 317, 320
Future X Cops 296

G

Game of Death 57, 58, 59, 61, 62, 67, 123, 124, 158, 214, 276, 294
Games Gamblers Play 229
Garner, James 45
Genghis Khan 24
Ghostbusters 310
Ghost Punting 165
Gibson, Mel 132, 216
Gidget 243
Gillard, Nick 274
Glickenhaus, James 131

Glimmer Man, The 266
Globus, Yoram 246, 247
Glover, Danny 216
Glover, Mary 39
Godenzi, Joyce Mina 163
Godfather, The 76, 89, 139
God of Cookery 310
God of Gamblers 226, 236, 309, 328
Godsick, Chris 189
Golan, Monachem 246, 252
GoldenEye 191, 277
Golden Gate Girl 39
Golden Harvest 46, 48, 50, 56, 61, 62, 73, 74, 77, 121, 123, 124, 125, 126, 127, 130, 135, 142, 155, 173, 229, 230, 268
Golden Needles 244
Golden Swallow 172
Golden Swallow, The 77
Golden Sword, The 172
Goldfinger 190
Goldman, Gary 254
Gong Li 195
Good Guys Wear Black 248, 249
Good, the Bad, and the Ugly, The 251
Gorgeous 149
Gosha, Hideo 244
Gossett Jr., Louis 252
Goyokin 244
Green Hornet 43, 44, 45, 46
Grey, Joel 249
Grier, Pam 263
Guenoden, Rodolphe 281
Gu Long 108
gyonshi 162

H

Hackman, Gene 265
Half a Loaf of Kung Fu 120
Half Past Dead 267
Hall, Arsenio 167
Hand of Death 118, 229
Hang 'Em High 248
Han Ying-chieh 47, 48, 53, 161, 315, 316
hapkido 57, 147, 159, 174
Hard Boiled 226, 235, 236, 259, 330
Hard Target 258, 259
Hard to Kill 263, 264
He Has Nothing But Kung Fu 159
Hellbound 253
Heller, Paul 52
Henriksen, Lance 259
Henson, Jim 269, 278
Herbeck, Bobby 269
Hero 87, 198, 207, 218, 219, 220, 241, 252, 259, 262, 275, 292, 300, 302, 303
Heroes of the East 97, 121, 122, 319
Heroes Shed No Tears 104, 230
Heroic Ones, The 175
Heroic Trio, The 170, 186, 187, 237, 330
Highlander 272, 302
High Risk 214, 215
High Voltage 301
Himalayan, The 174
Hiroyuki Sanada 177
Hitman 216, 253, 263
Holy Flame of the Martial World 110
Holy Virgin vs. the Evil Dead 299
Holy Weapon 192
Ho Meng-hua 76, 172

Selected Index

Hope, Bob 81, 103, 104
Ho Si-kit 30
Ho Sun-park 145
Hot Potato 245
Ho Tsung-tao 59
Hot The Cool and The Vicious, The 158
House of Flying Daggers 219, 292
House of Fury 304
House of Traps 87
Houston, Whitney 211
How Huang Fei Hong Vanquished the Twelve Lions 33
How Wu Song Killed His Sister-in-Law 30
Hsaio Ho 99, 100, 101, 103, 105, 107, 163, 320, 325, 327
Hsia Kuang-li 174
Hsu Feng 174. See Xu Feng
Hsu Hsia 128, 179, 320, 322, 326
Huang, Eva 312
Huang Fei-hong. See Wong Fei-hung
Huang Fei Hong Bravely Crushing the Fire Formation 80
Huang Fei Hong Vied for the Firecrackers at Huadi 33
Huang Feng 173, 174
Huang Hsing-hsiu 96
Huang Jang-li 61, 121, 122, 155
Huang Kin-lung 60
Huang Pei-chi 112
Hu Chien-chiang 200
Hudson, Ernie 66
Hui, Ann 189
Hui. Michael 126, 229
Hui, Ricky 230
Hui Ying-hung 99, 100, 101, 103, 105, 106, 173, 174, 322

Hu, Kelly 167
Hulette, Don 248
Human Lanterns 109, 323
hung gar 40, 89, 94, 95, 122, 162, 188, 213, 318
Hung Gar 27, 31
Hung His-kuan 94
Hung, Jackson 159
Hung, Sammo 49, 56, 118, 129, 130, 138, 142, 154, 155, 159, 162, 166, 172, 173, 179, 180, 182, 189, 204, 209, 215, 270, 274, 288, 293, 296, 298, 299, 303, 304, 306, 311, 321, 322, 323, 324, 325, 327, 328, 331
Huo Yuan-jia 48, 220
Hu Peng 30
Hurt, John 165

I

Ice Storm, The 192
I Kuang 48, 76, 113
Infernal Affairs 237
Inosanto, Daniel 49, 57
Inoue Umetsugu 172
Inspector Wears Skirts, The 181, 183
In the Line of Duty 4 186
In the Line of Duty 5 186
In the Line of Duty IV 299
Intimate Confessions of a Chinese Courtesan 108, 317
Invasion U.S.A. 252
Invincible Kung fu Legs, The 174
Invincible, The 60, 174
Invisible Target 295
Ip Man 20, 242, 288, 306, 307
Ip Man 2 20, 288, 307

Iron Chef America 273
Iron Giant 111
Iron Monkey 275, 300, 330
Ironside 45
Island of Fire 142

J

Jaa, Tony 288, 307
Jackie Brown 263, 275
Jackie Chan and the Kung Fu Kid 151
Jackie Chan Kung Fu Master 151
Jackson, Samuel L. 290
Jade Jungle, The 250
Japan 26, 28, 98, 127, 133, 139, 146, 182, 212, 228, 270, 280
Jaws 246
JCVD 261
jeet kune do 63, 119, 122, 245
Jeet Kune Do 44, 45
Jesus Christ Superstar 120
Jiang Hu 23, 76, 98, 108, 150, 176, 321
Ji Chun-hua 208
Johnson, Pat 269
Jones, Chuck 283
Jones, Tommy Lee 265, 266
Journey to the West 25, 29, 313
Judge Pao 87
Judgment of An Assassin 109
judo 98, 159, 241, 243
Jumping Ash 172
Just Heroes 233, 309
Justice My Foot 237, 310

K

Kage No Gunden 276
Kamen, Robert Mark 253
Kao Fei 106, 112, 134, 138, 158, 163
karate 77, 92, 98, 147, 159, 212, 217, 241, 243, 246, 248, 249, 252, 253, 257, 262, 273, 281, 297, 310
Karate Kid, The 151, 253, 254, 255, 269
Kato 43, 44, 51, 214, 307
Katzenberg, Jeffrey 278
Keaton, Buster 129, 137, 139
Kelly, Gene 34, 125, 139, 314
Kelly, Jim 53, 158, 244, 245
Kennedy, George 252
Khmara, Edward 64
Kickboxer 182, 184, 257
Kickboxer's Tears 182
kick-boxing 140, 213, 241, 257
Kid with a Tattoo, The 109
Kid With the Golden Arm, The 85
Kill Bill 275, 276, 290
Killer Angels 183
Killer Clans 108, 318
Killer Meteor 119
Killer, The 108, 119, 183, 185, 232, 237, 318, 328
Kim Tai-chung 61
Kindergarten Cop 310
King Boxer 70, 73
King Hu 34, 35, 47, 160, 172, 174, 194, 207, 279, 315
King of Beggars 310
King of Comedy, The 311
Kissinger, Henry 199
Knock Off 261
Kosugi, Sho 256

Selected Index

Ku Feng 112, 158, 176
Kuhn, Tom 54
Ku Ming 106
Kung Fu Chefs 296
Kung Fu Cult Master 209
Kung Fu Fighter 296
Kung Fu from Beyond the Grave 110
Kung Fu Hustle 288, 311–313, 332
Kung Fu Instructor, The 109
Kungfu Master, The 301
Kung Fu Panda 151, 241, 272, 278–286, 333
Kung Fu: The Movie 65
Kung Fu (TV series) 54
Kung Fu Warlords 83
Kung Fu Zombie 110
Kuo Chui 70, 82, 84, 85, 86, 87, 226, 319, 321, 323, 330
Kuo Nam-hung, Joseph 157
Kwan, Rosamund 135, 206, 215
Kwan Tak-hing 18, 31, 50, 89, 90, 121, 156, 221, 321

L

Lady Assassin, The 110
Lady is the Boss, The 105
Lady Kung Fu 173
Lady of Steel 172
Lady Snowblood 276
Lady Swordfighter of Jiangnan, The 171
Lady Warriors of the Yang Family 181
Lady Whirlwind 173
La Femme Nikita 184
Laird, Peter 269
Lam Chi-chung 312
Lam Ching-ying 154, 160, 161, 162, 322, 323
Lam, Ringo 142, 236, 261, 330
Lam Sai-wing 89
Lao-tze 22
Lao-tzu 283
Laser Mission 65
Last Hurrah for Chivalry 229
La Totale 213
Lau, Andrew 236
Lau, Andy 142, 144, 183, 236, 288, 296, 329
Laughing Times 230
Laughlin, Tom 240, 243
Lau, Jeffrey 309
Lauren, Tammy 167
Lau Shing-fung 185
Lawrence of Arabia 241
Lawton, J.F. 265
Lazenby, George 58, 77, 136, 174, 251, 295
Lee, Ang 192, 194, 332
Lee, Brandon 38, 64, 89, 272
Lee, Bruce 20, 31, 38, 39, 41, 42, 44, 45, 46, 48, 50, 52, 53, 54, 55, 56, 57, 58, 59, 60, 61, 62, 63, 64, 65, 66, 68, 71, 73, 75, 77, 91, 92, 110, 113, 117, 118, 119, 120, 122, 123, 124, 126, 131, 139, 140, 143, 152, 155, 158, 160, 161, 174, 180, 181, 192, 199, 202, 211, 214, 221, 231, 236, 243, 248, 251, 275, 282, 283, 294, 297, 301, 306, 307, 308, 309, 312, 315, 316, 317
Lee Choi-fong, Moon 182
Lee, Conan 254, 328
Lee, Daniel 214

Lee, Danny 60, 233, 309, 328
Lee Gam-ming, Tommy 158
Lee Hoi-chuen 39
Lee, Jason Scott 38, 63
Lee Jun-fan 39
Lee, Linda 53, 62
Lee, Moon 154, 182, 188, 205
Lee, Raymond 207
Lee Tso-nam 158
Lee, Waise 226, 234, 329
Lee Yuen-kam 39
Legacy of Rage 65
Legendary Weapons of Kung Fu 102
Legend of the Fist 307
Legend of the Seven Golden Vampires, The 73
Legend of the Wolf 301
Legend of Zu 261, 294
Leg Fighters, The 91, 174
Leon 310
Leone, Sergio 206, 233, 250
Lepke 263
Lethal Weapon 216, 217, 218, 262
Lethal Weapon 2 216
Lethal Weapon 3 216
Lethal Weapon 4 216, 218
Lettich, Sheldom 258
Lettich, Sheldon 257
Leung, Jade 184
Leung Siu-lung, Bruce 158, 312
Leung, Tony 218, 226, 234, 235, 291, 329, 330, 331
Leung Wing-hang 33
Lewis, Joe 43, 245
Libby, Brian 250
Li Hai-sheng 18, 96, 112, 125, 129, 154, 158, 176, 229, 325

Li Han-hsiang 76
Li Hsui-hsien 60
Li, Jet 20, 112, 143, 150, 188, 193, 198, 199, 201, 205, 206, 207, 209, 210, 214, 216, 217, 222, 223, 227, 242, 261, 263, 273, 275, 293, 294, 295, 297, 300, 305, 306, 307, 309, 324, 325, 326, 329, 331
Li, Lily 94, 106, 125, 134, 173, 174
Li Mei 75
Lin, Brigitte 133, 170, 175, 326, 330, 331
Ling Gar 27, 188
Li, Nina 218
lion dancing 30, 32
Lionheart 258
Lion in Winter 219
Little Tiger of Canton, The 118
Liu Chia-hui 70, 96, 97, 99, 101, 102, 103, 106, 145, 202, 244, 275, 319, 320, 321, 322, 325. *See* Liu, Gordon
Liu Chia-liang 70, 89, 91, 92, 94, 96, 98, 103, 105, 106, 107, 109, 112, 113, 119, 120, 121, 122, 131, 135, 142, 144, 155, 156, 165, 175, 177, 199, 200, 203, 205, 227, 229, 244, 254, 292, 294, 315, 316, 317, 318, 319, 320, 321, 322, 323, 324, 325, 326, 328, 331
Liu Chia-yung 70, 93, 97, 104, 105, 138, 163
Liu, Gordon 93, 95, 97, 99, 101, 103, 104, 113, 145, 202, 244, 275, 290, 295, 319, 320, 321, 322, 325
Liu Tak Wai 270

Selected Index

Liu Yung 111
Liu Zhan 89
Li Yi-min 157
Lloyd, Harold 129
Lock, Stock, and Two Smoking Barrels 275
Lo, Ken 141, 145, 310
Loke Wan Tho 71
Lo Lieh 70, 73, 75, 94, 100, 101, 113, 158, 276, 318, 321, 323
Lo Mang 70, 82, 84, 87, 88, 293, 319, 321, 323
Lo Mar 60, 110
Lone Wolf McQuade 240, 250, 253
Longest Yard, The 142
Long Kwan-wu, Mark 157
Long Sai-ga, Jack 157
Longstreet 45
Looking for Jackie 151
Loot, The 134
Lord of the Rings 292
Lost Bladesman, The 307
Love on a Diet 237
Lo Wai-kwong 124
Lo Wei 46, 48, 98, 118, 119, 120, 121, 123, 124, 130, 142, 172, 247, 316
Lu Chin-ku 110, 111, 235, 254, 307, 322
Lucky Stars Go Places 164, 165
Lu Feng 70, 84, 85, 88, 319, 321, 323
Luhrman, Baz 110
Lundgren, Dolph 66, 222, 258
Luo Guanzhong 22
Lyn, Vincent 140, 183, 184, 186, 299

M

Macchio, Ralph 253
Mad Detective 238
Mad Monk 310
Mad Monkey Kung Fu 100, 320
Mad Monk, The 76
Magic Blade, The 108, 318
Magic Crystal 183
Magnificent Bodyguard 120
Magnificent Butcher, The 18, 154, 156, 296, 321
Magnificent Seven, The 188
Magnificent Warriors 180
Magnum Force 248
Mai Te-lo 102, 105
Maka, Karl 165, 175
Mak, Alan 237
Mako 250
Malmuth, Bruce 263
Man Called Tiger, A 77
Manchurian Candidate, The 243
Mandylor, Louis 167
Mang Hoi 154, 178, 179, 182, 183, 205, 326, 331
Man with the Golden Gun, The 312
Mao, Angela 53, 172, 173, 175, 181
Mao Tse-tung 29, 199
Marco Polo 91
Marked for Death 264, 268
Marlowe 45, 49
Martial Arts of Shaolin 112, 203, 326
Martial Club 101, 322
Martial Law 166, 167, 272
Martin, Dean 45
Marvin, Lee 252
Masked Avengers 86, 323
Master Killer 107. *See* 36th Chamber of Shaolin

Master of the Flying Guillotine 78, 317
Master Strikes Back, The 109
Master, The 110, 204, 205
Matrix, The 191, 247, 273, 274, 305, 311, 331
Maximum Risk 261
McTiernan, John 256
Medallion, The 150
Melville, Jean-Pierre 233
Memoirs of a Geisha 195
Meng Fei 70, 81, 82
Message in a Bottle 149
Miao, Nora 52, 119
Michelle Yeoh 185
Michiko Nishiwaki 181
Mighty Morphin Power Rangers 271
Millionaireís Express 162, 236
Millionaire's Express 180
Miracle Fighters, The 156
Mismatched Couples 298
Missing in Action 252, 253, 255
Missing in Action 2 252
Mission, The 130, 175, 237, 259, 295
Monahan, Debi 66
Money Crazy 229
Money Talks 148
Monkey Fights Golden Leopard 29
Monkey King 25, 29, 307
Monkey Kung Fu 110
Moon Warriors 166, 274
Moore, Dick 54
Morita, Pat 253
Morricone, Ennio 134, 250
Mortal Kombat 272
Mosha 103
Most Dangerous Game, The 259

Mr. Canton and Lady Rose 139
Mr. Nice Guy 148, 215
Mr. Vampire 162, 182
Mr. Vampire 2 182
Mui, Anita 145, 170, 187, 330
Mummy 3 222, 295
Muppet Show, The 278
Murphy, Geoff 266
Murphy, Warren 249
My Fair Lady 101, 322
My Father Is a Hero 213
My Kung Fu 12 Kicks 312
My Lucky Stars 133, 154
My Son A-Chang 40
Mystery of Chess Boxing, The 157
Myth, The 61, 150
My Young Auntie 101, 105, 322

N

Naked Killer 185
Naked Weapon 267
Nash Bridges 166
Naughty Boys 133
Nelson, Jen Yuh 280, 281
Nero, Franco 246
New Legend of Shaolin 211, 214
New One-Armed Swordsman, The 78
New Shaolin Temple 293
Ngai Sing 211, 305
Ng Mei-lo 30
Ngor, Haing S. 163
Ng, Richard 133
Ng See-yuen 61, 80, 309
Ng Sze-yuen 119, 120, 123
ninja 87, 88, 98, 103, 159, 246, 247, 249, 256, 276

Selected Index

Ninja in the Deadly Trap 87
Ninja, The 87, 97, 177, 240, 246, 247, 254, 269
ninjitsu 241
Nixon, Richard 199
No Retreat No Surrender 177
No Retreat, No Surrender 255, 258
Norris, Chuck 38, 43, 51, 240, 247, 250, 251, 255, 256, 262, 263
Norton, Richard 163, 183, 245
Nowhere to Run 259

O

Ocean Heaven 222
Ocean Shores Limited 158
Octagon, The 240, 249
On, Andy 296
Once a Thief 235
Once Upon a Time in America 206
Once Upon a Time in China II 206
Once Upon a Time in China V 208
Once Upon a Time in China VI 216
Once Upon a Time in the West 206
On Deadly Ground 265, 266, 267
O'Neal, Ryan 165
One-Armed Boxer, The 77, 78
One-Armed Magic Nun, The 171
One-Armed Swordsman, The 76, 113
One Armed Swordsman vs. Nine Killers 78
One, The 76, 77, 78, 113, 171, 217, 275, 315, 331
Ong Bak 288, 307
On Her Majesty's Secret Service 58, 174
Operation Condor 140, 141, 181

Operation Scorpio 165
Opium and the Kung Fu Master 111, 325
Opium Trail, The 173
Orphan, The 41
Osborne, Mark 279
Out for Justice 264
Outlaw Brothers 181, 182
Outlaws of the Marshes 80
Out of the Dark 310
Ovitz, Michael 262
Owl vs. Dumbo 180

P

Package, The 265
Painted Faces 164
Painted Skin 305
Palmer, Bill and Karen 46
Pantyhose Hero 165, 166
Pao Hsueh-li 79
Paragon of Sword and Knife 171
Parker, Ed 43
Partners 165
Patriot, The 267
Paycheck 259
Peckinpah, Sam 233, 248
Pedicab Driver 165, 166, 270, 328
Peking Opera 18, 25, 26, 30, 34, 35, 49, 90, 112, 117, 122, 124, 125, 130, 131, 138, 156, 159, 160, 161, 162, 164, 175, 177, 201, 204, 205, 227, 231, 293, 316, 321, 326
Phantom Lover, The 221
Phantom Menace, The 273
Pink Force Commando 175

Plain Jane to the Rescue 230
Po Chi Lum 32
Pocketful of Miracles 139
Point of No Return 184
Police Academy 181
Police Story 116, 133, 136, 137, 142, 146, 150, 175, 186, 325, 327, 329
Pom Pom 133
Poon, Dickson 176, 178, 180
Post, Ted 248
Poteet, Jerry 63
Predator 255, 256
Pressfield, Steven 263
Pride of the Yankees 195
Prison on Fire 236
Prison on Fire II 236
Private Eyes, The 229
Prodigal Son, The 161, 162, 306, 323
Project A 116, 128, 129, 130, 131, 136, 137, 139, 146, 274, 298, 324, 327
Project S 170, 182, 187, 189, 296
Protector, The 131, 183, 249, 307
Proud Youth, The 109
Proyas, Alex 66
Pryce, Jonathan 191
PTU 237
Pulp Fiction 275
Pushing Hands 192
Pyun, Albert 256

Q

qigong 89
Queen's Ransom, A 77
Quest, The 260

R

Raffo, John 64
Raiders of the Lost Ark 134
Raining in the Mountains 172
Rain Man 236
Raise the Red Lantern 218
Rambo 249, 252
Rapid Fire 64, 66
Ratner, Brett 148
Reagan, Ronald 201
Rebel Without a Cause 75, 231
Red Cliff 242, 259, 291, 292
Reeves, Keanu 273
Reign of Assassins 195, 259, 292
Remo Williams 249
Rendezvous with Death 109
Reservoir Dogs 275
Return of Bastard Swordsman 110
Return of the Chinese Boxer 78
Return of the Jedi 273
Return of the One-Armed Swordsman, The 76
Return to the 36th Chamber 100, 321
Revenge of Angel, The 183
Revenge of the Sith 273
Reyes Jr., Ernie 269
Reynolds, Burt 251
Richter, W.D. 254
Ride with the Devil 192
Righting Wrongs 179, 326
Ritchie, Guy 275
Road Home, The 218
Rob-B-Hood 150
Robotrix 184
Rock, Chris 216

Selected Index

Rocky IV 255, 258
Rogers, Roy 267
Romance of the Three Kingdoms 22, 23
Romeo Must Die 217, 218
Roots 164
Rothrock, Cynthia 136, 163, 178, 180, 183, 188, 245, 326
Royal Tramp 310
Royal Warriors 177, 178, 179, 180
Running Man, The 62
Running on Karma 237
Running Out of Time 237
Running Scared 165
Run Run Shaw 72, 113
Rush Hour 116, 148, 149, 150, 167, 216, 241, 272
Russell, Kurt 254, 266

S

Sambrell, Aldo 140
Samourai, Le 231
Sapir, Richard 249
Satan Returns 301
Saturday Night Live 247
Saxon, John 53, 55
School on Fire 236
Schwarzenegger, Arnold 62, 213, 255, 259
Scorcese, Martin 233, 237
Seagal, Steven 179, 240, 262, 265, 268
Sebring, Jay 43
Secret Rivals, The 119
Secret Service of the Imperial Court 110, 307
Seetoo, James 29

Sense and Sensibility 192
Sentimental Swordsman, The 108
Serafian, Deran 257
Seven Black Heroines 175
Seven Brides for Seven Brothers 201
Seven Grandmasters, The 157
Seven Samurai 188, 194, 278
Seven Swords 261, 304
Sex and Fury 276
Shadow Whip, The 172
Shanghai 13 88
Shanghai Affairs 301
Shanghai Knights 149, 302
Shanghai Noon 149
Shaolin 288, 295, 334
Shaolin and Wu Tang 104, 202
Shaolin Intruders 111
Shaolin Invincibles 60
Shaolin Mantis 96, 175, 319
Shaolin Martial Arts 121
Shaolin Monk 160
Shaolin Prince 111
Shaolin Soccer 182, 241, 275, 308, 311
Shaolin Temple III 203
Shaolin Temple II: Kids from Shaolin 201–202, 325
Shaolin Temple, The 18, 95, 199–201, 204, 211, 295, 324
Shaolin vs. Ninja 97
Shaolin Wooden Man 119
Sha Po Lang 304, 305
Shaw, Alonna 257
Shaw Brothers 42, 57, 60, 71, 72, 74, 75, 90, 107, 109, 112, 121, 137, 162, 172, 173, 200, 221, 227, 229, 230, 245, 276, 322

Shaw, Robert 243
Shaw, Runme 76
Shaw Yuh-hsuen 71
Sheperd, Karen 179
She Shoots Straight 166
Shih Kien 33, 53, 90, 121, 125, 163
Shi Nai-an 80
Shinjuku Incident 151
Shin, Stephan 184
Shogun Assassin 276
Shoji Kurata 97, 158, 212, 227
Shoko Ikeda 141
Shou, Robin 272
Showdown in Little Tokyo 66
Shum, John 178
Shusett, Ronald 263
Siao, Josephine 171, 208
Sidekicks 253
Silent Flute, The 282
Silent Rage 20, 250, 251
Silliphant, Sterling 45
Silver Hawk 195
Sinatra, Frank 243
Siskels, Gene 67
Six-Fingered Lord of the Lute, The 171
Sixty Million Dollar Man 310
Smith, Will 151
Smith, William 55
Snake-Crane Art of Shaolin 119
Snake Deadly Act 174
Snake in the Eagle's Shadow 121, 320
Snatch 275
Son of the Incredibly Strange Film Show 135
Soo, Helen 159
Soong Sisters, The 189
South Pacific 243
Spawn 290
Spearmen of Death, The 86
Speed Racer 147, 247
Spider-Man 23, 305
Spielberg, Steven 104, 139
Spielman, Ed 54
Spiritual Boxer, The 92, 94, 98, 103, 120, 121
Spiritual Kung Fu 120
Spooky Encounters II 166
Spottiswoode, Roger 190
Spy Next Door, The 151
Stacey, Eddie 277
Stallone, Sylvester 132, 183, 222
Star Trek 147
Star Wars 134, 147, 166, 175, 273
Statham, Jason 222, 274
Stevenson, John 278
Stone, Mike 38, 43, 44, 59, 246
Stoner 174
Stony Island 251
Storm Riders, The 237
Story of Huang Fei Hong, The. *See*
Story of Ricky 182, 296
Street Fighter 143, 260
Street Fighter, The 78
Striker, Fran 43
Stunt Woman, The 166
Su Chiao-pin 292
Sudden Death 260
Suet Nei 171
Sun Chien 70, 82, 85, 87, 319, 321, 323
Sun Chung 108, 318, 320, 323, 324
Sunshine 195
Sun Yat-sen 107, 206, 307

Selected Index

Supercop 116, 142, 166, 182, 186, 187, 190, 192, 329
Super Power 110
Surfside Six 44
Swordsman 2 170, 176, 198
Swordsman 3 176
Swordsman of all Swordsmen 157

T

taekwondo 159
taichi 27, 42, 53, 89, 98, 122, 157, 192, 209, 210, 213, 264, 283, 288, 293, 294, 297, 313, 331
Tai Chi II 293, 294
Tai Seng 159, 182, 294, 308
Tam, Alan 135
Tang Chia 90, 91, 109, 111, 112, 315, 316, 317, 318, 320, 323, 325
Tang Kheng Heng 280
Tango and Cash 132
Tan Tao-liang 91, 158, 174
Taoism 22, 156
Tao Te Ching 283
Tarantino, Quentin 236, 263, 275, 290
Tarkinton, Rockney 53
Tattoo Connection, The 158
Taylor, Rod 53
Tea and Sympathy 243
Tei Wei, Dick 129, 138, 163, 179, 180
Ten Tigers of Kwantung 86
Terminator 187, 256
Thailand 25, 29, 46, 47, 56, 245
They Call Her One Eye 276
Thief in the Car 29
Three Men and a Baby 150
Throw Down 237

Thunderbolt 147
Tien, James 61
Tiger Cage 298, 299
Tiger Killer 112
Tiger on Beat 254, 328
Ti Lung 70, 73, 78, 79, 80, 81, 82, 86, 88, 92, 108, 109, 112, 119, 144, 145, 230, 316, 317, 318, 320, 325, 327
Time and Tide 261
Timecop 260
Ting Pei, Betty 58, 60
To Hell with the Devil 230, 235
To, Johnnie 236, 237, 330
To, Johnny 186
To Kill a Mastermind 109
To Kill With Intrigue 119
To Live 218
Tomorrow Never Dies 190
Tom Yum Goong 307
Tong, Stanley 142, 166, 187, 214, 329
Top Dog 253
Tops in Every Trade 109
Total Recall 263
Touch, The 195
Toxic Avenger, The 290
Transporter, The 275
Treasure Hunters 104
Trendle, George W. 43
Troum, Kenn 269
True Legend 195, 295
True Lies 213
Tsang, Eric 133, 163
Tse, Matthew 159
Tsui Chung-hok 171
Tsui Hark 142, 175, 178, 182, 205, 207, 215, 222, 230, 234, 254,

261, 279, 294, 295, 300, 304, 310, 326, 329, 331

Tsui Siu-ming 155
Tucker, Chris 148
Tung Wai, Stephen 56, 327, 331
Tuxedo, The 150
Twin Dragons 142
Twinkle Twinkle Lucky Stars 133, 162, 182, 245
Twins Effect, The 303
Tyson 290
Tyson, Mike 290

U

Ultimate Warrior, The 244, 245
Ultraman 270
Under Siege 265, 266
Universal Soldier 258
Unleashed 217
Untouchables, The 179
Urban Justice 268
Urquidez, Benny 130, 139, 245

V

Valiant Ones, The 160, 172
Van Damme, Jean-Claude 177, 255, 258
Vengeance 79, 238, 250, 316
V for Vendetta 247
Victim, The 159
Virgin Sword, The 171

W

Wagner, Raymond 251
Walker, Texas Ranger 253
Wallace, Bill 249, 289
Wall, Bob 43, 51, 53
Wandering Swordsman, The 174
Wang Feng 33
Wang Ing-sik 51
Wang In-sik 125
Wang Li 85
Wang Lung-wei, Johnny 70, 81, 99, 102, 106, 112, 142, 163
Wang Tao, Don 158
Wang Yu, Jimmy 70, 75, 76, 77, 78, 84, 88, 98, 99, 105, 119, 120, 130, 142, 160, 163, 172, 315, 316, 317, 318
Wang Zheng-quan 77
War 28, 35, 40, 44, 72, 75, 77, 180, 202, 222, 249, 275, 306
Ward, Fred 249
Warlords, The 83, 222, 227
Warrior from Shaolin 159
Warriors Two 154, 160, 162
Warrior, The 159, 261, 283, 284
Water Margin, The 73, 80, 229, 316, 317
Watson, Stephen 209
Wayne, John 62, 254
Way of the Dragon 50, 51, 57, 59, 247, 313, 316
Web of Death 108
Wedding Banquet, The 192
Weinstein, David 254
Weintraub, Fred 20, 52, 59, 62, 242, 244
Wei Pai 70, 85
Weird Man, The 88
We're Going to Eat You 205

Selected Index

Wells, Simon 281, 284
Whang In-sik 127
What's Up Tiger Lily 271
Wheels on Meals 130, 139, 245, 325
When Taekwondo Strikes 173
White, Michael Jai 275, 288, 289, 291
Who Am I 148
Wild Fire 75
Wild Geese, The 142
Wild Girl 109
Williams, John 134
Williams, Van 44
Willis, Bruce 132, 231
Wilson, Owen 149
Windtalkers 259
wing chun 40, 42, 89, 122, 161, 162, 188, 306, 323
Wing Chun 20, 27, 40, 170, 188, 192, 300
Winners and Sinners 130, 182
Winters, Shelley 252
Wise, Robert 108
Wonder Seven 188
Wong, Anthony 187, 330
Wong Fei-hung 30, 205, 206, 207, 208, 215, 216, 220, 295, 300
Wong Jing 143, 183, 185, 192, 207, 209, 211, 214, 236, 328, 329
Wong Kar-wai 166, 176, 331
Wong Kar-wei 306
Wong, Kirk 143
Wong Tao, Don 248
Woo, John 118, 195, 205, 226, 228, 230, 232, 237, 238, 242, 258, 259, 260, 261, 291, 292, 327, 328, 329, 330
World Northal 73

Wrecking Crew, The 45, 247
Wright, Tom 167
Wu Bin 289
Wu Chu-fan 41
wu dan 161, 173
wu de 33, 92
Wu Jing 145, 288, 293, 294, 295, 304, 331
Wu Ma 79, 176, 233
Wu Tang 104, 201, 202
wuxia 23, 72, 75, 76, 91, 104, 108, 176, 187, 192, 194, 195, 219, 222, 231, 235, 237, 279, 292, 316, 317, 330, 332
Wu Xia 307
Wu Yixiao 33

X

X Files, The 217
Xie Miao 211, 213
Xing Yu 312
xiu yang 92

Y

yang gang 76, 172, 231, 316
Yang Li-tsing 185
Yang Pan-pan, Sharon 174
Yang Sze. *See* Bolo
Yee, Derek 78
Yeh, Sally 175, 205, 232, 326, 328
Yeh Tse-man, Sally 175
Yellow Faced Tiger 247
Yellow River 204
Yen, Donnie 157, 186, 187, 188, 206, 213, 218, 288, 297, 306, 307,

329, 330

Yen, Klyster 297
Yeoh, Michelle 142, 170, 193, 195, 210, 218, 292, 293, 302, 326, 329, 330, 332
Yes Madam 176, 177, 178, 185, 229, 326
Yip, Amy 184
Yip Man 40, 306
Yip, Wilson 304, 305, 306
Young and Dangerous 237
Young Dragons, The 229
Young Sinner, The 243
You Only Live Twice 246
Yuan Hua 112
Yuan Pin 112
Yu Cheng-wei 200, 201, 203, 204
Yuen Baio 125, 129, 130, 133, 138, 154, 156, 160, 161, 163, 179, 180, 182, 204, 205, 293, 298, 321, 322, 323, 325, 326, 327, 328
Yuen Cheung-yan 124, 156, 157, 274, 331
Yuen Chun Wai 270
Yuen Kwai, Corey 157, 162, 163, 166, 176, 179, 183, 208, 211, 213, 218, 255, 275, 292, 299, 309, 326, 327
Yuen Mo-chow 269
Yuen Qiu 312
Yuen Shun-yi, Sunny 155, 156, 181
Yuen, Simon 116, 121, 122, 123, 155, 156, 157, 296, 320
Yuen Siu-tin 33
Yuen Wah 49, 138, 161, 163, 204, 312, 325, 327

Yuen Wo-ping 111, 121, 122, 124, 150, 155, 163, 175, 186, 188, 193, 195, 206, 209, 210, 212, 220, 273, 275, 292, 293, 295, 298, 299, 300, 304, 311, 320, 321, 329, 330, 331, 332
Yu Hai 200
Yukari Oshima 181, 188, 189, 296
Yuko Mizuno 97
Yung Wang-yu 94, 320
Yu, Ronny 176, 221, 330
Yu Tai-ping 85
Yu Zhan-yuan 117

Z

Zanuck, Richard 246
Zatoichi the Blind Swordsman 120
Zhang Jin-sheng 292
Zhang Yimou 218, 275, 292, 302
Zhang Ziyi 193, 194, 195, 218, 302, 332
Zhao, Vincent 198, 208, 295, 331
Zhao Wen-zhou 207, 295
Zibach, Raymond 280
Zu Warriors of the Magic Mountain 154, 175, 182, 205, 254
Zwart, Harald 151

www.ingramcontent.com/pod-product-compliance
Lightning Source LLC
LaVergne TN
LVHW051541070426
835507LV00021B/2360